D0939955

KIM STANLEY ROBINSON

MODERN MASTERS OF SCIENCE FICTION

Edited by Gary K. Wolfe

Science fiction often anticipates the consequences of scientific discoveries. The immense strides made by science since World War II have been matched step by step by writers who gave equal attention to scientific principles, human imagination, and the craft of fiction. The respect for science fiction won by Jules Verne and H. G. Wells was further increased by Isaac Asimov, Arthur C. Clarke, Robert Heinlein, Ursula K. Le Guin, Joanna Russ, and Ray Bradbury. Modern Masters of Science Fiction is devoted to books that survey the work of individual authors who continue to inspire and advance science fiction.

A list of books in the series appears at the end of this book.

KIM STANLEY ROBINSON

Robert Markley

UNIVERSITY OF
ILLINOIS PRESS
Urbana, Chicago, and Springfield

Library of Congress Cataloging-in-Publication Data
Names: Markley, Robert, 1952– author.
Title: Kim Stanley Robinson / by Robert Markley.
Description: [Urbana, Ill.] : UIP, [2019] | Series: Modern masters of science fiction | Includes
    bibliographical references and index. |
Identifiers: LCCN 2019006666 (print) | LCCN 2019015886 (ebook) | ISBN 9780252051616 (ebook) |
    ISBN 9780252042751 (hardcover : alk. paper) | ISBN 9780252084584 (pbk. : alk. paper)
Subjects: LCSH: Robinson, Kim Stanley—Criticism and interpretation. | Science fiction, American—
    History and criticism.
Classification: LCC PS3568.O2893 (ebook) | LCC PS3568.O2893 Z78 2019 (print) | DDC 813/.54—
    dc23
LC record available at https://lccn.loc.gov/2019006666

contents

ACKNOWLEDGMENTS

Writing a book about a contemporary author, especially one as prolific and fascinating as Kim Stanley Robinson, poses a fair number of challenges. Just when you think you have a handle on your narrative, a new interview, a new novel, or a new critical article forces you to insert here, expand there, and, in general, reorient your thinking. I am very grateful to Stan Robinson for his willingness to sit down with me for two interviews over the past twenty years and for responding to some emailed questions. As someone who works primarily in seventeenth- and eighteenth-century literature and science, I have to say that neither Daniel Defoe nor Robert Boyle answers emails.

Over the course of writing a book, one begins to pile up IOUs that can never fully be repaid, only acknowledged. Bill Regier, then the director of the University of Illinois Press, first encouraged me to write this study, and his patience and professionalism have proved extraordinarily valuable. My current editor, Marika Christofides, stepped in after Bill retired and helped me see this project to its conclusion. My research for this book was helped significantly by money from the Trowbridge endowment at the University of Illinois.

Over the years, I have benefitted from conversations with a number of scholars, friends, and students about science fiction, Robinson's fiction, and the cross-disciplinary field of literature and science. I would like to thank Rajani Sudan, Bruce Clarke, Carol Colatrella, Katherine Hayles, Stacy Alaimo, Ron Broglio, Melissa Littlefield, Spencer Schaffner, Ronald Schleifer, Hugh Crawford, Richard Grusin, Reynolds Smith, Lisa Yaszek, Doug Davis, Arielle Saiber, Laurie Finke, Rob Mitchell, Michael Simeone, Anne Brubaker, Jennifer Lieberman, Michael Black, Jeanne Hamming, Helen Burgess, Harrison Higgs, and the late Michelle Kendrick.

An early version of chapter 3 appeared in *Modern Fiction Studies* in 1997 and a revised version in my 2005 study, *Dying Planet: Mars in Science and the Imagination* from Duke University Press. The chapter has been substantially reworked for this book. Chapter 4 reworks my earlier article on the Science in the Capital trilogy in *Configurations* (2012). I am grateful to Johns Hopkins University Press for permission to reprint parts of these articles in *Kim Stanley Robinson*.

My family deserves more thanks than I can offer here. They keep me focused, as Robinson puts it, crabbing sideways toward the good. My daughter, Hannah Markley, is a terrific critic of literature, and I have learned a great deal from reading her work. My son, Stephen Markley, has embarked on his own brilliant career as a novelist. His fiction, again to borrow Stan's phrasing, is finer grained and wider ranging in its approach to how we live now than just about anything else on my bookshelf. Without the encouragement, incisive comments on this manuscript, generosity and good humor of my wife, Lucinda Cole, you would not be reading this book now. Her own award-winning scholarly work is an inspiration, and she makes my life better every moment. This book is dedicated to her.

KIM STANLEY ROBINSON

Kim Stanley Robinson emerged in the 1980s and '90s as a major crossover writer, a novelist who had a wide and enthusiastic following among readers of science fiction and who commanded serious attention from "mainstream" reviewers, readers, and literary critics. In the twenty-first century, Robinson has become not only an eloquent voice for the significance of science fiction but an important cultural commentator who has helped move the genre to the forefront of debates about literature's role in an ecologically and politically troubled world. In these and other respects, as I'll suggest throughout this study, Robinson has emerged as probably the preeminent writer of our era because his fiction both questions and expands the limits of what literature can and should be doing as our planet rapidly overheats. If literature, as Kenneth Burke suggested years ago, should be considered "equipment for living," then Robinson's work might be seen as equipment for living in a range of possible futures brought about by humankind's past errors, false starts, hopes, and fears.[1]

Over the years that I have been teaching Robinson's fiction, students repeatedly tell me that they are shocked when they realize that the author of *Red Mars* also wrote *Years of Rice and Salt*, or *Shaman*, or *Aurora*. While their reactions say something about the remarkable breadth of Robinson's work, they also testify to the complex ways that his novels weave together strands of ecological, utopian, and Buddhist thought. The history of literature, after all, is packed with writerly responses to environmental degradation, from elegiac laments for a lost, edenic world, to grim dystopian satires of humankind's catastrophic appetites for fuel, food, and wealth. In marshaling the science-fiction genres of alternative and future history to explore humanity's ongoing struggles toward a more just and environmentally stable world, Robinson's fiction escapes or transcends most of the convenient labels that critics use to describe contemporary literature. At the risk of overstatement, I suggest in this study that Robinson's fiction makes a strong case for seeing science fiction, and not traditional literary realism, as the truly significant genre for our current moment in human and planetary history.

In a world facing temperature and sea-level rises not seen in millions of years, old-style realism has its share of discontents. At the beginning of *The Great Derangement* (2016), Amitav Ghosh laments the lack of attention to the prospect of catastrophic climate change in "serious fiction" and "serious literary journals," and he concludes that its "mere mention . . . is often enough to relegate a novel or short story to the genre of science fiction . . . as though in the literary imagination climate change were somehow akin to extraterrestrials or interplanetary travel."[2] By cordoning off "serious" from science fiction, Ghosh reflects a larger cultural anxiety about the status of literature in a world where climate-enhanced disasters—like Hurricanes Harvey, Irma, and Maria in 2017—can make CNN or BBC footage seem like the trailer for a dystopian, end-of-the-world film. Although Ghosh has an important argument to make, his view of science fiction is, at best, stereotyped: what is at stake in Robinson's fiction is precisely the question of what we mean by "serious fiction" and "the literary imagination." As Robinson says in his introduction to *Green Earth* (his one-volume version of the Science in the Capital trilogy), "if you want to write a novel about our world now, you'd better write science fiction, or you will be doing some kind of inadvertent nostalgia piece; you will lack depth, miss the point, and remain confused."[3] Although science fiction hardly lacks for defenders, Robinson's claims for the genre's literary, cultural, and philosophical significance encourage us to entertain the possibility that sf has overtaken "realism" as a vehicle for "serious fiction," and that "seriousness" itself has to be redefined. Taken as a whole, his own work offers a range of responses to a question that resonates throughout his novels and short stories: How do we—as individuals, as a civilization, as a species—go forward from here?

As a study of Robinson's fiction, this book is neither a standard literary biography nor an introductory survey of his novels and short fiction. Instead, *Kim Stanley Robinson* investigates the significance of his work over the past four decades in reshaping contemporary literature and, in the process, encouraging readers to appreciate his expansive brand of "serious fiction." Like all great writers, Robinson resists being pigeonholed by critical truisms because his work always seems to slip out from under conventional labels and broad generalizations. Not surprisingly, then, this has proved a challenging but rewarding book to write because each of his novels (not to mention his short stories) is rich and complex enough to deserve full-length critical analyses of the sort one finds in *PMLA* or *Science-Fiction Studies*. In interpreting Robinson's fiction, I try to treat his major novels, like *The Years of Rice and Salt* (2002), with the kind of analytical commitment that, elsewhere, I have tried to bring to canonical works like John Milton's *Paradise Lost*, Daniel Defoe's *Robinson Crusoe*, and Jane Austen's *Pride and Prejudice*.[4]

If Milton, Defoe, and Austen still speak to the readers of Ghosh's "serious literary journals," Robinson's seriousness is of a different order. Robinson has worked within and across the generic boundaries within science fiction to emphasize his belief that "a literary life is an ongoing moral education, a complete geography of the human world."[5] He has authored groundbreaking alternative histories ("The Lucky Strike," *Years of Rice and Salt*), epic future histories (the Mars trilogy, *2312*, *Aurora*, *New York 2140*), and novels that either weave together multiple genres (*Galileo's Dream*) or resist generic labels altogether (*Shaman*). Robinson's many interviews and short pieces, in print and online, offer a running commentary on his commitment to science fiction as a critical component of contemporary literature, sociopolitical thought, and utopian speculation. In an article in *New Scientist* in 2009, Robinson called attention to Virginia Woolf's correspondence with, and debt in her late fiction to, the pioneering sf writer Olaf Stapeldon in order to argue that both writers shared the view that "scientifically minded people could . . . conceptualise novels as case studies or thought experiments, both finer grained and wider ranging in their approach to meaning than cruder genres such as religion, psychology or common sense."[6] This description provides a useful way to think about his own work and offers some insight into why he has emerged as a sought-after commentator on issues ranging from global warming to the absence of science fiction novels nominated for Britain's Man Booker Prize. If the best science fiction appropriates some of the techniques of realism to body forth the "finer grain[s]" of imagined societies, Robinson's work remains committed to "wider ranging" views of the transformations that technoscientific discoveries herald for human and planetary futures. In their ambitions to record a history of the Anthropocene that we do not yet know, his novels brilliantly chart imaginative topographies that encourage us to reassess our collective histories and imagined futures.

In his introduction to the anthology *Future Primitive: The New Ecotopias* (1994), Robinson describes science fiction as "a collection of thought experiments" or "historical simulations" that "form in our imagination a kind of consensus vision of the future."[7] His version of this "consensus vision" places questions of ecological stewardship and political economy at the center of his own thought experiments. In 1994 Robinson encouraged his readers to imagine alternatives to cyberpunk's dystopian "consensus vision" of humankind "as the last organic units in [the] denatured, metallic, clean, and artificial world" of a cyber-engineered future. In place of this denatured vision, Robinson asked his readers to explore the utopian possibilities of "cobbl[ing] together aspects of the postmodern and the Paleolithic" in what he called a "future primitive": a technologically sophisticated civilization living within the bounds of socioeconomic justice and ecological responsibility.[8] Twenty years later, in an interview with Gerry Canavan in their co-edited collection, *Green Planets: Ecology and Science Fiction* (2014), Robinson describes this "future primitive" in a different vocabulary by focusing on the three strands that he weaves together in his fiction: Marxism, ecology, and Buddhist thought. Rather than attempting a "synthesis" of these strands, he talks about "putting them together in various combinations, and tracing what happens" when Marxism, Buddhism, and ecology exist as a "bricolage" or "slurry."[9] In the chapters that follow, I trace how and why these "various combinations" structure his fictional worlds. If Robinson treats "science as a critical utopian leftist political action," he also insists that "we study and thus worship a sacred reality, which we [must] manipulate in order to survive," and, consequently, "science is already the best eco-religion" (*Green Planets* 256). Read in this context, his novels—from the Mars trilogy to *New York 2140*—offer a range of possible futures that chart humankind's uneven progress, often over centuries, toward critical utopias that are ecological, psychological, and spiritual.

To be clear, however, Robinson is hardly a typical utopianist. Rather than polished utopian societies, interstellar swashbuckling, or tub-thumping triumphs over world-weary dystopianism, he offers his readers futures that experiment in the greening of science, economics, and politics.[10] In all of his novels, Robinson is "remaking history" (to borrow the title of one of his short stories) by filtering our knowledge of the past and our imagination of possible futures through two superimposed lenses: the ecological fate of the Earth (or other planets) and the far-reaching consequences of moral, political, and socioeconomic decisions of individuals, often scientists and artists, caught up in world or solar-systemic events. In this respect, his fiction charts a collective struggle to think beyond the contradictions of historical existence, and, as the etymology of *utopia* suggests, beyond our locations in time, culture, and geography.[11] Utopian schemes in his novels are usually in the process, as he suggests in a chapter title of *Red Mars*, of "falling into history," sidetracked or undone by the gaps between the idealized visions of a stable sociotechnological society—the *Hidalgo* setting off for the stars in *Icehenge* (1984) or the ship headed to a seemingly Earth-like moon of Tau Ceti in *Aurora* (2015)—and the wear and tear of historical existence. Throughout Robinson's fiction his characters give voice to larger, though often inchoate, desires to transcend humankind's *originary* alienation—an alienation at once ecological, political, and psychological. His version of "critical utopian leftist political action" seeks to repair the breaches that sever us from nature, from others, and from ourselves.[12]

Robinson's commitment to countering the cynically packaged dystopianism of zombie apocalypses helps explain why his work frequently serves as a touchstone for literary critics and cultural theorists who do not write primarily about sf.[13] Throughout his career Robinson explores the complex relationships between science fiction and history, and, as Phillip Wegner astutely observes, his explorations of alternative and future histories overlap conceptually with the "radical theoretical work" of contemporary cultural theorists including

Slavoj Zizek, Jacques Derrida, Alain Baidou, and Judith Butler.[14] Along similar lines, Sherryl Vint argues persuasively that Robinson's sociopolitical and thematic concerns share some of the key insights, assumptions, and values of work in science studies by theorists such as Bruno Latour, Donna Haraway, and Karen Barad, among others.[15] Yet the range of Robinson's fiction, beginning with his early short stories and continuing through *New York 2140* (2017), recalibrates rather than passively reflects this "radical theoretical work." For this reason, other scholars—notably Fredric Jameson and Mackenzie Wark—argue that Robinson's fiction in itself constitutes an important theoretical intervention in contemporary utopian and Marxian thought.[16] If we consider science and literature as often complementary ways of knowledge making, we might think of Robinson's science fiction as thought experiments that push beyond the dystopian clichés of video-game survivalism.

More than a decade ago, Bruno Latour suggested that "critique"—the suite of analytic methods that had defined literary and cultural theory in the 1980s and '90s—had "run out of steam," and he called for developing "a powerful descriptive tool . . . whose import will no longer be to debunk but to protect and to care . . . to transform the critical urge in the ethos of someone who *adds* reality to matters of fact and not *subtract* reality."[17] In some ways, Robinson goes Latour one better. One of my working assumptions—and one shared by many of the critics I cite in this study—is that Robinson's science fiction *is* such a "powerful descriptive tool" because it not only offers us new insights into our contemporary situation but also expands our imaginative ability to chart possible realities to come. Another way of putting this is to suggest that his works help reorient contemporary literature away from confessional self-absorption by focusing on a collective utopian struggle for a just and equitable civilization. For Robinson, *struggle* is a crucial term: his imagined histories find his heroes and heroines fighting through repeated defeats, detours, and backslidings. Utopia, in his fiction, isn't for the faint-hearted.

While many readers are familiar with the future history depicted in the Mars trilogy, Robinson's novels offer different versions of the future that do not necessarily follow or conform to one another. By 2140 in the Mars trilogy, terraforming and colonization of the planet are well underway, but in *New York 2140* humanity is still earthbound; there are no space elevators made from high-tech materials, only "superscrapers" towering above northern Manhattan and other of the world's drowned coastal cities, refuges for the hyperwealthy in a society still struggling against the stranglehold of financial capitalism. If this recent novel asks us to imagine a version of our own time—life after the great recession of 2008–09—projected into the twenty-second century, its postcarbon future of solar and wind power has not (yet) led to the kind of political revolution glimpsed at the end of the Science in the Capital trilogy. The characters in *New York 2140* still must contend with a world economic system structured by hedge funds, computerized financial trading, and rampant speculation in real estate half-submerged under water. The different futures imagined in this novel, the Mars trilogy, and *2312* reflect different perspectives on our own time; they testify to Robinson's energy in continuing to experiment with his "bricolage" of socioeconomic, spiritual, and ecological thought.

In 2013 Kim Stanley Robinson described to me his ideal biography in six words: "Mountain walker, Mr. Mom, writes books."[18] In expanding a bit on these six words, I want to focus on how some aspects of his background, family life, and experiences percolate through his novels, and how Robinson's education and extensive reading have shaped his approach to science fiction. Robinson's father, Don, was born in Asheville, North Carolina, in 1925, and joined the navy soon after the outbreak of World War II. He was stationed at the Navy Pier in Chicago and, while there during the war, met his future wife, Gloria McElroy, who taught piano. After leaving the navy, Don received his BS in engineering at Illinois Tech. The novelist was born in 1952 in Waukegan, Illinois, the closest hospital to where the family lived in Zion, a town just south of the Wisconsin state line. In 1955 Don took a job at Hughes Aircraft, and the family relocated to Los Angeles. Several years later, they moved to unincorporated Orange County near Tustin. Robinson enjoyed, by his own admission, "an Ozzie and Harriet childhood" (2013) in Southern California, went to public schools, and graduated from El Modena High in 1970, already an avid reader of Shakespeare, the Romantic poets, and classic American novels like *Huckleberry Finn*. At the University of California-San Diego, Robinson studied literature and started reading deeply and widely in science fiction, encouraged by Jameson, one of his professors. He also began backpacking into the Sierra Nevada in California; he took his first trip there in August 1973 and says, "I never came down from that trip" (2013). The mountainous wilderness of California appears frequently in Robinson's fiction, from "Ridge-Running" (1984) to "Muir on Shasta" (1991) to *Sixty Days and Counting* (2007), and even mountaineering expeditions on other planets, like the ascent of Mount Olympus in his story "Green Mars" (1985), draw on his experiences backpacking through the Sierra.

After graduating from UCSD in 1974, Robinson traveled across country to Boston University to pursue his MA in English. The year he spent in Boston served as a platform for his future work, although his first winter in New England, Robinson admits, was a shock to his system and half-convinced him that New Englanders all had been driven half-mad by the cold, snow, and wan winter sunlight. In the summer of 1975 he attended the Clarion science-fiction writing workshop, then at Michigan State University, led by Damon Knight, and subsequently returned to UCSD to pursue a PhD in English. There he studied with Andrew Wright, Jameson, and Donald Wesling. Robinson's graduate career was atypical in that he continued to write—and publish—science fiction, encouraged by his professors. His first stories, "In Pierson's Orchestra" (1976) and "Coming Back to Dixieland" (1976), both appeared in Knight's edited volume *Orbit* 18, and "The Disguise" (1977) in volume 19. An early version of the third section of *Icehenge*, titled "On the North Pole of Pluto," was published in *Orbit* 21 (1980) as a short story.

Given the comparative freedom he enjoyed in pursuing his PhD at UCSD, it is not surprising that Robinson considers himself "well-treated" by academe, and, unlike many writers, "never felt alienated" (2013). During this period (1978–82), he was writing and rewriting drafts of *Icehenge*, *The Memory of Whiteness*, and *The Wild Shore*, the first volume of the Orange County trilogy. The composition of these very different novels was more or less simultaneous, according to Robinson; he would work on one manuscript, put it aside while he worked on another, and then return to revise the first. By the mid-1980s, with the publication of these novels, he already was among the most noteworthy of a new generation of science fiction writers.

In 1978, while working alternately on his dissertation and his own fiction, Robinson moved north to Davis, where he taught freshman- and sophomore-level writing classes at the University of California-Davis and worked odd jobs, including a stint in a bookstore. He completed his dissertation on Philip K. Dick in 1982 (later published by UMI Press in 1984 as *The Novels of Philip K. Dick*). In Davis he met Lisa Howland Nowell, an environmental chemist, and they were married in 1982. After publishing *Icehenge* and *The Wild Shore* in 1984 and *The Memory of Whiteness* (1985), he and his wife moved to Switzerland for two years, where she was doing postdoctoral work in environmental toxicology. They relocated to Washington, D.C., for four years while she worked for the U.S. Geological Survey and then, in 1991, returned to Davis, where they still live, and where they raised their two sons. Nowell's research concerns the buildup of pollutants, especially pesticides, in freshwater sediments and their uptake by fish and bivalves, and Robinson's detailed depictions of scientific conferences in *Green Mars* and the workings of the National Science Foundation in the Science in the Capital trilogy owe something to his firsthand observation of science in action.

Robinson's graduate study of literature and literary and cultural theory in the 1970s and his fiction have been entwined, in important ways, since the beginning of his career. His novels encompass a wide range of sociopolitical, cultural, and technoscientific concerns: the future of capitalism in an age of interplanetary expansion, climate change, ecological disaster, the complexities of gender in a coming age of genetic manipulation, the engineering of planetary environments, the rise of China as a world power, and species extinction, among others. At the same time, his novels are meticulously researched: the Mars trilogy draws extensively on the scientific literature of the 1970s and '80s on terraforming, *The Years of Rice and Salt* rewrites 650 years of world history, and the Science in the Capital trilogy has served, for many readers, as a primer on climatology. What unites Robinson's wide-ranging fictional worlds is, in his own words, his commitment to "a progressive course [of history] in which things become more just and sustainable over the generations."[19] Because, as Robinson has said, in the near future "we will be living on a quite different planet, in a significantly damaged biosphere, with its life-support systems so harmed that human existence will be substantially threatened," we face "a case of utopia or catastrophe." As a result, he suggests, "utopia has gone from being a somewhat minor literary problem to a necessary survival strategy."[20] If we think of Robinson's fiction as working toward this "survival strategy," we can begin to understand his appeal in and beyond the science fiction community.

The breadth and complexity of Robinson's fiction has guided my decision on how to structure this study. Rather than trying to discuss his short stories and novels chronologically, I have organized this book into five chapters and an epilogue with, as one might expect, extensive cross-referencing. My goal is not to write a "definitive" study of Robinson's still-evolving body of work but to offer a mid-career report that traces the developing concerns in his fiction as they morph from the short stories (many written in the 1980s), through his three trilogies, to his recent novels: *2312*, *Shaman*, *Aurora*, and *New York 2140*. Unless I benefit at some future date from the life-extension treatments that allow his characters in the Mars trilogy and *2312* to live for a couple of centuries, I will have to forego an extensive archival analysis of his short fiction, particularly stories that were incorporated into novels like *Icehenge* or that appeared in more than one version. My decisions on what aspects of his fiction to emphasize reflect my views—which I hope future critics of his work will debate—on why Robinson has emerged as one of the major writers of the late twentieth and early twenty-first centuries.

Chapter 1, "Falling into Other Histories," examines Robinson's alternative histories—mostly, if not exclusively, set on Earth—beginning with his early short fiction and concluding with *Years of Rice and Salt* (2002) and *Shaman* (2014). In stories such as "Remaking History," "The Lucky Strike," and "Sensitive Dependence on Initial Conditions" Robinson explores the ways that twentieth-century views of history face *both* back in time, trying to reconstruct a past from which its characters would like to see themselves descended, *and* forward, serving as rough guides to always speculative futures. He is less concerned with the shock value of alternative pasts than with the fundamental ethical and political questions they raise, such as Frank January's dilemma in "The Lucky Strike" about whether to drop the atomic bomb on Hiroshima. In *Icehenge*, three linked narratives that span centuries explore characters' efforts to recover—or debunk—the history of a rebellion on twenty-fourth-century Mars. While *Icehenge* could be discussed with the other novels of solar system colonization in chapter 5, its concern with the historical imagination—the thin, wavering lines among fact, hope, and belief—makes it a key work for understanding Robinson's alternative histories.

The Years of Rice and Salt is Robinson's most ambitious alternative history and one of the most far-reaching works in the genre. This epic novel begins with Europe depopulated by the bubonic plague in the 1350s and then reimagines the history of a world dominated by China, India, and the Islamic empires of the Middle East and Central Asia. Set at roughly hundred-year intervals in different regions of the world, its ten books follow the reincarnated souls of the novel's primary characters as they move through an alternative history of modernity in which benchmark events—the colonization of the Americas, the scientific and industrial revolutions, the world wars, and the advent of the nuclear era—are pried free from Western values and assumptions. In a world shaped by Tibetan Buddhism, where the struggles for justice transcend the temporal and spatial boundaries of individual lifetimes, characters find themselves, in incarnation after incarnation, trying to resist the disillusionment that mires humanity in the selfishness and violence that attend the pursuits of wealth, pleasure, and power.

In *Shaman*, Robinson pushes the generic boundaries of alternative history into a speculative past. The novel—a classic of what we might call pre-Anthropocene literature—focuses on a small pack of hunter-gatherers thirty-five thousand years ago, the artists who created the Chauvet cave paintings in southern France. Millennia before writing, agriculture, the domestication of animals, and permanent settlements shaped civilization, the shaman-in-training, Loon, can imagine the future only as extended moments of the present. Rather than struggling toward a utopian future, the hero and his teachers, Heather and Thorn, live an unrecorded history in an ice-age environment defined by the complex ecological relationships that tie the band's fate to the animals their shaman-artists depict. Thorn's and Loon's cave art reflects an artistic-ecological vision that extends beyond the parochial concerns of humankind.

Chapter 2 examines the Orange County, or Three Californias, trilogy (1984–90) that offers starkly different visions of twenty-first-century Southern California. Linked only by the single figure of Tom Barnard, a lawyer born in the late twentieth century, *The Wild Shore*, *The Gold Coast*, and *Pacific Edge* offer radically divergent histories of what is now our own era and radically different visions of landscapes transformed from the freeways and strip malls of 1980s Orange County. In *The Wild Shore* (1984), Henry Fletcher and the other survivors of a neutron-bomb attack live like postapocalyptic, nineteenth-century pioneers along the Pacific coast, occasionally foraging among the ruins of destroyed cities and suburbs. Tom preserves his own vision of a pre-apocalyptic past, shot through with myths, tall tales, and practical wisdom from a United States that no longer exists. In *The Gold Coast* (1986), Jim McPherson navigates an endless cityscape defined by the dystopian "condomundo" of cheap, cookie-cutter apartments and sprawling, triple-decker freeways. In trying to recover Southern California's socioecological history, he is often side-tracked and frustrated, and he struggles, as a writer and occasionally violent activist, to imagine how a more just and sustainable society might emerge. In *Pacific Edge* (1990), the concrete, asphalt, and electrical systems of *The Gold Coast* are recycled and repurposed to serve the goals of a utopian society materially and politically transformed by a commitment to social, economic, and environmental justice. Kevin Claiborne comes to recognize that utopia is an ongoing struggle against backsliding into the exploitative values and assumptions of resurgent capitalism. In a utopian solar- and wind-powered future, the land is never a passive backdrop but, as Kevin comes to recognize, an active force for sustaining the principles and practices of socioeconomic justice. Taken as a whole, then, the trilogy explores different socioecological futures and different paths that American civilization might take.

Chapter 3 turns to the Mars trilogy—*Red Mars* (1992), *Green Mars* (1993), and *Blue Mars* (1996)—in order to examine how Robinson uses the thought-experiment of terraforming an alien world to explore the complex relationships that constitute planetary ecology. At the center of the trilogy lies what Robinson calls "eco-economics," his challenge to the default assumption that economics means the exploitation, degradation, and eventual exhaustion of natural resources—and the subsequent pursuit of more resources to exploit. As terraforming transforms Mars over the course of the three novels, the planet becomes a site to imagine the possibilities of ecological and sociopolitical transformation and self-organization: the birth of a new planetary order that confronts head-on the obstacles to utopian progress—socioeconomic conflict, environmental degradation, racial and religious antagonisms, and state and corporatist violence and greed. As it undergoes its sea change from red to green to blue, Mars offers its citizens (and the novels' readers) a means to imagine a utopian future that replaces the politics of scarcity and desperation with hard-won forms of cooperation, ecological stewardship, and democratic diversity.

Chapter 4 examines the Science in the Capital trilogy (which Robinson condensed in 2015 to the one-volume novel, *Green Earth*). *Forty Signs of Rain* (2004), *Fifty Degrees Below* (2005), and *Sixty Days and Counting* (2007) were instrumental in defining the emergence of "cli-fi," fiction devoted to issues of anthropogenic climate change. Published a year before Hurricane Katrina, *Forty Signs* anticipates the sequence of natural disasters and political failures that plagued New Orleans during and after the flood; *Fifty Degrees Below* and *Sixty Days* explore how an altruistic utopianism might emerge from the ecological, political, and socioeconomic crises triggered by global warming. In subjecting Washington, D.C., to a climatological quasi-apocalypse, Robinson extends his exploration of human adaptation to extreme climates that had figured prominently in the Mars trilogy and his stand-alone novel, *Antarctica* (1999). In this regard, the Science in the Capital trilogy is less a traditional future or alternative history than a visionary reassessment of the assumptions and values that define contemporary science, from genetic engineering to paleoclimatology. In these novels, climate catastrophe profoundly unsettles traditional notions of ecology founded on metaphors of balance and harmony as Robinson weaves together an alternative ethics of political action and environmental stewardship. At Robinson's fictional NSF, oceanographers, atmospheric scientists, specialists in bioinformatics, mathematicians, sociobiologists, and physicians come to treat science as an ethical and spiritual approach to the world rather than a purely instrumental solution to environmental crisis. The eco-economics that Robinson describes in the Mars trilogy is brought down to earth in *Fifty Degrees* and *Sixty Days*: the struggle for a more just, equitable, and sustainable society becomes all the more compelling because no space colonies beckon and no off-world resources or technologies arrive to help revolutionize Earth.

In chapter 5, I discuss four novels from Robinson's early and later career, *The Memory of Whiteness* (1984), *Icehenge* (1984), *Galileo's Dream* (2009), and *2312* (2012), that anticipate or extend his concerns in the Mars trilogy with using the colonization of the solar system to think through the limits and challenges of our own terrestrial ecologies. These novels banish—or transform—sf staples of encounters with alien races and reject the tendency to treat interplanetary expansion as an escape from the political, economic, and ecological conflicts on a future Earth. Instead, Robinson explores the socioeconomic, cultural, ecological, and biophysical evolutions that stem from humankind's diaspora across the solar system: terraformed Mars, the domed and subterranean colonies on Jupiter's and Saturn's moons, the city-state of Terminator on Mercury, and terraria in hollowed-out asteroids offer a wide range of imagined futures.

Nonetheless, Earth's future remains central to Robinson's vision of the colonization of the solar system, and the crises of the late twentieth and twenty-first centuries shape his vision of our species' interplanetary future. *The Memory of Whiteness* set in the fourth millennium imagines artistic life in a universe of abundance made possible by breakthroughs in physics, energy generation, and even music. This version of utopia, however, stands in contrast to various characters' efforts in *Icehenge* to uncover the significance of a mysterious, Stonehenge-like structure on the surface of Pluto. In some ways a forerunner to the Mars trilogy, *Icehenge* marks the boundaries between utopian aspiration and oligarchic control, and between history and fiction. Written two decades later, *Galileo's Dream* weaves together different sf genres—time travel, an alternative history of the Scientific Revolution, and a future history of contact with alien intelligences—to reexamine the origins, uses, and consequences of scientific inquiry. Struggling against dogmatic forces in both the seventeenth century and the thirty second, Galileo, like Robinson's other scientist-heroes, confronts the problem of how to harness technoscientific progress to foster social, political, and economic justice in an often hostile world.

If the Mars trilogy is about the inhabitation of a terraformed world, *2312* emphasizes the ways that the thousands of human-constructed ecologies in the solar system redefine understandings of both nature and human nature. The novel recasts three traditions familiar to readers of late-twentieth-century science fiction: dead-end or dystopian planetary colonization (Dick's *Martian Time-Slip*), tales of the contacts among dispersed humanoid societies (Le Guin's Hainish trilogy), and interplanetary adventure across a *Star Trek* universe of seemingly limitless possibilities. Three centuries in the future, multiple gender identities, artificial intelligence, planetary terraforming schemes (this time on Venus), and the proliferation of micro-worlds in hollowed-out asteroids encourage readers to imagine what a diasporic civilization means for individuals and humankind as a whole. In this respect, *2312* explores the possibilities of biophysical, ecological, and computational diversity to reframe our understanding of the problems that confront humankind in our own, pre–solar-system era.

Chapter 6 considers Robinson's two most recent novels, *Aurora* (2015) and *New York 2140* (2017). *Aurora* drives a stake through the heart of intergalactic romance by depicting a failed version of the dream of a *Star Trek* civilization that extends far beyond the ecology of our solar system. Narrated in large measure by the spaceship's artificial intelligence, *Aurora* brilliantly experiments with the narrative structures of sf even as it explores the ecological and biogeographical limits of terrestrial life forms. *New York 2140*, in contrast, depicts the struggle for the city's political and environmental future when sea level is forty feet higher than today and rampant financial speculation still drives a capitalist economy. This struggle, however serious, is cast as a comedy about environmental resurrection and political revival in a postcarbon world. Throughout the novel, New Yorkers—from Herman Melville to H. L. Mencken—make cameo appearances, and Robinson uses their epigraphs and their views of the city to craft a futuristic tale of financial oligarchy run rampant and the ways that collective action might bring eco-economics down to earth.

If one were to construct a word-cloud for this book, my guess is that, in addition to the large-scale letters of "utopia," one would find clusters of verbs like "explore," "rethink," and "reframe." In shifting our frames of reference from the mundane to the speculative, sf is often about that prefix "re": the familiar made strange, and the strange—like a flotilla of oil tankers shooting salt into the Atlantic to restart the stalled Gulf Stream—seem like breaking news on CNN. Robinson has said that the world is a giant science-fiction novel we are all coauthoring, and this perspective makes reading his fiction seem like a kind of collaborative engagement. As a novelist, Robinson asks his readers not to marvel at his inventiveness but to see our own world and our paths to the future anew.

"I SAW THROUGH TIME":
FALLING INTO OTHER HISTORIES

From the beginning of his career, Kim Stanley Robinson has used the genre of alternative history to explore the ways that science fiction reframes crucial questions about politics, economics, and social organization. By the time he began writing fiction in the 1970s, alternative histories had spilled over from science-fiction classics, such as Ward Moore's *Bring the Jubilee* (1953), Philip K. Dick's *The Man in the High Castle* (1961), and, later, Bruce Sterling and William Gibson's *The Difference Engine* (1991), to "mainstream" bestseller lists with works including McKinley Cantor's *If the South Had Won the Civil War* (1962) and Philip Roth's *The Plot against America* (2004). Although there are surprising twists and turns and wrenching changes of perspective throughout his alternative histories, Robinson focuses less on the shock value of rewriting history for its own sake than with asking wide-ranging questions about how our stories of the past have shaped our sense of our possible futures. In such groundbreaking stories as "The Lucky Strike," "A Sensitive Dependence on Initial Conditions," "A History of the

Twentieth Century, with Illustrations," "Vinland, the Dream," and "Remaking History," and in novels such as *The Years of Rice and Salt* and *Shaman*, he explores how history writing faces both back in time, reconstructing the past to serve a variety of present purposes, and forward to challenge our assumptions about reshaping the future for characters who initially see themselves trapped by their individual and global crises. In his epic of an alternative world history, *Years of Rice and Salt*, Robinson expands the conventional limits of the genre by imagining a world marked by the sociopolitical dominance of Asian empires and the moral authority of Buddhist and indigenous ideas of tolerance and something approaching gender equality.

RETHINKING HISTORY

Robinson's early short fiction, published during the late 1970s and early 1980s, emerged at an important juncture for science fiction in the United States.[1] Two decades on, the countercultural movements of the 1960s seemed either a path not taken or a naïve form of escapism that had faded into history. In the wake of liberatory dreams deferred, critics such as Darko Suvin and Fredric Jameson argued for the significance of science fiction as a mode of critique of contemporary politics, culture, and economics. For Jameson, science fiction reverses the values and assumptions of classical historical fiction. If the historical novel, as the Hungarian critic Georg Lukács argued, emerged in the nineteenth century as a way to imagine "a determinate past" for the modern nation-state, Jameson maintains that science fiction imagines the present as "the determinate past of something"—a future or range of futures—"yet to come."[2] Robinson's early fiction brings pressure against traditional ideas of a "determinate past" in terms of alternatives to the history that we are living through and to the future histories that we cannot (yet) know. While many of his contemporaries between 1975 and 1985 turned to the dystopian chic of cyberpunk, Robinson offered a different perspective on Cold War tensions, endemic racism and gender discrimination, the loss of manufacturing jobs, and (in the years before graphic boards and the World Wide Web) the widespread adoption of personal computers.[3] Often focusing on the relationships between moral decision-making and the potential for utopian action, his short fiction asks readers both to reimagine the past and to rethink the possibilities for bettering the future.

In his remarkable short story, "A History of the Twentieth Century, with Illustrations" (1991), Robinson explores the enervating sense of being trapped in and by a dreary present. Frank Churchill, a popular historian suffering from depression in the aftermath of his divorce, is commissioned to write a coffee-table history of the twentieth century.[4] Working his way through various sources in the British Library, he grows obsessed with the violence and catastrophes of world wars, atomic bombs, and genocide, until he comes across a 1902 volume titled *A History of the Nineteenth Century, with Illustrations*. This book concludes with a burst of heroically naïve optimism: "I believe that Man is good. I believe we stand at the dawn of a century that will be more peaceful and prosperous than any in history."[5] Churchill leaves the British Library, rents a car, and drives north to Scotland, eventually taking the ferry to the Orkney Islands. There, on the windswept and wave-lashed coast, he visits the Neolithic ruins at Skara Brae and finds five-thousand-year-old stone houses, with stone shelves, cabinets, beds, and utensils. Although the inhabitants disappeared after six hundred years, Churchill realizes that what they have left "look[s] deeply familiar" and reflects "the same needs, the same thinking, the same solutions" as people in his own time (55–56). His experience of a neolithic history, before and oddly beyond the violence of modernity, brings him back from contemplating "end[ing] the pain and fear" by jumping off a cliff at "the End of Europe" (59). Instead, he recognizes intuitively that to live in the history of the present requires thinking beyond and living for the *difference*—the possibility—that the future holds. At the end of the story, makeshift camping in his car in a parking lot at the "End of Europe," Churchill writes a postscript to his reading notes for his coffee-table history of the twentieth century: "I believe that man is good. I believe we stand at the dawn of a century that will be more peaceful and prosperous than any in history" (62). This is (as Jacques Derrida might say) repetition with a difference: in citing the century-old historian, the hero finds not a faith *in* but a way *toward* a "good" that exists beyond the tyranny of the present.

"The History of the Twentieth Century, with Illustrations" is suggestive of the ways that Robinson's fiction distances itself from the kind of postmodernist ironies that abound in alternative histories written during the last decades of the century. As Philip Wegner and Jameson imply, postmodernism and modernism imagine the "good" primarily as a *negation* of the negative, alienated experience of the present, even as this negation often is treated cynically as a form of romantic rebellion or naïve complicity.[6] If postmodernism tends to reject master narratives as either bad-faith modes of repression or as confirmations of a broad and deep skepticism, it tends to cast the future as a projection or extension of its own cynicism.[7] In contrast, Robinson encourages readers to imagine the present as neither determined by the past nor determining a dystopian future. Instead, as *Years of Rice and Salt* suggests, the present itself is a kind of back formation—a *negation* of the utopian possibilities for a future potentially "more peaceful and prosperous than any [previous era] in history." In this regard, to look back at the present from imagined futures becomes an incentive to keep striving to make things better, what Cartophilus in *Galileo's Dream* describes as our efforts "to crab sidewise toward the good" (556).

In his early short fiction, Robinson shows us what is at stake in "Remaking History," the title of his engaging story that rewrites the Iran hostage crisis (1979–80) as parodic farce. In the twenty-first century a burgeoning film industry on the moon remakes Hollywood blockbusters in the surreal context of a low-gravity, space-suited environment. In updating a 1980s classic (starring Robert DeNiro, among others) about the successful rescue of the American hostages from Teheran in 1980, the actors wonder if the rescue and Jimmy Carter's subsequent reelection as president were all that important to late-twentieth-century history. One of them is not really "sure that Carter's reelection hinged on [the rescue of] those hostages anyway. He was running against a flake, I can't remember the guy's name, but he was some kind of idiot" (217). Although this sort of irony is familiar to readers of alternative histories, dating back to Murray Leinster's "Sidewise in Time" (1934), Robinson's dig at Ronald Reagan clarifies the political dimensions of his alternative histories. Rather than an after-the-fact analysis that makes Reaganism the irrevocable outcome of ostensibly larger forces at work in American politics and culture, the "real" history that we know becomes contingent: the writing of history forges random and unpredictable events into seemingly inevitable chains of causes and effects. In "Remaking History" the recognition that "actual events [emerge at] the nexus of multiple causal pathways and chance perturbations,"[8] however, does not entail a surrender to a world run by idiots but an opportunity to rethink both the past and present.

In this context, Robinson's linked stories, "The Lucky Strike" (1984) and "A Sensitive Dependence on Initial Conditions" (1991), create alternative histories of the dawn of the atomic age, reimagining the moral and ethical implications of the bombing of Hiroshima and Nagasaki. The earlier story is set in 1945 and begins with the bombardier selected to drop the first atomic bomb on Hiroshima waking from a nightmare about catastrophic destruction. Frank January realizes that "war breeds strange dreams," but his nightmares seem, at once, both inevitable (as his readers know) and tragically unnecessary. They are full of the horrors described by John Hersey in his nonfiction book *Hiroshima* (1946): blinded and faceless victims, a river clogged with corpses, and survivors struck deaf by the atomic blast. Hovering in January's future (and our collective past), the destruction of Hiroshima marks the horrific and logical extreme of technomodern violence. In the days leading up to the bombing run, January is enraged with both President Truman for ordering the strike and "the scientists who had designed the bomb" (81). To cope with his anger and guilt, he imagines alternative strategies—alternative futures—as a way to deal with the moral dilemma he faces. The generals, he daydreams, might arrange a demonstration blast, ordering January and his crew

> to go to Tokyo and drop the bomb in the bay. The Jap War Cabinet had been told to watch this demonstration of the new weapon, and when they saw that fireball boil the bay and bounce into heaven they'd run and sign the surrender papers as fast as they could write, kamikazes or not. They weren't crazy, after all. No need to murder a whole city. (79)

January tries to conjure into being a world of rational self-interest in which neither Americans nor Japanese warmakers are "crazy." This dream world of rational cause and effect—drop the atomic bomb in the harbor and watch Japan's inevitable "surrender"—is not the past that we know and ultimately not a future in which January can believe.

Written in the shadow of the Cold War doctrine of mutually assured destruction, "The Lucky Strike" foregrounds January's fears that endless war and insane violence are encoded in the DNA of the men who command him and the men in his crew. He realizes that "the war would always remain the central experience of their lives—a time when history lay palpable in their hands, when each of their daily acts affected it, when moral issues were simple, and others told them what to do" (83). Their nostalgia for this "central experience" of shaping history, he imagines, would lead a post–World War II military leadership "unconsciously" to "push harder and harder to thrust the world into war again" so that, in their minds, they might return in a future war and "magically be again as they were in the last [war]—young, and free, and happy" (83). In this psychosexual nostalgia for the "good" war of their youth, January imagines a nightmarish future with "more planes, more young crews like [his], flying to Moscow no doubt or to wherever, fireballs in every capital, why not? And to what end? To what end? So that old men could hope to become magically young again. Nothing more sane than that" (83). In the alternative timeline of 1945, January becomes an unwilling symbol of moral resistance to the institutionalized, multigenerational violence of the atomic age—a mindset dissected in Joe Haldeman's sf classic, *The Forever War* (1974). But where Haldeman's characters are caught in the paradoxes of time travel, fighting endlessly, although not mindlessly, against aliens, January takes (in)action by dropping the bomb too late to destroy Hiroshima. Initially, he lies about a supposed malfunction, but when he learns the generals have ordered another bombing run to destroy Nagasaki, he confesses that there "wasn't a malfunction" and justifies his disobedience by arguing that because the Japanese have witnessed the bomb's destructive force, "You don't *need* to do it, it isn't *necessary*" (92). Although he is proved right when the Japanese see the destruction near Hiroshima and the emperor orders his generals to surrender, January is executed for treason without knowing that he has saved countless lives and that his martyrdom sparks a global disarmament movement.

Yet even as January resists the logic of nuclear annihilation, Robinson emphasizes the unpredictable and unknowable consequences of his decision. In "A Sensitive Dependence on Initial Conditions," Robinson explores what he calls his own "second thoughts about the postwar alternative history" (383) described at the end of "The Lucky Strike" by focusing on the complex variables that affect individual actions and their consequences. His story stretches the generic boundaries of alternative history by filtering the politics of historiography—what Jameson calls "the political unconscious"—through the lens of Richard Feynman's "notion of a 'sum over histories'" in quantum theory.[9] As the narrator of "Sensitive Dependence" phrases the problem, Feynman's version of quantum theory "proposes that a particle does not move from point

A to point B by a single path, as in classical mechanics, but rather by every possible path within the wave" (102). This "path integral formalism," filtered, in turn, through the work of the mathematician Roger Penrose, means that "quantum effects in the brain take over" (108) and cycle the mind through an "extraordinarily large" number of "parallel and simultaneous calculations" before reaching a decision:

> And in the act of deciding, the mind attempts the work of the historian: breaking the potential events down into their component parts, enumerating conditions, seeking covering laws that will allow a prediction of what will follow from the variety of possible choices. Alternative futures branch like dendrites away from the present moment, shifting chaotically, pulled this way and that by attractors dimly perceived. . . .
>
> And then, in the myriad clefts of the quantum mind, a mystery: the choice is made. We have to choose, that is life in time. . . . And at the moment [of choice] the great majority of alternatives disappear without trace, leaving us in our asymptotic freedom to act, uncertainly, in time's asymmetrical flow. (108)

Quantum theory in this passage is less a metaphor for history or consciousness than the basis for both. The quest for covering laws, for ways to sift through all possible outcomes while recognizing the epistemological complexities of reaching a decision, is always quixotic. All of us, like January, are thrown back to the realization that initial conditions are never fully known: "The butterfly may be on the wing, it may be crushed underfoot. You are flying toward Hiroshima" (108). Robinson's shift to the second person "you" makes clear the stakes in alternative histories: our "asymptotic freedom" means that we are always condemned to make decisions without the impossible luxury of being able to foretell the consequences of our actions. Reader and character merge less through empathy or identification than in recognizing a shared dilemma: "You are the bombardier. . . . You know what the bomb will do. You do not know what you will do. You have to decide" (107). But, of course, any decision is contingent. The narrator offers us competing future histories that stem from January's decision not to bomb Hiroshima: by sparing the city, through a complex chain of events, the Hiroshima Peace Party bans nuclear weapons, an independent Palestine peacefully emerges, and the world enters a new era of prosperity. Or, the ban on nuclear weapons fails, and, by the mid-twenty-first century, January's decision results in a world that has "very little to distinguish [it] from the one in which January had dropped the bomb": massive social and economic inequality persists, "multinational corporations [rule] the world," and "gigantic sums of money [are] spent on armaments" (106). Robinson's "second thoughts," though, do not result in a dystopian re-writing of "The Lucky Strike" but in a new narrative that encourages readers to rethink what it means to confront alternative futures.

In this respect, Robinson's use of quantum theory to explore the complexities of both ethical decision-making and sociohistorical reality dovetails with the work of, among others, Karen Barad, a theoretical physicist and feminist cultural critic, who argues there is no sharp dividing line, no fundamental distinction, between quantum reality and lived experience: because path-integral formalism means that there is an infinity of all possible outcomes, the "asymptotic freedom" that troubles January is the inescapable condition of existence: we are all flying toward Hiroshima and all condemned to act freely without the ability to peer into alternative futures to foresee the consequences of our actions.[10] "History," says the narrator in "Sensitive Dependence," "is a particle accelerator. Energies are not always normal. We live in a condition of asymptotic freedom, and every history is possible. Each bombardier has to choose" (103). Certainty, it seems, is the first casualty of history.

Such questions of historical truth and individual responsibility are a focal point for Robinson's fiction in the 1980s and figure prominently in *Icehenge* (1984).[11] The novel examines the problems of memory, history, and autobiography in an age when people routinely live to be five hundred years old. It offers three linked narratives that deal with the consequences of a democratic uprising on twenty-third-century Mars: it begins with the story of Emma Weil, a systems ecogeneticist, who returns to devastated colonies on Mars in 2248 rather than join the remnants of the defeated rebels on a desperate voyage to colonize a habitable planet beyond the solar system; the second narrative follows Hjalmar Nederland, an archaeologist, who, in 2547, sets out to prove that the Martian rebellion against colonial authorities was more than anarchic rioting; and the third section, narrated by Nederland's great-grandson, Edmond Doya, centers on his efforts to prove that Icehenge, a Stonehenge-like megalith found on Pluto, is an elaborate hoax and not a monument erected by the rebels on their way out of the solar system.[12] At the beginning of the second section of the novel, Nederland muses that, at "three hundred and ten years old," he has outlived his memory: "most of my life is lost to me, buried in the years. I might as well be a creature of incarnations, moving from life to life, ignorant of my own past" (67). Nederland's sense of alienation extends over centuries and across alien topographies; it reflects a fear of losing his past and his sense of self.[13] His attempts to authenticate Weil's journal—the only firsthand evidence that a social-democratic rebellion did occur on Mars—lead Nederland and later Doya to fantasize about meeting Emma. But in their efforts to assert or debunk the belief that she led an expedition out of the solar system, both men turn the heroine of the novel's first section into an imaginative projection of an ultimate truth or knowledge, either a courageous pioneer or the brains behind an elaborate hoax.

The gap between Nederland's idealized quest for the truth and the realities he confronts focuses on the methodological problems of historical inquiry—an inquiry shaped by the limitations of memory and the experience of trauma. As a child, Nederland had survived the destruction of a rebellious Martian city by colonial authorities intent on bombing the revolution into oblivion. Unlike January, the Mars Development Group suffered no indecision while they were flying toward their own futuristic Hiroshima. Three hundred years after the destruction of New Houston, on an archaeological dig in the destroyed city, Nederland loses his temper when confronted by the bland reassurances of representatives of the oligarchic committee:

> "You may have been in the city [when it was destroyed]," Petrini said reassuringly, "but you can't possibly recall the incident—"
>
> "It wasn't an *incident*. It was war—a massacre, do you understand? They blasted the dome and came down on rocket packs and—and *killed* everybody! When I stood in this street I had an epiphanic recollection—you've all had those, you know what they're like—and I remembered it all. I was young then, but I remember."
>
> "Ridiculous!" Satarwal cried furiously. "Why should we believe somebody so biased—"
>
> "Because *I was there!*" (82)

This exchange pits individual experience—Nederland's "epiphanic" recall of the destruction of New Houston—against the authorized history of willed forgetting and denial. His determination to defend the political values of the revolution commits him to argue that Icehenge is genuine—a monument to the utopian aspirations of the surviving revolutionaries, the first explorers and would-be colonists to leave the solar system in search of a habitable planet. In contrast, Doya, a marginalized part-time academic, seeks to debunk the very politics of memory that motivate his great-grandfather.

Netherland, Doya, and others interpret Icehenge in the contexts of competing versions of the failed Martian rebellion and, by implication, of the historical traumas of the twentieth century. On one level, the novel implies that the monument was built by Emma (who reinvented herself and became a reclusive and mysterious billionaire) to commemorate the rebels and their voyage. But this theory is advanced at the end of the novel as only one of many reconstructions of the past. While Nederland believes that "history is made, because facts are not things" (89), his trust in the self-sufficiency of "things," like the archaeological artifacts he finds beneath the ruins of New Houston, is challenged by the controversies that swirl around Icehenge. He dreams about recovering an authentic history by excavating "one of the lost Martian cities" that he links to "all those cities that had been razed and abandoned by conquerors, Troy, Carthage, Palmyra, Tenochtitlan, [now] all resurrected by scientists and their work" (71). But his project gains a political authenticity only if this otherwise forgotten genocide on Mars can serve as a call to political action in his twenty-sixth-century present. His interpretation of Icehenge as a testament to the legacy that "once all the Martians revolted together, and broke spontaneously toward utopia" anchors his belief that such a revolution could occur again (138). "To love the past," Nederland contends, "is to become fully human" (165), but his love is uncritical and anticipates the questions that Robinson raises in his 1991 short story "Vinland the Dream" about our penchant for romanticizing a past that may well be manufactured.[14]

In this story, the Canadian minister of culture visits a purported Viking site in Newfoundland that may be a hoax. "History," she remarks, "is made of stories people tell. And fictions, dreams, hoaxes—they also are made of stories people tell. True or false, it's the stories that matter" (299). While Nederland's story offers him the hope of recovering his lost past by validating his dreams of Emma Weil, his great-grandson ends *Icehenge* by quoting a sensationalist author who claims that the monument was built by aliens: "In the beginning was the dream, and the work of disenchantment never ends" (262). The danger, at least for Nederland, is that by adding New Houston to his list of lost cities—"Troy, Carthage, Palmyra, Tenochtitlan"—the significance of its destruction becomes a target for "the work of disenchantment." If the quest to recover a lost, utopian truth in history perversely leads to the kind of cynical presentism that Jameson critiques, to give into disenchantment is to risk the future possibility of a collective "[breaking] spontaneously toward utopia." Nederland's view of utopia is undone by his belief in a romanticized revolution that *escapes* rather than *confronts* historical catastrophe. The challenge of Robinson's alternative histories is to transform the work of disenchantment—of critique—in our own time into the sophisticated utopianism that Wark locates in the Mars trilogy: "the invention of a grammar that might come after that of capitalist realism."[15]

THE YEARS OF RICE AND SALT: ALTERNATIVE MODERNITIES

As *Icehenge*, "The Lucky Strike," "Sensitive Dependence," and "Vinland the Dream" suggest, there is always a meta-dimension to Robinson's alternative histories—a self-conscious exploration of what "alternative" timelines mean for individual and political agency, moral decision making, and the contingency of history itself. In his epic alternative history of the last 650 years of civilization, *The Years of Rice and Salt*—arguably the most ambitious alternative history anyone ever has attempted—Robinson rewrites the bedrock values and assumptions of modernity.[16] The premise of this novel is that the Black Death in the 1350s wiped out 99 percent of Europe's population, and the narrative tracks the history of this alternative world from the end of Christendom to the present. Without the Christian West, the Islamic empires of the Middle East and China become the dominant world powers. The ten books of *Years of Rice and Salt* take place at roughly eighty-year intervals in different regions of the world. To unify this vast narrative, Robinson uses the literary strategy of reincarnating the souls of his primary characters—their fundamental psychological and moral constitutions—in new bodies and situations in settings ranging from Ming Dynasty China to the Islamic states of atomic-age Europe.

In brief, Robinson uses Buddhist accounts of reincarnation to solve the narrative problem of continuity across centuries—a problem that he addresses in *Icehenge*, the Mars trilogy, and *2312* with life-extension technologies.

Significantly, however, he treats reincarnation differently from those Western appropriations that translate the complex theological tradition of Tibetan Buddhism into self-help manuals or guides to the psychopharmacology of hallucinogenic enlightenment.[17] Rather than viewing spiritual enlightenment as a be-all and end-all, his characters experience the bardo (the realm of judgment between incarnations) as a point of stock-taking that—like the historical process itself—is open-ended, iterative, and contingent. The reincarnated souls relive, across the vast canvas of history, versions of the dilemma that January faces in "Sensitive Dependence": "You have to decide" (107) is expanded in Years into an alternative to Judeo-Christian views of history without the moral absolutes of salvation or damnation, good or evil, and heaven or hell.[18] In incarnation after incarnation, characters must reimagine what path to take toward a better future in the absence of either "factual" certainty or a traditional sense of novelistic self-knowledge.

Even as essential characteristics of these characters persist through the "intermediate state" of the bardo from one life to the next, reincarnation in Years is less a matter of faith than a "protopolitics" (Years 638) that holds open the promise of moral and socioeconomic progress. The major characters of the jati, or spiritual cohort, are yoked together by ties that extend across different existences and historical identities, even as their genders and biological and social relationships change. In the short interludes between their incarnations, they are judged, individually and collectively, in the chönyi bardo (or fifth of the six bardos), described in most Tibetan texts as the bardo of the luminosity of the true nature.[19] In the first of these interludes, the African-born eunuch, Kyu, killed by a mob in Beijing for his power-brokering at the court of the Yongle Emperor, encounters his longtime friend, Bold, a Mongol warrior who had discovered the ravages of the Black Death in a depopulated Europe and then had been captured by Arab slavers. As Kyu confronts his judgment by the Lord of Death, he realizes that "of all the worlds the bardo was one of the utmost reality" (74) because, as Bold tells him, it is only by working through the consequences of one's actions that one can begin to achieve the clarity needed to overcome the loneliness, egoism, pain, and despair of human existence. This clarity, however, is not a revelation but a journey: "We must try again," Bold insists, "we try and try again, life after life, until we achieve Buddha-wisdom, and are released at last" (76). "Release," in the novel, is the utopian horizon that hovers in view and recedes across centuries and across changing political landscapes. In encouraging us to jettison our default assumptions about Western hegemony, *Years of Rice and Salt* allows us to experience this quest anew.

In their subsequent incarnations, Bold, Kyu, and other major players in the narrative no longer exist as individual "characters" but embody spiritual and psychology types with traits, outlooks, and proclivities that change subtly from incarnation to incarnation. The "B" and "K" characters, in this regard, are defined by their different reactions to "try[ing] again," to navigating a world that is always dragging them back toward disillusionment, selfishness, and the transitory temptations of wealth, pleasure, power, and violence. At the end of the novel, the narrator makes explicit the ways that reincarnation marks, for the souls in the jati, the intersecting spiritual and political dimensions of historical change:

> In every group a Ka and a Ba, . . . Ka always complaining with the kaw of the crow, the cough of the cat, the cry of coyote, kaw, kaw, that fundamental protest; and then Ba always Ba, the banal baa of the water buffalo, the sound of the plow bound to the earth, the bleat of hope and fear, the bone inside. . . . The world was changed by the [Kas], but then the [Bas] had to try to hold it together. . . . All of them together playing their parts, performing their tasks in some dharma they never quite understood. (657)

In turn, these two figures always grow and develop, in complex ways within the dynamics of the jati. They become key figures, along with the "I" character—the scholar, philosopher, or scientist who seeks knowledge to point a way forward toward the good—in the more-than-historical process of helping others toward their "release."

Given its ambitions, *Years of Rice and Salt* is almost as difficult a novel to write about as it was for Robinson to compose. The idea for this novel first began to take shape in the 1970s, and Robinson said that writing it "broke my brain," because world history proved to be "so much bigger than Mars" (2013). In focusing on China, Robinson drew on a range of scholarly works by historians Joseph Needham, Jonathan Spence, Louis Levathes, William McNeil, and André Gunder Frank, as well as the classic Qing novel by Cao Xueqin (1715 or 1724–1764), *The Story of the Stone*, or, as it is sometimes known, the *Dream of the Red Chamber*.[20] In a variety of ways, these sources challenge histories of the modern world that celebrate the "rise of the West" since about 1500 by emphasizing its technoscientific superiority to China, India, and the empires of Central Asia.[21] *Years of Rice and Salt* transforms this revisionist scholarship into an alternative history of a modernity that develops in China, South Asia, and the Islamic empires of Central Asia. In jettisoning narratives of Western triumphalism, Robinson recasts the colonization of the Americas, the scientific revolution, and World Wars I and II (transformed into a seventy-year conflict between the Chinese and Islamic empires) and invites his readers to reconsider their ideas about the inevitable emergence of the Western-dominated world. The novel reframes humanity's quests for social and economic justice, scientific knowledge, and political democracy by recasting Western ideas of utopia in the Buddhist idioms of reincarnation and wisdom. In this respect, *Years of Rice and Salt* may be the first great quasi-prophetic novel of a Chinese-dominated twenty-first century: it envisions a global politics dominated by the economic power of China and the struggles within the Islamic world to modernize.

It is a long and circuitous road, however, through the violence and backsliding of history to Robinson's alternative modernity. In the novel's second book, "The Haj in the Heart," Bistami (the reincarnated B character) travels to al-Andalus (Spain) in the late sixteenth-century (CE), soon after the death of the Ottoman emperor Suleiman the Magnificent (1494–1566).[22] For Bistami, the Sufis of northern Africa offer a way of life that is, "among many other things, a refuge from worldly power" (129)—the authoritarianism that he had been accustomed to in India and Arabia. In their caravan across the Pyrenees, he and the scholar Ibn Ezra (the I character) ponder the role of divine providence in visiting the plague on Europe two centuries earlier and debate whether the plague will return to the "empty land" of al-Andalus. Some traditional scholars declare that the "Christians were exterminated by Allah for their persecution of Muslims, and Jews too" (130). This division of the world into good and evil, the chosen and the sinful, is, in one sense, precisely what Bistami seeks to escape; Ibn Ezra invokes *The Muqaddimah* (the great fourteenth-century history by Ibn Khaldun) to suggest that "plagues result from the corruption of the air caused by overpopulation, and the putrefaction and evil moisture" that foul the lungs and spread the disease (130).[23] He seizes on this explanation because it offers the kind of open-minded, scientific inquiry that he identifies with an expansive understanding of faith and toleration. As in their previous and subsequent incarnations, the B and I characters seek a vocabulary to explain, and rise above, human violence, prejudice, and misery. Rather than political revolution, Ibn Ezra takes seriously the internal transformations—the "haj in the heart"—that result in worldly progress. If, as he suggests, "this world is ours to prove ourselves devout or corrupt," the moral responsibility for both good and evil rests on humans' "free will" (133), on their willingness to move beyond the burdens of history. In this section of the novel, that goal shapes their efforts to rebuild the ruined Christian city of Bordeaux into Baraka, a tolerant, multiethnic haven led as much by the Sultana Katima, the K character, as by her husband.

In Baraka, the Sufis try to fashion "a new world" (150) shaped by Ibn Ezra's toleration and Katima's feminist take on Islamic theology, her strident efforts to "change the ways things worked, the way Islam worked" (155). In reinterpreting the Quran, she argues that "God spoke through Muhammad, and made it clear that women were souls equal to men, to be treated as such. They were given by God many specific rights, in inheritance, divorce, power of choice, power to command their children—given their lives" (155). Katima's feminism represents a challenge to Islamic authorities in the novel and to the default prejudices against Islam that Robinson's readers encounter on a daily basis. Baraka itself is less a religious refuge than an embryonic utopia sustained, for a time, by a collective belief in a better world. Katima's views, however, lead to inevitable conflicts with conservative Islamic authorities, and the town eventually is burned, although Katima and Bistami escape north across the Pyrenees. Once more in the bardo, Bistami tries to convince the skeptical Katima that their "haj in the heart" has led to "genuine progress": "I saw through time, I felt the touch of the eternal. We made a place [Baraka] where people could love the good. Little steps, life after life; and eventually we will be there for good, in the white light" (161). Bistami's claim that it is possible to see "through time" provides a spiritual rationale for ethical and incremental changes that cannot quite be experienced during his incarnations—the "little steps" of the jati—on a rough and tortuous historical road. As Years of Rice and Salt unfolds through time and across continents, the characters must contend with forces—tyranny, economic exploitation, gender inequality, intolerance, and racism—that threaten any sense of "genuine progress," the utopia that paradoxically is both on the verge of coming into being and always receding before them.

One of Robinson's boldest narrative moves in *Years* is to reimagine the colonization of the Americas (Yingzhou, or the "Ocean Continents") by the Chinese. The K character appears in book 3 as Admiral Kheim, chosen by the Wanli emperor (1572–1620) to lead a Chinese invasion of Japan. Becalmed once it reaches the China Sea, the Admiral's fleet drifts helplessly, carried by the northern Pacific current for four and a half months, until it reaches North America. In San Francisco Bay, the Chinese find friendly local peoples, and, as significantly, discover a sparsely populated and rich land radically different from Ming Dynasty China: "a whole country of animals, living together under a silent blue sky—nothing disturbed, the land flourishing on its own" (176). This discovery of this new world disorients the Chinese, especially the admiral, who realizes that

> he had taken China for reality itself. . . . And China meant people. Built up, cultivated, parceled off ha by ha, it was so completely a human world that Kheim had never considered that there might once have been a natural world different to it. But here was natural land, right before his eyes, full as could be with animals of every kind, and obviously very much bigger than Taiwan; bigger than China; bigger than the world he had known before. (176–77)

This barely populated land offers a glimpse of what we might think of as Robinson's "fourth" California—one before large-scale human inhabitation.[24] In this strange land, Kheim and his crew feel displaced in time as well as space: Yingzhou exists outside the bedrock sociopolitical values of Chinese civilization: class hierarchies, property ownership, agricultural production, a market economy, and a colonial tribute system. His disorientation in a land that challenges his understanding of the "completely . . . human world" of Eurasia becomes a refracted image of the reader's cognitive estrangement in encountering a colonial history without European aggression. Yet tragically Yingzhou also exists outside of the biopolitical order of Eurasian disease, and, despite their largely benign intentions, the Chinese soon realize that they have brought the smallpox virus with them. The microbial encounters between the "old" and "new" worlds become a driving force in history that neither the Chinese nor the indigenous tribes can understand or escape.

Leaving California for South America in a futile effort to limit the spread of the disease, the Chinese become reluctant, even inadvertent, agents of colonization. Captured by and then rescued from the Incas, Kheim is forced to resort to violence—gunpowder—to escape from his captors and sail back to China. He is neither Columbus nor Cortez, yet his expedition leaves behind a legacy of disease and death: Butterfly, the child of the California tribe's headman, is taken on board the fleet's flagship, but despite her acclimation to Chinese culture, she dies at sea, a victim of forces that no character fully understands. By rewriting the history of biopolitical contacts among the continents, Robinson recasts histories of colonization to emphasize the ecological and epidemiological consequences of encounters between Eurasia and the Ocean Continents.[25]

As Robinson's alternative history refocuses our understanding of colonization, it also opens a space for imagining modes of indigenous resistance to this biopolitical conquest of the demographic and natural landscapes of the "new" world. In book 5, "Warp and Weft," the nonhierarchical sociopolitical values of the indigenous peoples of the Yingzhou survive contact with Eurasia. The B character, Busho, is a Japanese *ronin*, a wandering samurai, who escapes the Chinese invasion of Japan, and, with other refugees, makes the transpacific journey to the gold fields of Yingzhou. Attacked again by the Chinese, the Japanese refugees are nearly wiped out, but Busho survives and spends years traveling east until he is rescued from the Sioux by warriors of the Hodenosaunee League, the six nations commonly known as the Iroquois.[26] Renamed "Fromwest" by the Hodensaunee, Busho—as a chief of his new clan and an agent of biopolitical technology transfer—works to preserve a culture that "is, in all this world, the best system of rule ever invented by human beings" (326). In contrast to the patriarchal cultures of China and Dar-al-Islam during a period equivalent to our seventeenth century, the Hodenosaunee embody the "genuine progress" of humankind toward justice and equality.

Fromwest's life with the Hodenosaunee allows the reader to imagine an *un*thinking (rather than a *re*thinking) of American history. During his vision quest on psychedelic "shaman's tobacco," Fromwest recalls a previous incarnation and describes how he had brought makeshift techniques of smallpox inoculation to Yingzhou by using the scab from his own infection to promote resistance to the disease among the indigenous peoples he encounters. This vision of his previous life also marks a way forward: Fromwest introduces Asian technologies—metallurgy and gun-making—that allow the Hodenosaunee to defend themselves against the Islamic colony in what we know as New York. Adopting and improving these weapons, the natives of Yingzhou resolve old differences, forge alliances, and unite in holding back Islamic advances from the east and Chinese advances from the west. The network of alliances among native peoples across the Great Lakes and Great Plains regions recasts the history of colonial violence in our world, preserving the values and sociopolitical structures of "the best system of rule ever invented by human beings" into a reimagined modernity. Amid the titanic conflicts between the Islamic and Chinese empires, the Hodenosaunee-led polity in Yingzhou embodies alternative history as a utopian counterweight to the horrors of technomodern warfare. It is significant, in this respect, that the jati's revolt in the bardo (336–40) occurs immediately after this book: waiting to be reincarnated, the characters pretend to swallow the wine of forgetting before they escape from the deity-guards back to the world and into their next incarnations. As a result, they retain dreamlike images of their past existences, and their imperfect but provocative recollections in book 6 serve as promissory metaphors for the collective memories of political-spiritual progress across time.

The spiritual dimensions of "genuine progress" require that traditional distinctions of class, gender, and religious belief become fluid: rather than an individual essence or self, "character" exists dynamically in individual and collective struggles toward politico-spiritual commitment. In late Qing China, the Widow Kang stands up for an itinerant Buddhist monk, Bao-ssu, accused of sorcery, but she cannot save him from being tortured and dying in prison during the soul-stealing scare of the 1760s CE.[27] This incarnation of the K character is among Robinson's most ambitious fictional creations, and the novelist has called the Widow Kang chapter "one of the best I've ever written."[28] Kang Tongbi adheres to Han Chinese rituals for widows, even as she writes poetry that gains her an admiring audience among the literati. Her poem on her husband's death is less an elegy than a meditation on the marginalized status of widows in Chinese culture, exploring the flows of time that subsume the individual:

We met and married; now you are gone.
Ephemeral life is like water flowing;
Suddenly we have been separated by death all these years.
Tears well up as an early autumn begins.
The one who has not yet died is dreamed of
By a distant ghost. (345)

Widow Kang engages in a mode of sanctioned introspection within Qing society yet challenges her socially prescribed alienation as the "one who has not yet died." Her subsequent marriage to a Muslim scholar reunites her with a member of the jati, the I character; Kang and Ibrahim share the half-remembered but powerful dreams of their past incarnations and the bonds that transcend their recollections: "They keep killing us. We keep getting killed" (370). Like Katima in Baraka, she recognizes that historical progress can come about only through and by a commitment to gender equality. Relocating to the frontier outpost of Lanzhou in a predominantly Muslim region of the empire, Kang recognizes that her art gains its power only through its commitment to redefining what women can achieve in patriarchal society, despite social, legal, and psychosexual constraints. The politics of gendered discrimination define the "they" against whom the K and I characters struggle throughout history.

The marriage of Kang Tongbi and Ibrahim brings together powerful ideas as well as exceptional individuals: poetry and history, activism and tolerance, action and knowledge. Ibrahim strives in his scholarly work to celebrate the progressive impulses of history—the moral and sociopolitical resonances of reincarnation—by describing what he terms "the basic underlying identity of the teachings of Islam and Confucius" (381). Yet his years of striving to achieve this synthesis take place in the shadow of Islamic jihads on China's western frontier, and Ibrahim comes to fear "that history itself has no such pattern to it, and that civilizations each create a unique fate that cannot be read into a cyclical pattern" (393). This possibility—of watching humankind backslide into chaos and warfare—echoes throughout Robinson's work: the fear that the limits of perception mark the limits of historical understanding. Ibrahim's intellectual struggle to discern progress amid the chaos of events is interwoven with his wife's, and her verse speaks both to the situation of women in Chinese society and to the significance of what she calls the "years of rice and salt," the imperative to improve individual lives: "Little steps, life after life" (382, 161).

In debating her husband about women's role in Qing society, Kang Tongbi suggests ways to recast spiritual beliefs in terms of the material and utopian values that her earlier incarnation, the Sultana Katima, had articulated in al-Andalus. Across centuries, the K characters envision a world that has moved beyond patriarchal philosophies and justifications. According to Kang, among all the

> religious figures of ancient times, only the Buddha did not claim to be a god, or to be talking to God. The others all claim to be God, or God's son, or to be taking dictation from God. Whereas the Buddha simply said, there is no God. The universe itself is holy, human beings are sacred, all the sentient beings are sacred and can work to be enlightened (398).

She interprets Buddhism in terms of her own experience, emphasizing the teaching "that one must pay attention to daily life, the middle way, and give thanks and worship in each daily action" (398). In reshaping her husband's universal history of civilization, Kang argues that a feminist critique of women's exclusion and dispossession is critical to what Ibrahim identifies as the "four inequalities" of world history: "the subjugation of farmers by warriors and priests . . . institutionalized [in antiquity], a subjugation that has never ended" (407); men's "general domination over women" (407); the extension of this gender inequality to familial relations so that "in each family, the control of legal power resembled the situation at large: the king and his heir dominated the rest" (407); and the "fourth inequality, of race or group, leading to subjugation of the most powerless peoples to slavery" (409). Kang and Ibrahim's critique echoes aspects of Marx and Engels's work in recognizing that these inequalities underwrite economic hierarchies: as "gathered wealth gathered more wealth," Ibrahim reasons, "something new" emerged, "a kind of cumulation of accumulations" (408, 409)—or, as we might say, capitalism. His analysis, however, gains force only in concert with Kang Tongbi's recognition that a grand analytics of history must recognize the ethics and politics of "the middle way."

Some readers of sf, by this point in the novel, may find themselves scratching their heads: rather than victorious Nazis or NASA successfully launching a Mars mission in the 1980s, *Years of Rice and Salt* insists—even more than the Mars trilogy—that readers take seriously the collective project of remaking history as a moral and spiritual imperative. Although one might argue that other of Robinson's novels (the Science in the Capital trilogy, *New York 2140*) speak more directly to contemporary problems of environmental catastrophe, *Years* explores the problems of re-enchanting the world, of imagining how to overcome Ibrahim's four inequalities, by turning alternative history into a mode of spiritual-materialist philosophy—the "bricolage" or "slurry" of Marxism, Buddhism, and environmentalism central to Robinson's fiction.[29]

On the western border of the Qing empire, Ibrahim comes to see Islam as a reaction against the material inequalities of the centuries after the Hegira: "In a world of growing inequalities, Islam spoke of a realm in which all were equal—all equal before God no matter their age, gender, occupation, race, or nationality" (408). In emphasizing this egalitarian tradition within Islam, Robinson asks us to think beyond the secularist tendency to reject religion as false consciousness or myth, or to see in non-Western theodicies a "primitive," if somehow "authentic" logic of inclusivity, rather than complex systems of belief.[30] "The Indian and Chinese description of the afterlife," Ibrahim contends, with its

> system of the six lokas or realms of reality—the devas, asuras, humans, beasts, pretas, and inhabitants of hell—is in fact a metaphorical but precise description of this world and the inequalities that exist in it, with the devas sitting in luxury and judgment on the rest, the asuras fighting to keep the devas in their high position, the humans getting by as humans do, the beasts laboring as beasts do, the homeless preta suffering in fear at the edge of hell, and the inhabitants of hell enslaved to pure immiseration. (411)

Ibrahim's analysis of history rests on this mirroring of political realities in theological doctrine—this "metaphorical but precise description" of spiritual hierarchies and material inequalities. In rejecting the idea (prominent in most treatments of the European Enlightenment) that secularization goes hand in hand with modernity, Ibrahim argues that divorcing spiritual growth from economic thought ensures that humanity "remain[s] stuck in some kind of prehistory, unworthy of [its] great spirit":

> All the inequalities must end; all the surplus wealth must be equitably distributed. Until then we are still only some kind of gibbering monkey, and humanity, as we usually like to think of it, does not yet exist. (411)

Utopian progress, as McKenzie Wark suggests, becomes the struggle to get to a point where utopian action can begin.[31] In Ibrahim's view, the yet-to-be history of humanity can emerge only in and through the (future, utopian) union of Islamic and Buddhist traditions. In the meantime, the "great spirit" of progress finds expression only in protest and art. For Robinson, the "little steps" toward utopia require a powerful analytics of our historical situation and a recognition of the power of alternative histories to encourage us to imagine how utopian change might occur.

In this respect, the Widow Kang section decouples egalitarian and feminist sociopolitical views from traditional narratives about Western ideas of progress from the Renaissance, through the Enlightenment, to modernity. This cognitive estrangement, Robinson implies, is critical to our ability to rethink history in universal but nonreductive terms. Kang's final poem captures the implications of this recognition that history can begin only after "all inequalities . . . end":

> Near the end of this existence
> Something like anger fills my breast;
> A tiger: next time I will hitch it
> To my chariot. Then watch me fly. (412)

These lines suggest how the trope of reincarnation describes an ideal of moral and political resilience. Throughout her incarnations, the K character (who had been a tiger) refuses to let go of her commitments to justice, equality, and collective responsibility, even when facing death. Kang's art defines the event horizon of political and ethical consciousness in Qing China; yet the recognition that her struggle will go on for "many generations" turns her belief in her incarnations-to-come—"next time"—into an apt metaphor for the possible futures that alternative history explores.

This looking forward to a "next time" resonates throughout the novel, reminding us that progress remains incremental and justice elusive. In seventeenth-century Samarqand (book 4), Iwang, a Tibetan lens grinder, and Khalid, a disgraced alchemist, become the lynchpins of the scientific revolution. After Khalid has his hand chopped off for faking the alchemical transmutation of lead into gold, Iwang dispels his friend's deep depression by convincing him that they can embark on a program of experimentation that "start[s] small": "We need to isolate one set of actions that we can see and control, and then study that, and see if we can understand it" (225). This intimation of the inductive method leads them to embark on a parodically fast unfolding of early modern science. The two ask the questions, conduct the experiments, and come to the conclusions that define the scientific revolution ushered in by Galileo, Robert Boyle, and Isaac Newton, among others. After inventing the telescope, Iwang and Khalid discover Jupiter's moons, develop the calculus, describe the inverse square law of gravitational attraction, and, ominously, to keep their experiments funded, improve munitions, including poison gas shells, for the bored and indifferent khan, Sayyed Abdul Aziz. Before succumbing to the plague at the end of book 4, Iwang challenges Khalid to seek the scientific knowledge that is the necessary—but hardly sufficient—condition to nudge humankind toward a more just and equitable future. Their story marks an important juncture in Robinson's work—a turn to the history of science, as in *Galileo's Dream*, that recasts technoscientific progress as utopian politics.

Two centuries later in book 7, the Kerala of Travancore unites the Hindus, Buddhists, and Sikhs in South Asia and defeats the Mughal, Safavid, and Ottoman Empires by using steamships, modern canons, and air transport against his enemies' traditional weapons. In ushering in a great age of industrialization, the Kerala establishes friendly relations with the Hodenosaunee League in North America, and his military victories and international alliances serve what he sees as a larger revolution, at once material and political. Like his earlier incarnation, the Sultana in book 2, he articulates a utopian vision of agricultural productivity and industrial progress that will lead to "plenty for all":

There will be no more empires or kingdoms, no more caliphs, sultans, emirs, khans, or zamindars, no more kings or queens or princes, no more qadis or mullahs or ulema, no more slavery and no more usury, no more property and no more taxes, no more rich and no more poor, no killing or maiming or torture or execution, no more jailers and no more prisoners, no more generals, soldiers, armies or navies, no more patriarchy, no more clans, no more caste, no more hunger, no more suffering than what life brings us for being born and having to die. (451)

The modernization of Travancore intensifies the rhetoric of utopian faith that has been the jati's quest and burden since the efforts of the Sultana and Bismati in al-Andalus. Rather than little steps, the Kerala describes progress in the grand rhetoric of other of Robinson's visionaries, like Arkady in *Red Mars*, for whom scientific discovery and technological progress stimulate the freedom to resist locally and dream globally. Yet as the Kerala's insistent repetition of "no more" suggests, his vision works only as a *negation* of the fallen conditions of injustice and repression that have preoccupied and motivated the K character throughout her or his incarnations: for the time being, the Widow Kang's "middle way," the "years of rice and salt," gives way to a vision of utopia as a decisive elimination of the "four inequalities" that drive history. But the Kerala's Travancore suffers the fate of most utopias: his assassination at the end of book 7 marks a return to the violence and repression that characterize book 8, "War of the Asuras," and defers into the future the justice and egalitarianism that the K character, in all her manifestations, seeks.

The Age of Progress is followed by the Long War that pits the Chinese empire against the united Dar-al-Islam, with the Travancori in South Asia and Hodenosaunee League fighting on the side of Chinese. The section describes in harrowing detail the nightmarish consequences of decades of trench warfare on the landscape near the Gansu Pass, where, almost two centuries earlier, Kang Tongbi and Ibrahim had sought to reconcile Buddhist and Islamic traditions: "What remained was a kind of disordered black ocean, ringed and ridged and cratered. . . . Land pulverized to bedrock . . . a perfect ideograph of the long war" (478). This vision of apocalyptic destruction dilates time so that history takes on the hallucinatory quality of a nightmare as though the alien landscapes of the Mars trilogy had been transported into an alternative history of the early and mid-twentieth century. After five years in this hellish existence amid scenes of devastation and hopeless excursions against the Islamic trenches a few miles away, the B character, Bai, can say only that the war "has to end someday. . . . Otherwise it will never end" (484). But K, reincarnated as Kuo, laughs that "this is not a logical war. This is the end that will never end" (484). Immediately before he is killed by a Muslim shell,

Kuo recognizes that the illogic has taken on a life of its own: "It's been forty years," he says, "since anyone on Earth has been sane" (486). The differences that the I character has sought to bridge in earlier incarnations—Ibn Ezra, Iwang, Ibrahim—return with an insane vengeance because progress is always contingent, and the forces of repression and violence are never truly defeated.

Yet even in this insanity of endless war, Iwa, the I character, voices yet again the values that had motivated him in his incarnations as Iwang and Ibrahim and strives to define what is at stake for the Chinese in fighting for "clarity, or whatever else it was that was the opposite of religion": an "attention to the real world, a kind of natural study" that ultimately "placed the greatest value on compassion, created by the enlightened understanding, created by the study of what was there in the world" (496). This is less an authorial endorsement of Chinese values than a reminder of the need to resist a technomodernist, cynical despair and to maintain a handhold on utopia amid a history of militarized insanity. The soul of Kuo returns to try to convince Bai that the hell of modern warfare *is* the bardo, to remind him of their previous lives, and to warn him that "dharma still commands right action . . . in the hope of small advances upward. . . . The whole world will have to be rebuilt" (501–2). After the Chinese finally win the war, Iwa joins Bai and a group of Indian soldiers in searching for fragments of the Bodhi Tree, the sacred fig tree under which the Buddha is said to have attained enlightenment. Rather than an escape to another life through reincarnation, Iwa reiterates one of the fundamental lessons of Buddhist thought: "[S]uffering is real. You have to face it, live with it. There is no escape" (503). Utopia is neither redemption nor transcendence but living on in and through the trauma of history. The scale of this rebuilding in the last sections of *Years of Rice and Salt* is brought home by the destruction of Islamic cities by the atom bombs that mark the end of the Long War: dozens of Hiroshimas, an alternative vision of the postapocalyptic world that we see in *The Wild Shore*.

The aftermath of the Long War underscores the prominence of women throughout the novel. Near the end of the novel, Zhu (the Z character), now age ninety, reflects on the history she has witnessed during what corresponds to our twentieth century: "[S]hould we describe history as being the story of women wresting back the political power they lost with the introduction of agriculture and the creation of surplus wealth? Would the gradual and unfinished defeat of patriarchy be the larger story of history?" (634). This long view of history suggests why Robinson considers *Years of Rice and Salt* more ambitious, "so much bigger," than the Mars trilogy, and why his concerns in this work resonate across his other novels. In charting the efforts of the K, I, and B characters to put the destruction wrought by the Long War into context, the final sections of the novel explore the survival of the utopian impulse in and through apocalyptic devastation, recalling the efforts of other of Robinson's activist-historians, like Nederland in *Icehenge*.[32] But in Islamic Nsara (on the Atlantic coast of France) after the war, the moral and scientific projects of knowledge-making falls to three women—the scientist Idelba, her niece Budur, and Budur's teacher, Kirana, who takes up the critique of Ibrahim's "four inequalities" by emphasizing how the Koran's commitment to gender equality has been corrupted by "generations of patriarchal clerics" inventing "falsified authorities" and "rebuilding an unjust tyranny" (524). Kirana attributes the ultimate defeat of Dar-al-Islam in the Long War to the fact that China and Travancore recognized women's rights and drew on their abilities to overcome a more conservative enemy. Gathering around her Islamic veterans of the Long War and women chafing under the stultifying rule of male clerics, she and the "old soldier," Naser Shah, envision strengthening "the most Buddhist parts of Islam" by retaining "the best of the old to make a new way, better than before" (537). In their minds (anticipating the intertwining of Buddhism and science in the Science in the Capital trilogy), an Islam of "mercy and compassion"—of tolerance and equality—is fundamental to the investigation of world history and their own political situation. Budur, who escapes from her family's harem to follow her aunt Idelba to Nsara, brings together feminist and scientific traditions in order to promote the new science of archaeology as a force for making the understanding of the past a means to articulate "a sense of the future" (576). This future—a counterstrike against the forces of political and religious oppression—is ultimately brought about by peaceful protests against the corrupt Nsaran regime and a (mostly) bloodless revolution aided by the appearance in the harbor of the Hodenosaunee fleet.

In their final incarnation (a half-century after the end of the Long War), the Chinese revolutionary leader Kung is assassinated for his efforts to reform a corrupt, militaristic regime. His final words to his disciple Bao, "Go on" (625), might be the mantra for all of Robinson's utopianists, who persist, even in the face of death, precisely because they come to recognize that the "pulse of history's long duration was much slower than an individual's time" (626). Throughout his life, Bao strives to "go on," working for the "League of All Peoples" in the "Agency for Harmony with Nature" in Pyinkayaing [Burma], then, after he retires to Yingzhou, continuing to fight to reduce disparities in wealth and status and mitigate ecological devastation. In this incarnation, he confronts the dilemmas that, as we will see, characters face in Robinson's solar system novels, alternative futures in which life-extension treatments allow people, like Nederland, to outlive their memories. At seventy, Bao feels that "he could remember a great many things that had happened—it was the feeling for these things that was gone away, leached out by the years. They were as if they had happened to someone else. As if they had been previous incarnations" (632). Experience passes into history, and, as Zhu suggests, the only hope for the future is to reimagine history as *always* alternative—always open to the intersections of "residual elements of past cultures" and "emergent elements" that, in their interference patterns, might "suggest ways forward" (640). As *Years* comes to its close in an alternative version of 2002, utopia remains a way rather than a destination. During his last conversations with Zhu about "What Remains to Be Explained," Bao jots down a wide range of questions about possible alternative histories of his world's past and more general queries about human existence: "How can we give to our children and the generations following a world restored to health?" (642). His own actions serve as a response, not quite an answer, to this question. Like Nirgal in *Blue Mars*, Bao, "crisscrosse[s] the world, meeting and talking to people, helping to put certain strands into place, thickening the warp and weft of treatises and agreements by which all peoples on the planet were tied together" (642). Whether wandering into plague-ravaged Europe circa 1352 CE or teaching in Yingzhou more than six centuries later, the B character recognizes that the quest for a just future never ends.

SHAMAN: HISTORY BEFORE HISTORY

If *Years of Rice and Salt* marks a milestone in the genre of alternative history, *Shaman* pushes the boundaries of sf from a different direction. *Years* invites comparisons between what we read in the novel and what we know about world history: the more one has read, the more rewarding the novel is likely to be. In *Shaman*, however, history no longer exists as a narrative that explains the past, real or imagined, in order to serve the needs of the present. Instead, we are immersed in a history *before* history—before writing, before agriculture, before sophisticated technologies of calculation, and before socioeconomic hierarchies. The novel is set during the ice age that enveloped much of the northern hemisphere between thirty thousand and forty thousand years ago, and we encounter this ice-age world through the eyes of the individuals and clans responsible for creating the Chauvet cave paintings in Southern France during that period.[33] The narrative enriches our senses of individual and social psychology by reimagining the ways that memory, art, and craft knowledges shape experience. Instead of lives extended by the longevity treatments of the Mars trilogy or the "protopolitics" of reincarnation, *Shaman* compresses human existence to the short lifespans, around "two twenties," of a prehistorical tribe surviving the harsh conditions of one of the last great ice ages. In emphasizing the complexity and sophistication of a prehistoric socio-climatological world, Robinson explores in *Shaman* the possibilities—sociocultural and psychological—of a steady-state culture that sees its environment as the natural, cyclical, and timeless state of the world.[34] Even as parts of the novel recall the polar scenes in *Antarctica* and *Fifty Degrees Below*, *Shaman*'s prehistoric societies exist without the framing narratives of a seemingly apocalyptic environmental crisis and without the utopian striving by "little steps" toward the good. Instead, the novel unwrites the values and assumptions that we know as history.

The narrative follows the hero's life for a few years after his initiation ritual at age twelve. Loon is the reluctant heir-apparent to the tribe's shaman, Thorn, a role forced on him after the death of his father. Loon and thirty or so other members of his pack exist within a culture that survives by adapting, amid a host of challenges, to the seasonal rhythms of southern Europe in an age of mammoths, aurochs, and saber-tooth tigers. The problems of getting, preparing, and storing food define the complex social structures of the group. Eating organizes culture. Schist, the tribe's chief,

> was always talking food: cooking and fishing with Thunder [his wife] and the women, hunting and trapping with the men. He had dug their storage pits himself, and was always lining them with new things. He spoke with people from

other packs to see what they knew. He and Thorn had worked out an accounting system . . . using clean lengths of driftwood to notch marks for their pokes of animal fat, bags of nuts, dried salmon steaks, smoked caribou steaks; everything they gathered to eat in the cold months was stored and marked down. He knew how much every person in the pack would eat, based on the previous winter's markings and adjusted by everyone's summer health, by how much fat they had put on, and so on. He knew better than you how hungry you would be. (72)

Schist's methods of accounting, calculating, and remembering suggest what is possible—even essential—for a culture with neither alphanumeric writing nor agriculture. The arts of prediction and probability—the notches on drift-wood—mark Schist's knowledge of bioclimatology: "He knew better than you how hungry you would be." In an ice-age environment, hunting, scavenging, and gathering are, at once, strategies, crafts, and modes of technoscientific knowledge that structure the life-or-death calculus of food acquisition and storage. The novel is filled with scenes of hunting and trapping, and the pack's social organization is structured by the craft knowledges centered on the problems of securing, preserving, storing, and rationing the food they need to accumulate before the onset of the "hungry months" of late winter and early spring. Counting is the bioclimatological offspring of scarcity.

As a shaman-in-training, Loon must absorb the lessons taught by Thorn and the herbalist Heather, but he lives in a world without hierarchy and without metaphysics. Thorn is not a spiritual leader but a walking repository of knowledge that Loon must learn by listening, watching, memorizing, and reinterpreting. Within this prehistoric culture, Robinson explores the complex conflicts and synergies between different modes of knowledge that character-ize his fiction: Loon is caught between Thorn's fascination with artistic and philosophical questions and Heather's experimental and craft knowledges. Except for Thorn's cave painting, Loon is more interested in "what Heather wanted him to know": "He could see her things, touch them, put them cau-tiously to his tongue. Thorn on the other hand was always going off into the realm of numbers, stories, poems, songs, and all of it to be memorized, sometimes word for word. Words words words!" (194). While Heather shares the outlook of Robinson's scientists, Thorn is obsessed with preserving knowl-edge beyond individual lifetimes, and, in his world, the problem of historical memory is also the problem of narrative. If the genre of alternative history challenges our notions of causality and historical inevitability, Thorn wants to link experience across time—in "numbers, stories, poems, songs"—so that history can come into being.

History in *Shaman* emerges, then, like experimental knowledge, in the patchwork strategies of individuals that must be passed down through generations. Like Galileo and Sax Russell in the Mars trilogy, Heather experiments, observes, and tries again, but her trials rely on complex webs of interspecies identification that invert modern notions of technoscience as a form of mastery over the natural world.

> Heather used her cat as an herb tester. She would leave some meats the cat liked most with a sprig of a strange new plant in it, and when the cat ate it Heather would watch to see what happened. She didn't think any plant would kill the cat, because if it did not agree with the little beast it would quickly cough it back up.
>
> When Heather saw this happen, she would shoo the cat away and go to the vomit and inspect it closely, even take dabs of it between finger and thumb and taste it with her tongue.
>
> Now as she did this Loon said, —Heather, you're eating cat vomit.
>
> —So what? I can taste tastes that are like other tastes I know. It gives me ideas how this flower might be put to use.
>
> —What if it kills you?
>
> —Cats have very delicate stomachs. It won't kill me. (126–27)

For Heather, the inductive method of herb-testing turns the cat into a collaborator rather than an experimental subject. Rather than erecting boundaries between the human and nonhuman world, this exchange makes the vomiting cat an actor in a sophisticated mode of synergistic knowledge production. Throughout the novel, Loon's training as a shaman is shaped by a range of complicated and symbiotic relationships with the animals his pack hunts and that he eventually represents on the walls of the Chauvet cave. In some respects, this ur-relationship of human and animals serves as the half-glimpsed ideal behind the efforts of Swan and Amelia Black to re-wild the earth in the futures that Robinson depicts in *2312* and *New York 2140*.

Heather's cat embodies a set of interspecies relationships in an environment where distinctions between wild and domesticated animals do not exist.

In fact, the idea of domestication is only beginning to be realized by the jende, a tribe who live on the frigid shores of the Atlantic. While the jende use captive, semi-domesticated wolves to hunt, Loon describes the canine-human relationship in terms of social and ecological reciprocity:

> Wolves and humans were cousins, just like bears and porcupines, or beavers and muskrats. Wolves had taught people to hunt and to talk. They were still the better singers by far, and hunters too for that matter. What people had taught wolves in return was a matter of dispute, and depended on what stories were told. How to be friends? How to double-cross and backstab? The stories were divided on this. (140–41)

Humans, in effect, are the butt of the joke in collective "stories" that offer alternative views of humankind's effects on the environment. Like Heather's experimental cat, Loon's wolves share a familial relationship with humans as teachers, rivals, and "singers," and their perceived negative qualities—their very wildness—seem lessons they have absorbed from humans. In complex ways, then, the wolves are, in Donna Haraway's sense, a companion species, although the nature of such companionship is redefined in the novel: in a pre-agricultural society without domesticated livestock and without the economies of land ownership and grain storage, animals exist as "cousins" instead of being classified as property or threat.[35] Cats and wolves, in this regard, help to define oral and folk knowledges of science, climatological adaptation, and collective existence without the soul-trying struggle toward the good that Robinson describes in *Years of Rice and Salt*.

Shaman, in short, stands history-as-progress on its head. Loon and his pack confront the challenges of negotiating an unrecognized utopia, and their way of life resists the entry into a nascent, "civilized" history that the jende—with their captured slaves, semi-domesticated wolves, and sophisticated methods for preserving frozen fish and bags of seal fat—embody. Captured by these "northers" on his quest to free his wife, Elga, Loon is "startled by the sight of [the jende's stored food that] would feed the camp's people for two or even three winters. He had never seen anything like it. These people were rich" (255–56). The trade-off for this food-wealth is a society hardening into the hierarchies of class, gender, species, and tribal differences. In contrast to the loosely matriarchal social structures that Loon knows from living in a pack without a headman, the jende anticipate the social stratification to come millennia in the future.

To live before history, *Shaman* suggests, is to navigate different coordinates of time and space. The traveler Pippiloette entertains Loon's pack with a song about a man he encountered who decided to walk east as far as he could to see how big the world was. After twelve years, the man returns, having realized that the "world was just too big" (215). When Pippiloette asks the traveler, "What will you do, now that you're back?" the man responds, "[T]o tell the truth, I'm thinking I may take off east again" (215). These long-distance journeys into unknown territory are, of course, a staple of science fiction and figure prominently in Robinson's work, notably in the travels of John Boone and Nirgal across the changing planetscape of Mars. Pippiloette's traveler, however, is not on a quest for knowledge; he is not trying to escape, like Genly Ai and Estraven fleeing across Winter in Le Guin's *The Left Hand of Darkness* (1969); and he is not venturing into unknown worlds like science-fiction heroes and heroines have done since Jules Verne's *Journey to the Center of the Earth* (1864). Instead, the man who walks east travels beyond the local, embodied knowledges of the members of the Chauvet pack and their neighbors. As the languages of the peoples to the east become unintelligible, as the topography and climate grow strange, the traveler reaches the limits of what one individual can comprehend. He walks off the edge of the cognitive maps of experience and memory. What he brings back, according to Pippiloette, is the realization that knowledge is a form of multilayered dislocation.

Throughout the novel, the temporal and geospatial coordinates that locate us within history and civilization disappear into Robinson's imagining of preliterate modes of memory and knowledge. In a key passage, Thorn recalls the climatological crisis—"the ten years' winter"—that his pack barely survived. His song turns art into a life-or-death vehicle for fostering collective memory and social identity. As a record of climatological anomalies, such artful knowledge prepares his listeners to recognize future crises by etching into their collective memories the strategies that might allow them to survive future crises:

. . . nothing but winter, yes winter for TEN LONG YEARS.
And if it were not for the great salt sea
Everybody everywhere would have died and been dead . . .

We ate what lived through ten years of winter,
Meaning whelks and clams and mussels and sea snails,
Meaning seaweed and sandcrabs and limpets and eels.
We ate fish when we could catch them,
We ate shit when we couldn't. (85–86)

The memories that fade over the centuries in Robinson's future histories are preserved by the shaman's art. Thorn's song challenges idealized notions of hunting and gathering—Stone Age peoples living in harmony with or sustainably in nature—by voicing the struggles and uncertainties that mark pre-agricultural existence: "We ate shit." Millennia removed from the deteriorating ecologies on the spaceship in *Aurora*, Thorn's history, as collective memory and art, defines a horizon of past knowledge and a mode of technoscientific disaster preparedness: forget hunting or gathering, head to "the great salt sea." In deromanticizing the past, Robinson explores the experiential and psychic lives of the Chauvet cave painters by reimagining their knowledge practices as art for survival's sake.

At the annual gathering the packs call "eight by eight" (the eighth day of the eighth month), Thorn joins shamans from other packs for their "corroborees"—part social gathering, with fermented liquors and psychoactive mushrooms, and part scientific exchange devoted to trying to reconcile the vagaries of the lunar and solar years by comparing notations in their notched sticks. In addition to strategies for marking time, they make elaborate topographical maps of their region of the Urdrecha (modern day Ardeche in France) in sand. Once these maps are completed, debated, and modified they are swept away. Their notched sticks and maps are experiential, not representational, embodying different relations to time and topography. Time in *Shaman* is always embodied time, and it is experienced, in part, through the prosthetic memories of craft, art, and song. But the friendly communications and nonhierarchical affiliations among packs are threatened by the intrusion of newfangled assumptions about violence and ownership: the jende's kidnapping of Elga. But even that conflict ultimately is resolved by Loon's designing and making new snowshoes to trade to the wood-poor jende as compensation for his having rescued her from captivity. This peaceful resolution hinges on a complex set of horizontal, rather than hierarchical, relations among packs, and it also underscores the significance of techno-climatological adaptation to the environment: better snowshoes are more important than additional forced labor. While Loon's recognition that his improved snowshoes will be valuable for the "northers," his innovation remains a form of craft knowledge rather than a step in a grander narrative of progress.

If Loon and his pack have never been modern, they also have never been political, and Robinson asks his readers to consider what it would mean to live in a utopian topography cut free—temporally and conceptually—from history. Loon understands time as successive, but describes it as mineralogical rather than organic:

> The world would scrape [Loon] down just like he scraped this chunk of rock. It would go on until Thorn died, and then the pile of granules that was Loon would replace him, and do all the things Thorn had done, including scraping down some apprentice of his own; then he would die, and the apprentice would go on and do it to his apprentice, and on and on and on and on and on and on and on and on and on and on and on it would go, the earthblood and their own blood ground up together under the sun. (86)

For Loon, time is neither progressive nor cyclical: he does not complain about a history to come or an alternative that could be; instead, he sees himself embedded in a shamanic succession without larger contexts or consequences. Late in the novel, nearing his death, Thorn voices his near-despair at the prospect of dying when he is "only two twenties old" (417). In insisting that Loon pass on his knowledge, the dying shaman laments that after Heather, apparently near eighty, is gone, there will be no one left in the pack "old enough to know everything you need to know" (419). This knowledge is at once practical and extraordinarily fragile: "There are no secrets, there is no mystery," says Thorn. "It's all right there in front of us. You have to have enough food to get through the winter and spring. That's what it all comes down to" (418–19). Art and science, knowledge and experience. In some ways, Thorn gives voice to a form of presentness that harks back to hard-won insights that Bao recognizes at the end of *Years of Rice and Salt*. Science—whether before history or progressing asymptotically toward a utopia at the "end" of history—is a web of strategies that preserve, across generations, the realization that "it's all right there in front of us."

At the same time, though, Thorn knows that collective knowledge is "fragile. . . . It's gone every time we forget. Then someone has to learn it all over again" (419). Art and song, like science, are his only bulwarks against the forgetting that confronts the major characters in *Years of Rice and Salt*, who, as they re-gather in the bardo between incarnations, struggle to understand what they have learned and what can be preserved across history. Thorn recognizes that knowledge is a mode of collective responsibility, yet he fears that the craft knowledge accumulated during his forty years is "going to be lost" (420) as soon as he dies. If Heather's experimental method and herbal knowledge can be passed on to Loon, Thorn's quest to understand the time represented by the notches in his year-stick speaks to the dreams of a utopian, if world-bound, knowledge: "I wanted to know everything," he tells Loon. "I remembered every single word I ever heard, every single moment of my life, right up to a few years ago. I talked to every person in this whole part of the world, and remembered everything they said. What's going to become of all that?" (419). Loon's response suggests that at age fifteen or so he is indeed ready to become a shaman: "We'll do what we can" (420). This quest for a knowledge of "everything," even in a preliterate world, resonates with Robinson's probing of epistemology in other novels, from the Mars trilogy to *Aurora*. But in *Shaman* the narrative resolution—if not the philosophical "answer"—to Thorn's question awaits Loon during his three days of painting in the Chauvet cave.

Working without regard to day or night, Loon adds to the remarkable art work of the cave and "signs" it with multiple palm prints, with his crooked finger, on the walls. "Dropped into the lonely world of the shaman, deep into dreams and visions, always alone, even when in the pack" (435), he becomes both the medium for cultural succession—the transmission of a visionary, aesthetic knowledge—and an existential figure seemingly outside of time: the artist who reimagines his or her world. Loon reworks and extends the paintings left by Thorn and his predecessors, providing a way to think beyond the "on and on and on" of a successive time without history. His art ensures that the embodied experience of history can be transmitted into and by a visionary act. In the world of dreams and visions, Loon's art—his contributions to the collective pictorial memories of the pack's ongoing present—redefines time itself.

In going back before history in *Shaman*, Robinson provides an alternative to a world of science and science fiction: our contemporary culture is obsessed by trying to account for, and profit from, what will happen next: the latest investment strategies for the intertidal in *New York 2140*, hedge fund managers' indices, and the futures market in commodities, weather forecasting, and climatic change. If his alternative histories remind us how large the world is and how deep time has been, Robinson's three trilogies and his future histories of solar system exploration and settlement remind us how profound questions have resonated across human experience. Thorn's question—"What's going to become of all that?"—echoes throughout his fiction and asks his readers to imagine what is going to become of us when we must confront the near- and long-term consequences of socioeconomic inequality, sexual repression, and political deadlock.

CHAPTER 2

THREE FUTURES FOR CALIFORNIA:
THE ORANGE COUNTY TRILOGY

Robinson wrote the Orange County or Three Californias trilogy over the course of almost a decade as he finished his PhD, spent two years in Switzerland, where his wife held a postdoctoral fellowship, and taught as an instructor at the University of California, Davis. The three novels—the postapocalyptic *The Wild Shore* (1984), the dystopian *The Gold Coast* (1988), and the utopian *Pacific Edge* (1990)—established Robinson as a major voice in twentieth-century science fiction.[1] Linked by the single figure of Tom Barnard, a lawyer born in the early 1980s, the novels offer radically different histories of our own era, and, from the reader's perspective in Ronald Reagan's America, radically different visions of the future. By having Tom, roughly eighty years old in each of the novels, retell the history of the early twenty-first century to his grandchildren's generation, the trilogy explores the potential consequences of the political, social, and economic problems of the late twentieth century. In this respect, each novel asks us to imagine two future eras: the early 2000s (when Tom is a young man), and the more distant future in the mid-twenty-first century (2047 in *The Wild Shore*, 2065 in *Pacific Edge*) when his readers will be either as old as Tom or themselves a part of history. All of these future histories of Southern California are carved into and cemented onto the land. The settings for the novels situate readers in landscapes radically transformed from the freeways and strip malls of 1980s Orange County: the built environment has been left in rubble by a nuclear attack in *The Wild Shore*; the endless cityscape has metastasized into a nightmarish "condomundo" in *The Gold Coast*; and the concrete, asphalt, and electrical systems of late capitalist California have been recycled and repurposed in *Pacific Edge* to serve a utopian society materially and politically transformed by a collective commitment to social, economic, and environmental justice.

It is telling, then, that each of the novels begins with an archaeological expedition through the ruins of late-twentieth-century California. In *The Wild Shore*, Henry Fletcher and his friends head north from their home in San Onofre (the hills near Camp Pendleton) to scavenge silver from the gilt handles of coffins in the graveyards located "in the ruins of Orange County" (WS, 6). *The Gold Coast* begins with Jim McPherson and his friends excavating the ruins of the El Modena Elementary School, built in 1905 and "razed in the 1960s" (GC, 4), buried beneath layers of concrete. Jim's desire "to see, to touch, to *fondle* some relic of the past" (4) marks his sense of alienation from "condomundo" (4) and motivates his own narrative (told in short interludes between the chapters) of California's transformation, over eons, from a pristine wilderness to the "autopia" of the mid-twenty-first century.[2] This opening scene—literally digging up the past—resonates throughout *The Gold Coast*: the archaeological strata of Southern California's history testify to the political and economic stratification that marks a world of triple-decker highways crisscrossing above the tiny, cramped apartments of Orange County. If Jim's vision of his world is defined by "the layers of OC's lighting, decade on decade, generation on generation" (GC, 3), the transformation of Kevin Claiborne's environment in *Pacific Edge* turns the excavation of the concreted past into a socioeconomic and ecological restoration project: digging up—and recycling—the detritus that produced these "layers of . . . light." The building materials of Kevin's utopia are salvaged from "four-lane asphalt streets, white concrete curbs, big asphalt parking lots and gas stations"; they include, says his friend Gabriela, "a traffic light box," "telephone lines, power cables, gas mains, PVC tubing, the traffic light network—and . . . another gas station tank" (*PE*, 2). In unearthing and recycling the infrastructure of late-twentieth-century California, the utopianists in *Pacific Edge* recognize that a sustainable society depends on both acknowledging the limits of its resources—particularly water and undeveloped land—and holding fast against those willing to compromise with the reemergent forces of capitalist development. In each novel, then, digging up the past introduces us to the lives, values, and worldviews of their heroes.

By looking backward from the future to the history of the 1980s, the trilogy encourages its readers to recognize that their own present—the brutal inequalities and military threats of the Cold War era—is haunted by these different visionary futures. As Christopher Woodward suggests, "When we contemplate ruins, we contemplate our own future," and Robinson's three Californias, in different ways, remind us that figuratively we all are flying toward Hiroshima, forced to confront history-altering political and moral decisions.[3] Each novel, as Tom Moylan astutely argues, "gives us a self-reflexive meditation on its own conditions of production," particularly in the ways that the narratives written by Henry in *The Wild Shore*, Jim in *The Gold Coast*, and Tom in *Pacific Edge* rework the generic traditions of science fiction.[4] These narratives of apocalyptic destruction, capitalism run wild, and socioecological restoration invite readers to imagine futures radically different from the "realist" presumptions that sociopolitical, ecological, and economic conditions will persist, more or less as they are, into the future.

In its socioecological commitments, Robinson's trilogy distances itself from the quasi-hallucinogenic technofutures of 1980s cyberpunk that defined the fiction of many of his contemporaries, among them William Gibson in the Sprawl trilogy (*Neuromancer* [1984], *Count Zero* [1986], and *Mona Lisa Overdrive* [1988]), Pat Cadigan in *Synners* (1991), and Bruce Sterling in *Islands in the Net* (1988). Rather than twentieth-century gadget culture metastasizing into a dystopian cyberfuture, Robinson downplays visions of a digitized technonarcissism that Gibson explores in his more recent fiction: *Pattern Recognition* (2003), *Spook Country* (2007), and *Zero History* (2010).[5] The Orange County trilogy remains critically engaged with, but distanced from, speculations about futuristic technologies: a key plot element in *The Gold Coast* hinges on a telephone message that awaits on an "answering machine" (212); in *Pacific Edge* Kevin has trouble communicating with his sister in Bangladesh (118–19), even though he talks to his parents (Tom's daughter and her husband) who live and work on an orbiting solar array for energy generation. In the same novel, Doris and Kevin laboriously print out and photocopy municipal records to uncover why Alfredo is so intent on purchasing extra water for El Modena. In all three novels, Robinson explores alternatives to data-drenched, posthumanist futures that redefine identity in terms of collecting, storing, and managing information. Instead, as Moylan suggests, they adapt a familiar literary strategy—a history written within a history—to describe archaeologies of knowledge, memory, and information: Henry's first-person, coming-of-age narrative in *The Wild Shore*; Jim's ecocultural history of Orange County in *The Gold Coast*; and Tom's fragmentary notes on utopia in *Pacific Edge*. These narrative strategies, like twentieth-century answering and copying machines, locate Robinson's imaginative futures within an American, and specifically Californian, literary tradition. By downplaying the technofuturism of his contemporaries, Robinson signals his commitment to exploring in the trilogy the socioeconomic, ecological, and political implications of his culture's westward expansion to the Pacific and into the future.[6]

At the beginning of *The Gold Coast*, Jim McPherson offers his cynical take on talk of manifest Californian destiny, declaring that the "sunset tropism" of "the great late surge of corporate capitalism" has turned Orange County into "the end of history" (3). Although his critique becomes more nuanced later in the novel, his view suggests why an archaeology of the past must go beyond sifting through the detritus of the twentieth century. In *Pacific Edge*, the town attorney, Oscar Baldaramma, recently arrived from Chicago, writes to a friend in the Midwest that he is reading his way through "a stack of 'California writers'" as he "struggle[s] to . . . cut through the legends and stereotypes, and get to the locals' view of things": "Mary Austin, Jack London, Frank Norris, John Muir, Robinson Jeffers, Kenneth Rexroth, Gary Snyder, Ursula Le Guin, and Cecelia Holland" (*PE*, 269).[7] With the exception of Le Guin, these writers are not (primarily) science fiction authors, and Oscar's list suggests that the trilogy as a whole needs to be read within a shared tradition defined by "Muir's 'athlete philosopher,' his 'university of the wilderness'" (*PE*, 269). These "California writers" extend a Thoreauvian tradition of nature writing and sociopolitical critique in emphasizing the foundational value of the land: valleys, deserts, coast, and mountains are neither scenic backdrops for human drama nor parcels to be surveyed, subdivided, mined, paved over, built on, bulldozed, and paved over again. The ecosystems of California, for Robinson, are as crucial to the trilogy as his characters. Political ecology in Orange County is destiny.

THE WILD SHORE: INTO THE RUINS

The Wild Shore's opening expedition "north into the ruins of Orange County" (6) in 2047 locates the novel within a tradition of postapocalyptic science fiction, defined in the twentieth century by such classics as George R. Stewart's *The Earth Abides* (1947), Walter A. Miller's *A Canticle for Leibowitz* (1959), Roger Zelazny's *Damnation Alley* (1969), Kate Wilhelm's *Where Late the Sweet Birds Sang* (1976), and David Brin's *The Postman* (1985). All of these novels feature arduous journeys across the devastated, postapocalyptic landscapes of North America, ravaged by disease, nuclear war, and/or catastrophic climate change. In different ways, these works explore collective as well as individual responses to the destruction of twentieth-century civilization.[8] In *The Wild Shore*, a surprise neutron bomb attack has destroyed cities across America, and, without the skills or knowledge to live off the land, the survivors in Southern California, as Tom recalls, "fought each other and finished the murder off" for the attackers; within a year, "more people died than had been killed by the bombs . . . [u]ntil there were so few left there was no need to fight anymore, no one to fight" (295). As a survivor from the "old time," Tom assumes the roles of teacher, unofficial historian, and sage, much like Stewart's hero, Isherwood Williams, in *Earth Abides*. Although "as the oldest man in the valley legends naturally collected around him" (72), Tom is only slightly more successful than Stewart's hero in preserving the past. By the end of *Earth Abides*, Ish awakes intermittently from the fog of old age to recognize that his descendants have little use for the rusted and malfunctioning detritus of industrial technologies and value old coins only because they can be filed down to arrowheads. Tom, in contrast, preserves some remnants of preapocalyptic life in tales that weave together fact and fantasy.

Tom's fascination with the American president (or generals) who chose not to launch a counterstrike after the nuclear attack sets him apart from those characters in the novel who look nostalgically back to Ronald Reagan's vision of American exceptionalism. At backcountry swap meets where salvaged books, pre-war utensils, and rusty tools are traded, other survivors from "the old time" maintain that if President Eliot had launched a nuclear counterattack or a preemptive strike against the attackers—alternatively claimed to be the French, Vietnamese, South Africans, Japanese, or Russians—the United States "wouldn't be in this fix right now . . . we would be the strongest nation on Earth" (43). In fashioning an alternative universe where Eliot had pushed the nuclear button, the old-timers—except Tom—remain rooted in visions of a past that yokes national greatness and military power; worldwide destruction, in their minds, would have benefited the United States because it would have left other nations "in the same boat" (44). In contrast, Tom tries to preserve a sense of a cultural past that reflects the complexities and tensions of a preapocalyptic world—a world that Henry's generation knows only through the prisms of memory, belief, and ideology.

Using mildewed books that he has found or acquired at swap meets, Tom teaches Henry and his friends how to read and write, has them memorize passages from Shakespeare and Milton, and tries to re-create for them a sense of history through his fanciful reminiscences, tall tales, and impromptu lessons. Early in the novel, Henry recites for Tom a passage from book 1 of Milton's *Paradise Lost*—Satan's speech as he looks around for the first time at Hell:

> "Is this the region, this the soil, the clime,"
> Said then the lost Archangel, "this the seat
> That we must change for Heaven?
> —this mournful gloom
> For that celestial light?" (*WS*, 24)

For readers familiar with Milton, this passage filters the worldview of San Onofre's survivors through Satan's defiance of divine power. Without fully understanding this passage, Henry recognizes intuitively that it speaks to the conditions that he and his small community face: a devastated landscape; the frustration of having no way to combat the continuing surveillance by Japanese satellites and patrol boats; and impotent rage at the unseen powers that hinder communications, prevent Americans from venturing too far offshore in their fishing boats, and ensure that they do not repair the railroad tracks between San Onofre and San Diego. For Henry, Tom's lessons and his salvaged books themselves constitute barriers to knowledge: "That was all we heard about: the past, the past, the God-damned past. The explanation for everything that happened was contained in our past" (71). American history in San Onofre is not a living tradition but the vehicle for a series of commands and cautionary injunctions that announce rather than justify the constraints that hedge in the characters' lives. Even as Henry writes his own narrative—the novel itself—he remains caught between the demands of the past and the realities of a postapocalyptic world.

As his complaint about the "God-damned past" suggests, Henry's sense of history is bound up with the ruins and relics of a destroyed civilization: "big buildings . . . falling down every way possible; windows and doors knocked out like teeth, with shrubs and ferns growing in every hole; walls slumped; roofs piled on the ground like barrows" (8). In part because readers see this devastated landscape through Henry's eyes, the narrative develops as a bildungsroman that uses his Huck Finn–like experience to rework the tradition of postapocalyptic science fiction. *The Wild Shore* strips society of modern technologies and reimagines a nineteenth-century settler community dependent on fishing boats, moldy books, and handcars on railway tracks. This enforced state of technocultural primitivism cuts the survivors in Orange County off from both futuristic technologies (the satellite-based weapons systems arrayed against them) and from their own history. As Tom puts it, in the novel's postapocalyptic world "the United States of America is *out of bounds* . . . we are *beyond the pale*" (22) of technomodernity. In this respect, the "United States of America" is, at best, a spectral fiction that exists only in fragments—the memorized, decontextualized passages of *Paradise Lost* and *King Lear*—that define and haunt Henry's senses of time and history.

A zombie-like fiction of national identity, however, remains alive in the ruins of San Diego where the mayor and his cohorts, using a radio and a skeletal electrical grid, dream the demagogic dream of resurrecting the United States as a military and economic power. Sounding like Ronald Reagan in 1980 or (unnervingly) like Donald Trump in 2016, Mayor Danforth wants "to make America great again, to make it what it was before the war, the best nation on Earth" (104). These visions of national resurrection, however, quickly turn out to be a rationalization for the mayor and his cohorts to assert political control over San Onofre. Nonetheless, with Japanese satellites destroying the survivors' half-built rail links along the coast, and Japanese patrol boats protecting their base on Catalina Island, "America" exists only in the shadows of its lost modernity. In San Diego, Tom acquires a copy of a postapocalyptic novel, "*An American around the World: Being an Account of a Circumnavigation of the Globe in the Years 2030 to 2039*, by Glen Baum" (170).[9] This picaresque fiction is taken as gospel by some of the San Onofrean teenagers who take turns reading it aloud, with Henry's friends, Steve and Mando, "angrily" denying the charge that "the whole book is made up" (253). When Henry calls it "a bunch of lies," Steve insists that, by escaping to Catalina, he will "make it true" (332). In treating fiction as history, in weaving Baum's far-fetched adventures into his own worldview, Steve represents what has been lost in the postapocalyptic world of *The Wild Shore*: any sense of critical disengagement from the narratives that shaped the world of the late twentieth century. While the San Diegans want "to make America great again," Tom recalls existence in Reagan's America as "a stupid life" when people "struggled at jobs in boxes so they could rent boxes and visit other boxes, and they spent their whole lives running in boxes like rats" (221–22). This indictment of a vanished consumerist culture, however, does not mean that either Tom or Henry romanticizes post-attack life. What Henry comes to realize, in a way that Steve never does, is that history involves far more than distinguishing truth from lies.

For Tom and Henry, the postapocalyptic world of 2047 remains haunted by the past. Yet, at the same time, the reader's experience of the novel—whether in 1984 or 2019—is haunted by a future history that questions our cultural faith in progress itself. Jacques Derrida terms this complex relationship between past and present a "hauntology," punning on the term ontology, the study of the nature and structure of being and physical reality. His neologism registers the uncertainty and disorientation that come with recognizing that our seemingly bedrock assumptions and values are based on fictions and misapprehensions about individual identity, social existence, and material reality.[10] Taking his cue from the opening sentence of Karl Marx's *Capital*, "a specter is haunting Europe," Derrida argues that our perceptions of reality and history are haunted by ghostly apparitions—like Hamlet dealing with the ghost of his father—that mark the limits of what we can know and constrain how we can act. These apparitions reflect the complexities of alternative history—and the simulations of science fiction more generally—because they suggest, as the narrator says in "Sensitive Dependence on Initial Conditions," we "live in a condition of asymptotic freedom, and every history is possible" (103). Each of these possible histories is haunted by what it is not—what might have been different in the past (neutron bombs destroy the United States), what could be in the future (the postapocalyptic society of San Onofre), and what other forms the twenty-first century might take: the different futures of *The Gold Coast* and *Pacific Edge*. In *The Wild Shore* both the characters and the ecologies of Southern California are haunted by their pasts, even as the reader's experience is haunted by the novel's vision of the future.

Henry inhabits an environment radically altered by the climatic changes wrought by the neutron bomb attack—a world sliding into the nuclear winter that Jonathan Schell theorized would result from the particulates ejected into the upper atmosphere in the aftermath of planet-wide devastation.[11] In *The Wild Shore*, sociopolitical and economic collapse is carved into the landscape and roils the atmosphere, marking the failures of late twentieth-century society to make progress toward the utopian possibilities of socioeconomic and environmental justice.[12] After escaping from San Diego, Henry and Tom trudge along a destroyed interstate highway in a snowstorm, as though the Southern California coast has become a refracted vision of the New England frontier two centuries earlier. The colder climate, which Tom and the author of *An American around the World* link to the nuclear attack, resonates symbolically with the loss of "modern" communications and transportation technologies.[13] Cursing the "Snow in July," Tom "wonder[s] if we've kicked off another ice age" (159). These disruptions of global weather patterns turn postapocalyptic Orange County into a strangely haunted vision of the forested landscapes of preindustrial New England. In ways that recur and develop throughout Robinson's career, alternative histories are haunted by the prospects of such radically altered climates.

In this landscape of summer snowstorms, Tom's tales of the past weave together fact and fiction, memories and tall tales. Tom is part historian, part fabulist, part teacher, and part bullshit artist, repeatedly revising what he has told Henry and the others born after the attack, and ultimately admitting that his "stretchers," as he calls them, are like Baum's novel: they may not be true, but, in reshaping the past, they shape present understandings. He tries to explain that the fiction of "an American around the world" serves an essential function: "We needed it even if it was a lie, understand?" (292). Like Nederland in *Icehenge* surveying the archaeological dig at the destroyed Martian city of New Houston, Tom lives a divided existence as a survivor from the "old time" (214) whose very identity has been riven by unthinkable devastation.

In a key scene in *The Wild Shore*, Tom tells a tale of picking up a hitchhiker in the desert who turns out to be his doppelgänger:

> Sure enough, we were the same Tom Barnard. Born in the same year to the same parents. By comparing pasts all through the years we quickly found the time we separated or broken in two or whatever. One September five years before, I had gone back to New York City [where he was a lawyer], and he had gone to Alaska. (215)

Several years later, Tom meets himself again on a Mt. Whitney climbing trail on the day of the nuclear attack. "I was still a lawyer, older and slouchier than ever," Tom tells Henry, living "a stupid life" that makes any nostalgia for preapocalyptic America and fantasies of rebuilding the United States into a world power seem hollow. As Tom and his doppelganger watched the explosions—"fifty suns all strung out and glowing . . . up and down the California coast"—they "melted together" and he "remembered both [his] pasts" (221, 223). But this narrative—of life in New York boxes and a working life in Alaska—underscore the parable-like quality of Tom's narrative, captured in his remark that "'you couldn't live a whole life in the old time'" (223). These alternative histories of Tom's past lives bring him to the same place—Mt. Whitney—but as he finally admits on his deathbed, he was only eighteen when the bombs exploded, making him eighty-one in 2047, and not, as he had claimed, well over a hundred. This admission makes Tom in 1984 roughly the same age as Henry, and many of his impressions of preapocalyptic life seem retrospective efforts to make sense of inexpressible devastation.

Neither a lawyer nor a rebel who headed to Alaska to escape a "stupid life in boxes," Tom admits he "only grew up in the old time. . . . Not for long, and without understanding it at the time, but [he] was there." In recasting history, he is not "lying outright. Just stretching" (292). The past, for Tom, becomes a postapocalyptic tall tale that ties him to an American culture that is disappearing with the memories of the few men and women who can remember

1984. When Tom falls ill and has to be carried from his cabin down to Doc's "hospital," he calls himself "the last American" (247). "The Last American" is the title of the third and final section of Stewart's novel *The Earth Abides*, and, like Isherwood Williams, Tom finds that his legacy, his efforts to preserve what he can of the past, are hedged in on all sides by life in a postapocalyptic society. The teenagers he tries to teach can envision technomodernity only as the subjugating powers of the Japanese or as the wreckage of an incomprehensible history.

For Henry, Tom's "stretching" reflects a fundamental ambivalence that extends beyond describing "the old time" and shadows the lessons that "the last American" has tried to teach. While Henry learns for himself the dangers posed by the San Diegans and their failed mission to attack the Japanese, he remains "confused" by Tom's outlook that "Onofre was primitive and degraded, but we weren't to want for the old time to come back either, because it was evil" (360). This confusion extends to his own narrative:

> The old man told me that when I was done writing I would understand what happened, but he was wrong again, the old liar. Here I've taken the trouble to write it all down, and now I'm done and I don't have a dog's idea what it meant. Except that most everything I know is wrong, especially the stuff I learned from Tom. (376)

Henry's perspective remains limited because neither the future, represented by Japanese patrol boats and an industrialized world beyond the wild shore, nor the past suggest a way forward, a way to make sense of the post-1984 gravestones in San Onofre's cemetery that register deaths from radiation-induced cancer, infections, birth defects, and unidentifiable diseases. Writing is not knowing. Henry's response, in this respect, voices the dialectic at the heart of postapocalyptic fiction: the hope of the survivors' beginning again to remake history along utopian lines, and the fear that this remnant, like Steve and the San Diegans, will fall back into the violence and shortsightedness of a fallen world, haunted by their own dreams of reanimating the past.

AUTOPIAN FUTURE: *THE GOLD COAST*

The future history in *The Gold Coast* projects Cold War–era social tensions, technological trends, and political conflicts into the late twenty-first century.

Robinson's Southern California in the second volume of the trilogy is an over-built and overburdened extension of the region's 1980s environment, a consumerist world grafted onto a sprawling military-industrial complex that overwhelms Orange County physically and psychically. This reality is "everywhere, it fills all realities, even the insane ones" because "its caking of concrete and steel" (353, 151) represents corporatist efforts to bury political alternatives along with the natural landscape. Throughout the novel, scenes of all-night partying, designer drugs, and smuggling intersect with a layered, complex plot centered on high-tech corporate espionage, infighting among defense contractors, and a violent but futile resistance than envelops Jim McPherson. Even as the narrative focuses on the mall sprawl, triple-decker highways, and loss of personal and political freedoms in California's "autopia" (a future vision of what J. G. Ballard called "autogeddon" in *Crash* [1973]), the novel subjects this dystopia to a withering critique. If the bureaucratic military-industrial complex is dehumanizing and corrupt, some of those trapped within its nightmarish, Orwellian history nonetheless search for ways to imagine and forge a different version of the future.

At the beginning of the novel, Jim is alienated and underemployed, a struggling poet who, as his father Dennis puts it, "is still hanging out in Orange County, teaching night classes and working in a real estate office part-time" (13). Jim lives in a tiny apartment under a three-tiered highway and drifts from party to party, drug to drug, and, for a time, from woman to woman, without a coherent plan either to make more money or to try to change the political landscape of the 2060s. Instead, he devotes himself to trying to "creat[e] an aesthetic life, one concentrating on the past" (41). In this respect, *The Gold Coast* narrates his journey from disengagement to activism to violence and, ultimately, to imagining a future that goes beyond the Hobson's choice of either art or violence. If the labyrinthine corporate culture of the novel seems at times almost as bleak and paranoid as Philip K. Dick's postapocalyptic world in *Do Androids Dream of Electric Sheep?*, Jim's ecocultural history of Orange County, stretching back to the Neolithic era, offers a counternarrative to the novel's future history. Throughout *The Gold Coast*, short interludes from Jim's ecohistory implicitly track the stages of his own journey, transforming his experience into a prequel for utopian political action.

Jim's counternarrative is all the more important in *The Gold Coast* because Tom Barnard is neither the survivor of the "old time" nor the retired, if reclusive, hero of utopian change that he is in *Pacific Edge*, but a bed-ridden old man, stashed in a dingy nursing home, "a jail for the old, a kind of concentration camp" (77), waiting to die. His memories are anecdotal, even fragmentary, and he seems to his nephew, Jim, beaten down by his time as a public defender: "Bald freckled pate. Ten thousand wrinkles. A turtle's head" (73). Yet Tom's comments on his life are telling. He became a public defender because, as he says, "this isn't a just society and that was one way to resist it" (75); his switch from the present tense ("isn't") to the past tense ("was") indicates that nothing has changed for more than half a century, that his resistance has not made his society any more "just." In a dystopian world, the future follows relentlessly from the present and the past deadens to the concretized environments of "autopia" and "condomundo" (77). Tom himself is an artifact, like the wreckage of El Modena elementary school, and his infirmity suggests that the resistance to militaristic corporatization he represents, too, is on life support. The dystopian present of Robinson's twenty-first-century projects the tensions of the 1980s and its consumerist excesses eighty years into the future.

Against this backdrop, Jim grapples with the problem of writing an eco-cultural history that resists the temptation to backslide into self-reflexive, quietist poetry. Even as he tells himself, "he *is* a poet, he is he is he is," he finds himself torn between "slavishly" imitating older poets—"Shakespeare, Shelley, Stevens, Snyder, shit!"—and a tired postmodernism "moldering in its second half century" (67). In both cases his efforts to write make him aware that he may have nothing to narrate except the kind of fragmentary images and half-voiced memories that now characterize Tom's end-of-life existence. His challenge, as he slowly discovers, in writing the history of Orange County becomes to craft a creative-political response—creativity *as* critique—that leads from a dystopian vision toward a future that gives voice to his and his society's need for progressive action. Yet this recognition is hard-won. Jim soon is drawn to Arthur Bastanchury's increasingly violent actions against defense contractors and a militarized society that is fighting small wars from Bahrain to Indonesia. And he quickly finds himself caught up in a network of friends intent on expanding their drug- and weapon-smuggling operations. During a nighttime drive back from one of these meetings about sabotage raids on military-corporate installations, Jim "dreams of a cataclysm that could bring this overlit America to ruin, and leave behind only the land, the land, the land . . . and perhaps—perhaps—a few survivors, left to settle the hard new forests of a cold wet new world, in tiny Hannibal Missouris that they would inhabit like foxes, like deer, like real human beings" (151). This irruption of the world of *The Wild Shore* into Jim's reveries in *The Gold Coast* suggests how dreams of resistance can shade into fantasies of a romanticized apocalypse as the only alternative to a corrupt society. But Jim quickly realizes the limits of this dark nostalgia for an idealized, Huck Finn past: "There is no way back; because there is no way back. History is a one-way street. It's only forward, into catastrophe, or the track-and-mall inferno, or . . . or nothing. Nothing Jim can imagine, anyway" (152). If his fragmentary history of California's past becomes a way to "imagine" an alternative to "the track-and-mall inferno," his manuscript, fragment after fragment, asks readers to chart for themselves the fog-shrouded intersections between history and a utopian commitment to sociopolitical change.

After Jim commits his first act of sabotage, he realizes that "resistance" is more about changing one's "perception" than accomplishing anything substantive (115). The narrative then turns to the section of his history that describes the lifestyle of the hunter-gatherers who once inhabited Newport Bay: "[T]heir village life went on, year after year, generation after generation, existing in an unobtrusive balance with the land, using all of its many resources, considering every rock and tree and animal a sacred being—for seven thousand years. For seven thousand years!" (117). Rather than a factual anthropology, this description calls for an act of imaginative projection on the reader's part, a view that anticipates, in some ways, the world of *Shaman*: "See them, in your mind's eye, if you can, living out their lives on that basin crowded with life." But once we are engaged by this vision, we are asked to recognize that, with the coming of Europeans and their weapons—"a band of men . . . looking kind of like crabs, wearing shells that they could take off," who "could kill from a distance with a noise"—"History began" (117). Because history begins with "kill[ing] from a distance," its "one-way street" leads inexorably to Jim's present, to the defense contractors whose plants litter what, millennia ago, had been an idyllic land. The fate of the original inhabitants at the hands of well-meaning missionaries becomes part of the refrain that ends each section of the history: "Within fifty years [of the missionaries' arrival] all of [the natives] were dead. And all that went away" (117). This refrain, "All that went away," points not only to successive devastations of the landscape but also to the logic of dystopian fiction that, as Moylan suggests, testify to Jim's efforts to "giv[e] life to the estranging and enlightening perspective of the long view of history."[14] Jim's "long view" centers on the land as much as on the succession of peoples who have inhabited it, devastated its ecologies, and eventually paved it over.

This view allows readers to put into context Robinson's critique of the moral, political, and economic corruption that disfigures both the land and social life of Orange County. Jim's father Dennis works for Laguna Space Research, a firm competing for a lucrative Defense Department contract for an antiballistic missile system. Nested within corporate bureaucracies, Dennis nonetheless "doesn't like to reflect on how fully American strategy is entangled in nuclear weapons; the situation repels him" (16). His dilemma— working against his own moral inclinations—is emblematic of Robinson's strategy of projecting the nuclear standoff of the Cold War into the mid-twenty-first century. In key scenes in *The Gold Coast* Dennis comes to realize that his company's proposal has been sidelined by a corrupt general who has awarded the antiballistic missile contract to a competitor, whose lowball bid means the system has no chance of actually working. Dennis's colleague, Dan Houston, describes "the waste, man, the waste" inherent in the cutthroat bidding by defense companies that renders collaborative scientific and technological progress a bad joke: "All their lives used up in meeting deadlines for these [defense] proposals. And for five out of six of them it's work wasted. Nothing gained out of that work, nothing made from it. Nothing *made* from it. . . . Whole careers. Whole lives" (221) are sacrificed to "the power struggles of certain people in Washington" consumed by "personal ambitions, personal jealousies" (335). In the dystopian world of *The Gold Coast*, the utopian science that Robinson explores in the Mars and Science in the Capital trilogies are perverted to fruitless and self-destructive ends. Dennis, like Howard the Duck, is trapped in a world that he hasn't made.

It is hardly surprising, then, that Dennis and his son are at loggerheads throughout the novel, even though, in their final argument, he concedes sardonically that Jim is right: "The world is on the brink of a catastrophic breakdown. You think I haven't *noticed*?" (344). Although Dennis tries to distinguish between nuclear weapons and the "guidance systems" he works on, he acknowledges that he is complicit in a system he fundamentally distrusts. He knows full well that "nuclear weapons are crazy" but believes that his actual job in antimissile technologies "is to try and stop them. I wish they were gone, and maybe someday they will be" (343). His embittered self-defense—victimized by his job yet forced by Jim to defend his life's work—leads him to insist that the endemic "corruption" he confronts is "not the system" and that "the system is there to be used for good or bad. And it's not all that bad. Not by itself" (344). In rejecting his father's distinction, Jim ensures that they cannot find common ground, and their final argument sends him off on his vandalism spree. The ultimate dystopia is the fear that both father and son, in different ways, have internalized: "there's no way back" (151) to the life that existed before "autopia."

In the context of a looming "catastrophic breakdown," Jim's manuscript history seems a compensatory stand-in for the narratives Tom provides in *The Wild Shore* and *Pacific Edge*: a vision of the past and notes toward a utopia of the future. Inspired, in part, by his growing attraction to Hana Steentoft, a feminist artist who teaches in the classroom next to his, Jim recognizes the need for the writer, as Albert Camus and Athol Furgard maintained, "to be a *witness* to one's times" (259). The acid test for his work—and for the novel as a whole—is cast in terms of repurposing his literary education:

> [Jim] recalls Walter Jackson Bate's beautiful biography of Samuel Johnson, the point in it where Bate speaks of Johnson's ultimate test for literature, the most important question: Can it be turned to use? When you read a book, and go back out into the world: *can it be turned to use?* (261)

In an important sense, this question informs much of Robinson's work beyond *The Gold Coast*: Can novels about terraforming Mars, global warming, or humankind's expansion into the solar system *"be turned to use"* in helping us find a way forward through the crisis years of the twenty-first century? In another, it focuses on the problems of the use-value of literary education and offers an alternative to Tom's having the children of San Onofre in *The Wild Shore* memorize passages from *Paradise Lost* and *King Lear*. Rather than a model to emulate—"Shakespeare, Shelley, Stevens, Snyder, shit!"—literature becomes a form of action, a moral and sociopolitical intervention. At the end of the novel, Jim wonders, "How to decide what to do? How to know how to act?" (379), and his questions, as we will see in chapter 4, resonate with those posed in the Science in the Capital trilogy: "How to go forward?" What Jim has learned, in effect, is that "every action takes place in . . . a network of circumstances" (379) and that there are no simple escapes from condomundo. Utopia, in its embryonic stages, works toward a plan of action, toward understanding the uses to which history and literature might be put.

In this sense, it seems significant that the novel does not end with Jim's night of "idiot vandalism" against the real estate office where he works, against Laguna Space Research, where his father works, and against a "closed Fluffy Donuts" shop (389). For much of the novel, it seems as though utopia can emerge only as the *negation* of a negation, a rebellion against the "concrete and steel" of knotted highways where "only the car remains constant, and the hours spent in it each day. The real home, in autopia" (347). But Jim's ecohistory of Orange County suggests that an instinctive sense of connection to the land remains. Near the end of *The Gold Coast* the narrative turns to an extended scene of mountain climbing in the Sierra Nevada that recalls (or anticipates) other scenes in mountains in Robinson's stories "Ridge Running" and "Muir on Shasta." Jim leaves condomundo for the mountains with his friend, Tashi, who lives in a tent on a condo roof, considers surfing "an ecstatic melding with" the universe, and believes "the less you are plugged into the machine, the less it controls you" (97, 98). Far away from autopia, the two men ascend an old glacier bed above Owens Valley, and Jim finds that, in "concentrate[ing] on the work [of climbing]," he has found "that this endless upward struggle is the perfect analogy for life. Two steps up, one step back. . . . The goal above seems close but never gets closer. Yes, it's a . . . very stripped-down model of life—life reduced to stark expansive significance" (360). Rather than a romanticized return to a pristine natural world, Jim's climb emphasizes the physical work of mountaineering and the bodily effects of "a strange, physical rapture" that comes from "discovering a world he never knew existed—a home. He had thought it a lost dream; but this is California too, just as real as the rock underneath his sore butt" (364). In recognizing this "stripped-down model of life," Jim redefines his sense of "home"—an existence that offers a perspective beyond the view from inside the cars of autopia.

Jim's recognition that the mountains are "California too" suggests a way to negotiate the tensions that exist back in "condomundo." If Orange County is "the ultimate expression of the American Dream," it exists outside the traditional narratives of Horatio Alger individualism and reimagines existence as the intersections among vast interconnecting systems of capital, information, influence, weapon systems, automobiles, and drugs. There can be no biographies in autopia because, as Jim puts it, "there aren't any great individuals in OC's history, that's part of what OC means, what it is" (261). Instead, his history, *Torn Maps*, pieces together a fragmentary vision of the land and its peoples that, by the end of the novel, gestures beyond the dystopian horizon of Orange County. At the end of the novel, he is on his way to give his history to Hana, and he characterizes his narrative in collective rather than individualistic or autobiographical terms: "It's not a big book, nor a great one; but it's his. His and the land's. And the people who lived here through all the years; it's theirs too, in a way" (388). In one respect, this characterization of his book focuses our attention on Samuel Johnson's question about its use. *Torn Maps* gestures beyond seeing California as "the tired end of postmodernism" (259) to the seldom-glimpsed utopian impulses of those who "did their best to make a home of the place—those of them who weren't actively doing their best to parcel and sell it off, anyway" (388). His book, in one sense, extends the impulses that led him and his friends at the beginning of the novel to excavate the ruins of an old school: an effort to uncover and move beyond with a seemingly forgotten past.

PACIFIC EDGE AND THE POLITICS OF UTOPIA: "ON THIN ICE, SKATE FAST"

If *The Gold Coast* suggests that there can be no bystanders in dystopia, *Pacific Edge* undertakes the enormous challenge of casting off the nightmarish, corporatist bureaucracies that engulf Jim and Dennis McPherson and, in their place, envisioning a democratic-utopian system of social and economic justice. Robinson's third California is set in the utopian community of El Modena in the 2060s, a society that places communal checks on powermongering and economic aggrandizement. As utopian fiction, the novel includes elements of a traditional "anatomy" of an ideal society, but it focuses as much on the land as the site of a home-grown California utopianism as it does on describing El Modena's socioeconomic principles. At times, *Pacific Edge* reads as though Scott and Helen Nearing had stepped into the future and across the continent from their farm in rural Maine.[15] Because Kevin Claiborne finds himself at odds with much of the community in his battle to save Rattlesnake Hill, one of the last wild areas in the county, from development as a multipurpose business center, the novel explores what utopianism entails when it is confronted by the day-to-day practicalities of the stewardship of the land and its inhabitants. To this end, Robinson creates a different kind of temporal framing than he does in *The Gold Coast*. Rather than devoting passages between the major chapters to an ecohistory of Orange County, *Pacific Edge* interlaces Kevin's utopia with entries from Tom Barnard's early twenty-first-century journals—fragmentary efforts to outline a utopian project during his internment by a neofascist society.

Pacific Edge imagines a utopian future as a *negation* of the anti-ecological and antidemocratic value systems, policies, lifestyles, and economics of late-twentieth-century capitalism.[16] The narrative focuses, often at length, on the day-to-day running of El Modena, recasting local bureaucracy as participatory democracy. Kevin's duty as a citizen offers a localized version of the utopia in Ursula K. Le Guin's *The Dispossessed*. Where Le Guin imagines a quasi-anarchist, planet-wide system of collective labor on Anarres—a utopia orchestrated by work and living assignments—Robinson concentrates on a different kind of township utopia: Kevin's efforts to save Rattlesnake Hill from being sold to developers, while battling his romantic rival, Alfredo, a charismatic, insinuating capitalist, who envisions El Modena reintegrated into a semi-resurgent, profit-based economy. Given its focus on water usage, land development, and Kevin's job in repurposing the architecture of condomundo into bright, communal, and environmentally friendly living spaces, *Pacific Edge* reimagines the road to utopia as a series of eco-managerial solutions to late-twentieth-century problems. A carpenter and softball star, dedicated to "renovat[ing] that sleazy old condo of a world" (22), Kevin inhabits an affective utopia as much as a sociopolitical one, where he seems to himself (at times) "nine years old forever" (65). In this respect, Robinson tries to convey an embodied sense of utopian experience: the physical sensation of lacing a double to left field works synecdochically to suggest how utopia changes both bodies and minds. But his struggles to counter Alfredo and win back his sometime girlfriend, Ramona, force Kevin to reexamine many of the values and assumptions he has always taken for granted. In focusing on Kevin's struggles, *Pacific Edge* explores the psychological and interpersonal registers of utopian social existence.

In a latter-day Emersonian moment early in the novel, Kevin daydreams about the kind of holistic vision—unalienated labor, a sense of oneness with the natural world—that characterizes traditional versions of utopian life:

> God existed in every atom, as [his friend and coworker] Hank was always saying, in every molecule, in every particulate jot of the material world, so that he was breathing God deep into himself with every fragrant breath. And sometimes it really felt that way, hammering nails into new framing, soaring in the sky, biking through night air, the black hills bulking around him. . . . He knew the configuration of every dark tree he passed, every turn in the path, and for a long moment rushing along he felt spread out in it all, interpenetrated, the smell of the plants part of him, his body a piece of the hills, and all of it cool with a holy tingling. (32)

This passage hinges on the temporal, even transitory, nature of Kevin's experience: "sometimes it really felt that way." Utopia is sensed more than articulated, and as Robinson's first major utopian experiment, *Pacific Edge* is more concerned with imagining the day-to-day experience of living—softball games and all—rather than with charting the progress of El Modena's transformation from a fossil-fueled, consumerist wasteland into a latter-day Emersonian society. Like many of Robinson's 1980s short stories, then, this novel remakes history, although without trying to provide a detailed roadmap from the present to the future.

In 1998 at a session on utopian literature at the MLA convention, Robinson responded to a question about El Modena's transformation to a utopian society by invoking the old saying: "On thin ice, skate fast."[17] In one respect, this "thin ice" takes the form of the white spaces on the printed page that stand in for the half-century between the short excerpts from Tom's journal and his old age in the 2060s. These fragments recount his expulsion from Switzerland because his visa has expired, his politically motivated detention at a concentration camp for people with AIDS, and his awareness, after his release, that he has "to do something. Not just write a utopia, but fight for it in the real world" (299). This fight, however, is seen only in retrospect, his brief allusions to the legal and legislative battles, over two generations, that broke up large corporations, "set limits on the more extreme forms of greed," and "nationaliz[ed] energy, water, and land" as "common property" to serve society's "more long distance self-interest" (284). The fragmentary passages from Tom's journals sketch the outlines of a future utopian history—the challenge that Robinson takes up in the Mars trilogy. Written in the early twenty-first century, these notes try to imagine the history that ultimately leads to El Modena's utopian society.

At the beginning of the novel, the elderly Tom is far removed from his activist past, mourning his dead wife, and emotionally almost as isolated as he was in his incarnation in *The Gold Coast*. His psychological suffering marks the alienation that troubles even utopia. "We live with disjunctures," he reflects bitterly, and his life now seems to him surreal, even fictive: "[H]e had never done any of it; just as likely to have been raising bees in some bombed-out forest, or lying flat on his back in an old folks' home, choking for breath. Incarnations too, no doubt, following other lines. That he had carved this line to this spot, that the world had spun along to this sage sunlight and the great solitude; impossible to believe" (63). This allusion to Tom's "incarnations"—his alternative selves in *The Wild Shore* and *The Gold Coast*—reflects both his past commitment to his having "carv[ed] this line" to utopia and the personal toll that his struggle exacts. This "disjuncture" from his own activist past is what Tom has to overcome before his death at the end of the novel: he must rekindle his faith in the struggle against the resurgent forces of capitalist development. As he writes in one of his journal entries, "Utopia is when our lives matter" (181).

Tom, in his eighties, embodies both the fears and hopes that Robinson harbors for the millennial generation that comes after his: what legacies are the children of the Cold War passing on to the next two generations? Because his journal entries sketch a utopian traverse across thin ice by focusing on the generic difficulties of writing, or imagining, a utopia, Tom arguably becomes a more compelling figure in this narrative than the storyteller of *The Wild Shore* or the dying old man of *The Gold Coast*. In *Pacific Edge*, having been released from detention in 2012, Tom imagines utopia in the experiential terms that had characterized his youth in late-twentieth-century Orange County, then "a child's paradise [where] he was healthy, well fed, well clothed, well housed":

> While I was growing up in my sunny seaside home, much of the world was in
> misery, hungry, sick, living in cardboard shacks, killed by soldiers or their own

police. I had been on an island. In a pocket utopia. It was the childhood of someone born into the aristocracy, and understanding that I understood the memory of my childhood differently; but still I know what it was like. I lived it and I know! And everyone should get to know that, not in the particulars, of course, but in the general outline, in the blessing of a happy childhood, in the lifelong sense of security and health. (300)

In Tom's retelling, the child is father to the utopian activist. His commitment to fighting for utopia is grounded in an ethical imperative to extending his "happy childhood" beyond the privileged enclaves of "pocket utopia[s]." In returning to his childhood past, Tom rediscovers his embodied sense of utopia—"the lifelong . . . security and health" that he sees as a fundamental human birthright—by helping Kevin, his grandson, try to save Rattlesnake Hill from development.

This struggle to preserve the green space above El Modena interweaves a political plot—fights over water rights, urban expansion, and international capital trying to weasel its way back into utopia—with Kevin's romantic triangle: his love for Ramona and his rivalry with Alfredo. The threat to utopia surfaces in the endemic tendency among some of his fellow citizens to revert to the very growth-oriented, anti-ecological policies that were restricted by legislation earlier in the twenty-first century. El Modena always could drift back to the highways and gas stations of its gold-coast past because, as Tom recognizes, "saving the land for its own sake goes against the grain of white American thought, and so it's a fight that will never end" (107). Utopia, in this sense, becomes a reinhabitation of the land by the spiritual, if not ethnic, descendants of the indigenous peoples who, as Jim describes them in *The Gold Coast*, existed "in an unobtrusive balance with the land" (*GC*, 117) for seven thousand years. For Kevin's generation, the enemy in this fight is not oppression but the seductions of what we would now call "sustainability"—the ethical and ecological confusion that comes from assuming that both first-world lifestyles and the environment can be mutually sustaining.[18] Alfredo asks the El Modena community to imagine "a center [on Rattlesnake Hill] that combine[s] high tech labs and offices with restaurants, an open deck with a view, a small amphitheater for concerts and parties and just looking at the view" (267). Alfredo's is a utilitarian, managerial future that reshapes the natural world in terms of the "goal[s] of city planners" and the lure of a lifestyle that redefines utopia in terms of its "restaurants," "concerts and parties," and scenic views: the leisured world of the 1 percent. He defines the natural world in terms of its use-value: "More people," says Alfredo in nailing down his argument, "would use the hill than ever do now" (267). But the narrative makes clear that his is a self-interested argument because he is in league with "black banks" intent on circumventing laws against the concentration of wealth. At stake in his debate with Kevin are their radically different visions of utopia—upscale restaurants versus unspoiled wilderness—and whether they can somehow coexist. The question that *Pacific Edge* poses is whether "major growth [can] start again" (267) without upending the safeguards that Tom and Kevin see as the foundation of utopia.

Over the course of the novel, Kevin is poised to lose both his romantic and political contests. Ramona dumps him for Alfredo, and he ends up fighting with members of his own Green Party who want to trade Rattlesnake Hill for a population cap in El Modena and a backcountry plan to preserve more remote areas of wilderness. His refusal to go along with his party's compromise is tainted, in the minds of many of his friends and coworkers, by their suspicions that his differences with Alfredo stem from jealousy, not principle. Ultimately, Kevin and his friends preserve Rattlesnake Hill after Tom's death by making a grove of trees on its summit—trees that Tom had planted as a boy—a shrine to his memory. The memorial plaque, cast by his friend Doris, is inscribed "There Will Never Come an End to the Good He Has Done" (311). While this inscription pays tribute to the radical utopianism that Tom first voices in his journals and then fights for as a lawyer, the "Good" depends on Kevin's realizing that he can use Tom's memory to stop El Modena from drifting away from its principles of socioeconomic justice and ecological balance. Kevin's season-long hitting streak in softball ends on a spectacular catch by his friend Hank, but Hank's eulogy for Tom suggests that "the weird emptiness of the future" (316) that El Modena faces does not have to be filled by a cynical backsliding toward corporatism.

Although some critics have seen *Pacific Edge* as less successful than Robinson's other Californias, the novel works as an experiential utopia that offers readers the possibility of recognizing the narrative and political shape that a progressive or redemptive future might hold.[19] At a key point in the novel, Kevin finds that in telling the story of his breakup with Ramona, "he gained a sort of control over it, a control he had never had when it happened . . . shaping the experience, deciding what it meant, putting other people in their proper place" (255, 256). In structuring this personal narrative, he comes to realize that "he had been out of control, living moment to moment with no plan, at the mercy of other people" (256). This recognition of the power of narrative to shape experience stands as a useful way to think about *Pacific Edge* and, more broadly, the trilogy as a whole. *The Wild Shore* gives narrative form to the postapocalyptic nightmares that have haunted science fiction since H. G. Wells's *The War of the Worlds*. In turn, *The Gold Coast* offers readers a vision of what might happen if they succumb to the "cynical reason" of late capitalism and do little or nothing to counteract their complicity in the forces that make the 2060s a version of Reagan-era America on steroids.[20] For its part, *Pacific Edge* asks its readers to consider the possibility of whole-scale renovations of what they know about Southern California, late-twentieth-century capitalism, and human nature itself. Kevin describes his work in "blast[ing] some space and light" into the dingy "little tiny white-walled rooms with cottage cheese ceilings, cheap carpet over plywood floors" of condomundo as "changing bad to good" (127). If the communal living and collaboratories of El Modena may not seem like utopian fulfillment to some readers, Kevin's belief in "seeing homes as organisms" and treating them as "a work of art that you live in" (128) speaks to the possibility of repurposing the present. Imagining utopia is a project, as Tom and Kevin learn, requiring both hard work and a dedication to multiple forms of inhabitation: living in one's own body as part of a community and part of the natural world.

The future in *Pacific Edge* requires assembly but little machinery: from the human power gliders at the beginning of the novel to the great sailing ship that ultimately proves to be Tom's grave when it sinks in a storm, the postindustrial twenty-first century is, in a very real sense, elemental. Wind, sun, and rain define Orange County and shape the people who are trying to "scale back" (267) the population and its ecological footprint so that humankind and the natural world can exist in a dynamic balance. While the climate of Southern California may seem well-suited to visions of utopian existence, the land is never a passive backdrop for the characters but an active force in a solar- and wind-powered future. In this respect, *Pacific Edge*, like *The Wild Shore* and *The Gold Coast*, asks its readers to rethink their bedrock ideas about the modern exploitation of the natural world and its resources. And by the time Robinson had finished writing this first utopian novel, he already was turning to a new world—Mars—that required expanding the values of an imagined El Modena to a planetary scale.

TERRAFORMING AND ECO-ECONOMICS
IN THE MARS TRILOGY

Since its publication in the 1990s, Robinson's award-winning Mars trilogy—*Red Mars* (1993), *Green Mars* (1994), and *Blue Mars* (1996)—has become a touchstone for critics who argue that science fiction about planetary ecology, in the words of Lindsay Thomas, can "cultivat[e] a feeling for the ongoingness of change" at the "different [temporal] scales" that lie beyond human experience.[1] This tendency to use the trilogy as a template for thinking about larger climatic and environmental issues underscores the novels' significance as a thought-experiment about terrestrial ecology and suggests why they appeal to a wide readership in and beyond the science-fiction community. Although the term "Anthropocene" was not widely used until 2000, the Mars trilogy is among the most important works of contemporary fiction to focus on the complexities of ecological—or anthropocenic—responsibility.[2] Robinson explores the fundamental aspects of this responsibility by creating a world where every human intervention in a nascent biosphere registers the entangled responsibilities of ecological, ethical, and scientific action. In reworking and adapting both a long tradition of science fiction set on Mars and late-twentieth-century scientific literature on the prospect of terraforming the planet, Robinson conjures into being a planetary future that resists both dystopian and idealistic visions of humankind returning to a pristine nature. In the Mars novels, then, the Anthropocene emerges neither as a series of management crises nor as a nostalgic idealism for an unspoiled world but as a set of responsibilities that extend throughout and beyond earthly ideas of a biosphere.[3]

This politics of anthropocenic responsibility leads Robinson to explore the consequences of Martian colonists struggling "to yoke together impossible opposites" (GM, 229): mind and body, spirit and matter, nature and culture, and biosphere and technoscience. In different ways, this process of yoking "impossible opposites" characterizes the struggles depicted in Robinson's later solar system novels like 2312 that I discuss in chapter 5. But in the Mars trilogy, the epic undertaking of creating a biosphere from scratch offers a way to think through the constitutive ideologies of modernity: the radical separation of nature from culture and the celebration of modern technoculture at the expense of a devalued, primitive past. In challenging these ideological presuppositions, Robinson's Mars trilogy reframes the boundaries and possibilities of utopian thought. Taken together, Red Mars, Green Mars, and Blue Mars demonstrate, more so than Pacific Edge, the significance of utopian thinking as "a necessary survival strategy" to get humanity through the sociopolitical and environmental crises of late modern culture.[4]

DYING PLANET: THE TRADITION OF SCIENCE FICTION

Robinson began thinking about a terraforming trilogy set on Mars in the early 1980s, and his novels mined one of the richest veins of twentieth-century science fiction. Before the Mariner (1965, 1969, and 1971) and the Viking (1976, 1977) missions to the red planet, Mars was the setting for roughly three-quarters of interplanetary sf—largely because it had a long and complex interaction with the scientific understanding of the planet.[5] This long history—beginning with visions of dying civilizations and late-Victorian utopias on a canal-laced surface—is too rich, varied, and complicated to explore in depth here, and that is why I devoted a book-length analysis (Dying Planet) to what Carl Sagan called "the continuing dance between science and science fiction" about the red planet.[6] Nonetheless, a quick sketch of the tradition is important for understanding how and why Robinson refashioned a century of fiction.

By the late nineteenth century, Percival Lowell's theory of Mars as a dying world, home to an advanced civilization that had engineered canals to channel water from the polar regions to the equatorial deserts, dominated scientific debates about extraterrestrial life.[7] For science-fiction writers, the planet became a favored site for thought experiments about alien evolution, alternative societies, and battles against the hostile conditions of an aging world slowly losing its atmosphere and water. To write about Mars, even in the mid-twentieth century pulps, was to imagine how intelligent beings—human and nonhuman—coped with the "slow violence" of ecological catastrophe.[8] The more Lowellian the planet seemed, the greater the temptation became for writers to use advanced Martian civilizations to critique the shortcomings of Western society or to consider how more technologically advanced Martians might treat the less-evolved human species on Earth. During the 1890s H. G. Wells crafted the first great novel of interplanetary invasion, *The War of the Worlds*, but other writers took different approaches to imagine what kind of beings Martians might be and what their contact with humans might entail.[9] Kurd Lasswitz's novel *On Two Planets* (1897) explores the consequences of an ostensibly benevolent colonization of Earth, as an advanced society on Mars assumes the interplanetary White Man's burden of civilizing the reluctant inhabitants of late-nineteenth-century Europe. A decade later, in *Red Star* (1908) and its prequel, *Engineer Menni* (1913), the Russian revolutionary and physician Alexander Bogdanov recast the tradition of previous Martian utopias by depicting the red planet as a socialist paradise.

Wells, Lasswitz, and Bogdanov were all educated as scientists and seized on the idea of Mars as a dying planet to think through the evolutionary implications of an inhabited Mars. All three also were left of center politically: Wells was a socialist, a supporter of women's rights, and a critic of British imperialism; Lasswitz a liberal philosopher and historian whose politics may have cost him a university position; and Bogdanov a committed revolutionary who worked closely with and, at times, bankrolled Lenin. If Mars offered these novelists the chance to imagine possible futures for European civilization, their differing visions share a conceptual basis in Lowell's vision of a dying world in unending ecological crisis: Wells's Martians escape a dying planet to invade earth; Lasswitz's liberal, neo-Kantian Martians try to colonize, more or less benignly, an Earth whose "primitive" inhabitants are reluctant to share the planet's abundant sunlight and water; and Bogdanov's utopian race idealizes the triumphs of collective labor over a hostile environment. While these turn-of-the-last-century novels define the generic limits imposed on fiction by Lowellian Mars, we need to recognize how critical a role such texts played in revolutionary thinking.

A conservative environmentalist convinced that the desertification of its equatorial regions meant that "Earth [was] going the way of Mars," Lowell emphasized the connections among a degraded environment, politics, and social organization that science-fiction novelists—and many of their readers—exploited.[10] In 1920, Wells visited Moscow and interviewed Lenin at the Kremlin. Lenin told Wells that if life were discovered on other planets, there would be no need for revolutionary violence, and he explicitly tied progress to what he termed the "earthly limit"—that is, the material and environmental constraints on human progress. "Human ideas," Lenin reasoned, "are based on the scale of the planet we live in [and] on the assumption that the technical potentialities, as they develop, will never overstep 'the earthly limit.' If we succeed in making contact with the other planets, all our philosophical, social, and moral ideas will have to be revised, and in this event those potentialities will become limitless and will put an end to violence as a necessary means of progress."[11] As Richard Stites argues, utopian fiction played a significant role in shaping Russian and then Soviet conceptions of historical and political progress, and behind Lenin's comments about the effects that extraterrestrial civilizations might have on "human ideas" lie assumptions that, in some ways, anticipate the utopian strivings in Robinson's trilogy.

In *Molecular Red*, McKenzie Wark explores the entwined strands of Marxian—and post-Marxian—thought and fiction that weave their way from Bogdanov's conviction that Marxian economic theory had to be brought into line with advances in organizational and physical science by a tektology of *"comradely cooperation,"* through the feminist materialisms of Donna Haraway and Karen Barad, and ultimately to Robinson's trilogy.[12] Wark's analysis of the complex entanglements of labor, politics, ecology, and knowledge help explain why Mars remains a favored site to explore what Robinson, in defining science fiction, calls "the history that we cannot know."[13] If Mars has, as

Robert Crossley suggests, a "literary history" in twentieth-century science fiction, it also continues, as Wark, Thomas, and others suggest, to serve as an imaginative site to think through the problem of catastrophic climatic collapse.[14]

In *Dying Planet* I explored at length the interwoven histories of planetary science and science fiction devoted to Mars, and these histories appear in different ways in Robinson's Mars trilogy. The Viking images of the planet's surface sent back in the late 1970s turned the Martian surface into what Robinson has called "a giant, mountainous wilderness" that could be reimagined—without canals, dying civilizations, bizarre life forms, or ancient ruins—as the site on which humankind, since Wells and Bogdanov, has projected its fears of ecological devastation on Earth and its hopes for the future.[15] Lowellian Mars offered fictional analogues for—and even uncanny anticipations of—the crises that confronted millions of people worldwide in the twentieth century: food shortages, massive unemployment, drought, the dust bowl, forced migrations, political turmoil, violence, and belated efforts, such as WPA projects, that sought to preserve the productivity and beauty of the natural world. In the age of pulp fiction, works such as P. Schuyler Miller's "The Cave" (1943)—a classic story of planetary hard times—imagines that an entire planetary ecology has deteriorated to a point that Mars's "surface had been desert for more millions of years than anyone [on Earth] had yet estimated."[16] This vision of a world on which "all living things [are] united in the common battle for existence against a cruel and malignant Nature" (125) makes explicit, with a vengeance, the ecological implications of Lowellian Mars: human (or Martian) agency and heroism are defined by their stoic resistance to nature's implacable hostility.

By the McCarthy era of the 1950s, this vision of ecological disaster had assumed the burden of what Paul Carter has termed science fiction's "trenchant social criticism": Judith Merril, the science-fiction novelist and anthologist, claimed bluntly that during the McCarthy era the genre was "virtually the only vehicle of political dissent."[17] In her collaborative novel *Outpost Mars* (1953), coauthored with C. M. Kornbluth and published under the pseudonym "Cyril Judd," she offers a sardonic view of capitalism and corruption, and a bitter condemnation of humankind's self-destructive tendencies in bringing to Mars the problems of "damned, poverty-ridden, swarming Earth! Short of food, short of soil, short of water, short of metals—short of everything except vicious, universal resentments and aggressions bred by other shortages."[18] Such passages should remind us that, a generation before Robinson's trilogy, Mars served as a vehicle for critiquing the brutal inequities of postwar culture as well as for utopian alternatives to Earth's looming eco-disaster. The best of postwar Martian science fiction, like Ray Bradbury's *The Martian Chronicles* (1950), often gives voice to the then-marginalized views that the evils of colonization and ecological devastation betray the principles of American democracy. In British and European science fiction of the postwar era, these critiques morph into dystopian visions of space colonization in D. G. Compton's Kafkaesque novel *Farewell Earth's Bliss* (1965) and in Ludek Pešek's bleak and often terrifying description of the first human mission to Mars in *The Earth Is Near* (1971). Both of these novels deheroicize space exploration and subvert easy identifications among the final frontier, national pride, and masculine identity so crucial to the first years of Soviet and American manned missions.[19]

Yet despite the postwar turn to dystopian critique and the blasted dreams of an inhabited planet, Mars remained, as Arthur C. Clarke put it in his introduction to Jack Williamson's *Beachhead* (1992), "the hope for science fiction" in the late twentieth century where humankind would have to confront a truly alien "natural" world and its own destiny as a space-faring civilization.[20] In this regard, the photographs sent back to Earth by the Viking landers in the late 1970s offered two different invitations to the human imagination: on the one hand, Mars became *ahuman*, evoking an areography—ancient flood plains, immense canyon systems, and gargantuan shield volcanoes—that extended history four billion years back in time. But this ahuman quality also reinforced the tendency to project human desires and meanings onto this alien landscape—to reimagine Mars yet again in the image of a primordial Earth. The Viking photographs inspired a generation of science-fiction writers to recast the old-fashioned, planetary adventure novel as a high-tech confrontation with the unearthly nature of vast canyons, ancient riverbeds, and massive craters. After 1976 the future mission novels—Williamson's *Beachhead*, Ben Bova's *Mars* (1992) and *Return to Mars* (1999), Stephen Baxter's *Voyage* (1997), Gregory Benford's *The Martian Race* (1999), and Andy Weir's *The Martian* (2011), among many others—depict the exploration of Mars as part epic journey, part heroic quest, and part realistic cliffhanger about the best-laid plans gone awry as astronauts encounter crisis after crisis on an alien world. Such novels, most written by Americans and many by scientists, declare their faith in the future of space travel while offering cautionary tales about the perils astronauts face on Mars and the dire consequences for humanity if we fail to open a new frontier on the red planet.[21]

Among this rich tradition of Martian science fiction, the most significant for understanding Robinson's Mars trilogy is the idea of terraforming—a science fiction trope that began to migrate to science journals and into serious scientific consideration in the 1960s. Recognizing in the post-Mariner era that Mars likely was a dead or near-dead world, science-fiction writers began to speculate that, given its chemical makeup—notably the water and oxygen locked in its polar caps—the planet could be engineered into a habitable environment for future colonists, holding open the possibility of a god-like redesign of the red planet. Terraformed Mars, in this sense, offers the hope of redressing sociopolitical and environmental failures on Earth by harnessing the destructive technologies that threaten humanity—nuclear weapons in the 1950s and 1960s, greenhouse gases thereafter—to warm and hydrate the red planet and thereby sow a new utopian ecology on its surface.

Pulp fiction writers in the 1940s, notably Jack Williamson, had raised the possibility of engineering entire planetary environments, and after Robert C. Heinlein described the terraforming of Ganymede in *Farmer in the Sky* (1950), other writers—including Arthur C. Clarke, Isaac Asimov, and Walter M. Miller—depicted a near-future Mars in the process of being converted to an earthlike home for colonists. In Clarke's *The Sands of Mars* (1952), terraforming marks a new beginning for the human race, morally as well as scientifically, a chance to resolve the environmental problems and political conflicts that beset Earth. On a planet defined by its "cold, lack of water, lack of air" (86) the problems of labor and self-sufficiency reflect Clarke's "realistic" speculations about the prospects for settling Mars. But rather than a straightforward saga of human technological prowess conquering a hostile world, *Sands of Mars* raises ethical concerns about terraforming the planet: the novel cautions that humankind must not simply repeat the mistakes of its terrestrial past. The discovery of an indigenous race of animals with well-developed cognitive capabilities leads Clarke's settlers to conclude that terraforming Mars depends on humankind's "duty always to safeguard the interests of its rightful owners"

(199). This language of property rights and ownership remakes terraformed Mars in the image of an idealized commonwealth. For Clarke, enhancing the conditions for life becomes a measure of humankind's moral fitness, an indication that understanding and justice have progressed hand in hand with space-age technology.

Asimov in "The Martian Way" (*Galaxy*, 1952) places the politics of water at the center of future conflicts between colonists on Mars and Earth. His story describes the heroic venture to capture an ice asteroid from the rings of Saturn and return it to Mars so that the colonists no longer will have to import expensive water from Earth. The following year Walter Miller's "Crucifixus Etiam" in *Astonishing Science Fiction* offers the first—and one of the most thought-provoking—explorations of the values that drive the dream of terraforming Mars and the sacrifices that such a project requires. A generation later in 1990, Paul Verhoeven's film, *Total Recall* (loosely based on Philip K. Dick's short story, "We Can Remember It for You Wholesale" [1953]) makes terraforming a fantasy solution to the problems posed by two antithetical traditions in post-Mariner science fiction: the discovery of the technology of an advanced (usually long-vanished) race, and "scientific" speculation about colonizing and terraforming Mars. This film has received a fair share of attention from critics, who argue that its overt concerns about political freedom, individual identity, exploitation of labor, and invasive governmental interference mask the contradictions within the logic of late capitalism.[22] Scientifically, however, the terraforming of Mars is much less serious: it occurs instantaneously as a result of magical alien technologies and becomes a cartoonish way to evade—rather than think through—the implications of Earth's environmental degradation.

ROBINSON'S TRILOGY

In its focus on terraforming as a way to think about environmental problems, *Red Mars*, *Green Mars*, and *Blue Mars* offer an alternative to the scientific and ideological sleights of hand that characterize *Total Recall*. As Wark suggests in *Molecular Red*, Robinson's touchstone in the trilogy is the utopian systems theory of Bogdanov's *Red Star* (1907) and, I would add, the complex tradition of writing about Mars as a vehicle for social and ecological critique in works such as Kornbluth and Merril's *Outpost Mars*. Beginning with two short stories, "Exploring Fossil Canyon" (1982) and "Green Mars" (1985), and continuing after the trilogy in his collection of stories, sketches, and poems, *The Martians* (1999), Robinson uses the idea of terraforming to explore the complex relationships between planetary ecology—the interlocking, auto-poietic systems that sustain the conditions that allow life to flourish—and political economy, the distribution of scarce resources among competing populations and interests. At the center of this thought experiment about terraforming is what Robinson calls "eco-economics," his challenge to the assumption that economics depends on the exploitation, degradation, and eventual exhaustion of natural resources. The utopian speculations in *Pacific Edge* about what a just society would be like expand in the Mars trilogy into an epic future history that spans the transformation of a world over more than two centuries. On a planet where the biosphere itself is being manufactured, the idea of value, Robinson argues, must be rethought: *quantitative* measures of labor and capital need to be brought into balance with *qualitative* contributions to socioecological health—what we now call sustainability. This is, in part, the struggle and promise of a utopian science, embodied in the trilogy by Sax Russell, who spends almost two hundred years doing his part for this "stupendous Parthenon of the mind, constantly a work in progress, like a symphonic epic poem of thousands of stanzas being composed by them all in a giant ongoing collaboration" (*BM*, 527). Eco-economics makes possible this "ongoing collaboration" by offering an alternative to an economics of self-interest and aggrandizement.

The trilogy depicts Mars as a vast geological wilderness, encouraging readers to imagine the experience of "red rock red dust the bare / mineral of here and now" (*Martians*, 385). In "Fossil Canyon" a tourist hiking through the canyon systems of Valles Marineris finds lava pellets that he initially mistakes for fossils. After the guide, Roger Clayborne (who reappears in two subsequent stories), correctly identifies these "pseudofossils" as pellets from the eruption of Olympus Mons, Eileen Monday feels "a loss larger than she ever would have guessed. She wanted life out there as badly as . . . the rest of them did" (52). Roger and Eileen voice what appear in the trilogy as the "red" and "green" positions on colonizing Mars: the reds want to leave Mars in a nearly pristine—and lifeless—condition; the greens want to terraform the planet to make it habitable for humans. Within their ranks, however, the greens represent a spectrum of technological and political positions, giving voice to competing versions of planetary inhabitation: an ecotopia that harks back to the science-fiction paradises of the 1890s: a vast mining colony, a tourist haven, or even a new world that will supersede a worn-out Earth. The reds range from those who try, by appealing to the ecological courts in *Blue Mars*, to preserve the nearly airless and dry conditions on the higher elevations that remain almost the same as they did before terraforming, to ecoteurs who sabotage terraforming projects long after the planet has turned green and then blue. The kind of political conflicts that Robinson depicted in *Pacific Edge* expand, in the Mars trilogy, to planetary scale.

In exploring the utopian possibilities of terraforming, Robinson distinguishes his work from the science-fiction traditions he has inherited. His contemporary sf authors, like Larry Niven in *Rainbow Mars* (1999), continue to populate the fourth planet with a century of imagined Martians, from H. G. Wells's octopoid cannibals to Burroughs's giant green warriors, or to imagine, like Ben Bova in *Mars Life* (2008), a fanciful genealogy that ties humans to vanished Martian ancestors. Robinson distances his approach from these traditions of Mars as a living planet. Standing on the surface of Mars, Eileen recognizes that the experience of "red rock red dust" lies outside the literary and philosophical territory of modern planetology:

> All the so-called discoveries, all the Martians in her books—they were all part of a simple case of projection, nothing more. Humans wanted Martians, that was all there was to it. But there were not, and never had been, any canal builders; no lamppost creatures with heat-beam eyes, no brilliant lizards or grasshoppers, no manta ray intelligences, no angels and no devils; there were no four-armed races battling in blue jungles, no big-headed skinny thirsty folk, no sloe-eyed dusky beauties dying for Terran sperm, no wise little Bleekmen wandering stunned in the desert, no golden-eyed golden-skinned telepaths, no doppelgänger race—not a funhouse mirror-image of any kind; there weren't any ruined adobe palaces, no dried oases castles, no mysterious cliff dwellings packed like a museum, no hologrammatic towers waiting to drive humans mad, no intricate canal systems with their locks all filled with sand, no, not a single canal; there were not even any mosses creeping down from the polar caps every summer, nor any rabbitlike animals living far underground; no plastic windmill-creatures, no lichen capable of casting dangerous electrical fields, no lichen of any kind; no algae in the hot

springs, no microbes in the soil, no microbacteria in the regolith, no stromato-lites, no nanobacteria in the deep bedrock . . . no primeval soup (*Martians*, 53).

This litany of science-fiction creatures and doppelgänger races depopulates twenty-first-century Mars, from Burroughs and Dick down to the eco-niches that some scientists suspect may still harbor biological relics of the planet's habitable past.[23] Without these generations of fantastic Martians, the planet of "red rock red dust" becomes a site to explore how humankind might respond to an alien world that could be injected with life. In theory, terraforming Mars would force humanity to calculate—and take responsibility for—all the biogenetic and chemical interventions that create and sustain living environ-ments. Eileen's Mars is a thought-experiment that never can be performed on Earth but that has to be the starting point for considering how and why to transplant humans and other earthly biota to an alien planet. In this respect, Robinson's trilogy becomes the site for rethinking the values and assumptions that underlie our ideas of ecology and sustainability.

In "Green Mars," Roger and Eileen meet two hundred years later (thanks to the longevity treatments that play a critical role in the trilogy) on a climbing expedition up the escarpment of Olympus Mons. Mars has been terraformed, and Roger treats the loss of the "red rock red dust" as "the visible sign of a history of exploitation," the reshaping of the planet to conform to human "his-tory" rather than to its native "topography" (192). In contrast, Eileen invokes Heidegger's "distinction between *earth* and *world*" in order to suggest that *all* experience is mediated: "'*Earth* is that blank materiality of nature that exists before us and more or less sets the parameters of what we can do. . . . *World* then is the human realm, the social and historical realm that gives earth its meaning'" (144). "Green Mars" fictionalizes a dynamic accommodation that emerges between these positions. In the Mars trilogy, Robinson encourages us to rethink this distinction between "earth" and "world"—and to consider how the idea of terraforming challenges and transforms our fundamental values and assumptions about our environments. As he suggests in the poem in *The Martians*, "Canyon Colour," the idea of bioengineering a planetary landscape resists earth-bound categories: "There, on a wet red beach—/ Green moss, green sedge. Green./ Not nature, not culture: just Mars" (364). In an epic that resonates with the questions posed within the domain of the cultural study of science, readers confront a world that resists being reduced to the imposition of human desires on a "blank" landscape, to the "projection" of human desires that Eileen analyzes in "Fossil Canyon."[24]

Mars, in this respect, becomes a way to reimagine a tradition of American nature-writing that has shaped many readers' senses of their environments. The mountain-climbing scenes that figure prominently in Robinson's fiction, from "Muir on Shasta" and "Ridge Running" to *The Gold Coast* and *Sixty Days and Counting*, are extended and defamiliarized on the red planet. At nineteen, on a Mars just beginning to be terraformed, Roger has an epiphanic moment in the wilderness on "the great northern desert of Vastitas Borealis":

> Light leaked over the horizon to the southeast and began to bring out the sand's dull ochre, flecked with dark red. When the sun cracked the horizon, the light bounced off the short steep faces of the dunes and filled everything. He breathed the gold air, and something in him bloomed, he became a flower in a garden of rock, the sole consciousness of the desert, its focus, its soul. Nothing he had ever felt before came close to matching this exaltation, the awareness of brilliant light, of illimitable expanse, of the glossy, intense *presence* of material things. ("GM," 145)

This passage and others like it in the trilogy are less concerned with moments of psychological self-awareness than they are with the experience of an unearthly environment that deconstructs barriers between self and an alien "nature." Yet as the hiss of the oxygen regulator reminds him, there is no fantastic return to an idealized or pristine nature, no choice to make that could sever Earth from World. There is only an ethics of responsibility, of the values that the characters bring to the ascent of Olympus Mons. Roger's experience of "what it *feels* like to be in such wilderness" (206) is recaptured when he and Eileen finally reach the caldera of the tallest volcano in the solar system. Their experience of finding themselves "in the middle of such an heartless immensity" provokes very different feelings from what we might expect from a tradition of writing that pits "man" against "nature." Robinson's citing of Herman Melville's *Moby Dick* is suggestive: where Pip is driven mad by being left alone on the sea, Roger and Eileen see the negotiation between self and "wilderness" as an opportunity to be explored rather than a battle to be fought or a horror to be avoided. Rather than the hostile Martian environment envisioned by science-fiction writers like Schuyler Miller in the 1930s and Pešek in the 1970s, Robinson offers what Oliver Morton calls the "most textured and varied evocations of a mapped Mars that literature has to offer."[25] This imaginatively "mapped Mars" explores how the radical alterity of science fiction can enrich understandings of planetary ecology.[26]

As sf authors and their readers have realized for a century, Martian ecology is invariably a means to think about *political ecology*—what we might call notes toward a utopian future.[27] As Robinson puts in a poem in *The Martians*, "in the/ Attempt to imagine Mars I came to see/ Earth more clearly than ever before" (382). Part of this move toward clarity in the trilogy takes the form of Robinson's eco-economics—a key concept that extends into his later novels, including *Antarctica*, *Sixty Days and Counting*, and *New York 2140*. Having established themselves on the fourth planet in *Red Mars*, the First Hundred—the initial party of scientists sent to colonize the planet—fragment politically, socially, and geographically. After several years, a scientific team led by Vlad Taneev and Marina Tokareva develop a process to retard the onset of aging, then turn their attention to eco-economics as a means to integrate ecology and "its deformed offshoot, economics" (*RM*, 297): their goal is to formulate a way to account for the feedback loops among production, distribution, and consumption on a planet where terraforming literally manufactures the resources—air and water—essential for life. In contrast to traditional economics, "people arbitrarily . . . assigning numerical values to non-numerical things," as Vlad puts it, eco-economics defines "efficiency [as] the calories you put out, divided by the calories you take in." An ethical imperative follows: "Everyone can increase their ecological efficiency by efforts to reduce how many kilocalories they use" (*RM*, 297, 298). Restricting consumption becomes a far more effective means to increase one's value to the system than accelerating production because production inevitably strains scarce resources. Eco-economics, in this regard, calls into question the logic of capitalist production and, more generally, the ongoing exploitation of nature as the primary means to generate value. As a utopian simulation, it suggests experimental alternatives to ever-increasing cycles of resource extraction and environmental degradation.

Robinson's fragile ecology-in-the-making on Mars, in this context, serves as a fictional projection of late-twentieth-century eco-economic crises—a virtual space in which to imagine a society struggling through and toward "some kind of universal catastrophe rescue operation, or, in other words, the first phase of the postcapitalist era" (*BM*, 63). His trilogy works in a variety of ways to imagine the conditions under which capitalism will evolve—haltingly, violently, uncertainly—toward an eco-economic future. What distinguishes his novels from other late-twentieth-century speculative fiction about humanity's future on Mars is his emphasis—evident as well in *2312*—that the unending profits envisioned by late (and future) capitalism require infinitely exploitable resources in order for humankind to outrun the diminishing returns and declining living standards of intensification. As William Fort, the head of a metanational corporation that eventually evolves into an umbrella of semi-autonomous collectives, declares in *Green Mars*, "Capital is a quantity of input, and efficiency is a ratio of output to input. No matter how efficient capital is, it can't make something out of nothing" (81). If this statement describes a fundamental relationship between economics and the natural world, then the principles of eco-economics require, as Wark suggests, a "tektology" (Bog-danov's term) that mediates encounters among "otherwise *incommensurable* kinds of knowledge organization: science, both pure and applied, engineering, design, politics, culture, religion, folklore, and so on."[28] Terraforming Mars, in other words, evokes entangled forms of stochastic self-organization that cut across disciplinary divisions of knowledge. Eco-economics, as a revisionist tektology, then, might be read as Robinson's response to the obstacles that frustrate many utopian aspirations: social unrest, economic competition, psychic crises, national rivalries, racial hatreds, violence, greed, stupidity, and environmental degradation. As an eco-economic landscape, Robinson's Mars explores the involutions of fictional and scientific simulations of terraform-ing, even as it encourages readers to question the values on which scientific speculations about planetary engineering rest.

TERRAFORMING AS SCIENTIFIC SPECULATION

In reworking the tradition of Martian science fiction, Robinson relied on a burgeoning scientific literature on terraforming, an offshoot of semi-official planning for the human exploration of Mars in the aftermath of the Viking missions in 1976.[29] As the hypothetical "process of planetary engineering, specifically directed at enhancing the capacity of an extraterrestrial plane-tary environment to support life," terraforming encouraged science geeks to speculate about how "to recreate an unconstrained planetary biosphere emulating all the functions of the biosphere of the Earth."[30] In the case of Mars, the consensus candidate in the solar system for such planetary engineering, the grandchildren of Elon Musk have their work cut out for them. The planet's atmosphere is 95 percent carbon dioxide; its atmospheric pressure is about 6 millibars (less than 1 percent of Earth's); and its mean surface temperature is –56°C. Mars has no surface water (with some infrequent and temporary exceptions), and because it has only trace amounts of oxygen, it has no ozone layer, so its surface is bathed in ultraviolet radiation. Some years after the Mars trilogy was published, the robotic exploration of Mars detected high levels of perchlorates in the regolith that potentially pose risks to human health by inhibiting thyroid function.[31] Despite the grim prospects for all forms of life on Mars, beginning in the 1960s scientists such as Carl Sagan, Joseph Burns, and Martin Harwit took what they knew about the planet and started playing with ideas of how to thicken its atmosphere and warm the planet in order to create an earthlike biosphere.[32]

In the aftermath of the Viking missions to Mars in the 1970s, scientists developed a better idea of Martian areography and began to define the planet in terms of its potential resources for future colonists. Citing "compelling evidence that Mars has a permafrost that is rich in water," Thomas Meyer and Chris McKay suggest that "it is possible to prepare breathable air, water, rocket propellant, fertilizer, and other useful compounds and feedstocks" from gases in the Martian atmosphere.[33] Such in situ resource utilization (ISRU) would allow future colonists to relax "the need for tight closure, total recycling and complex toxicogenic filtering of the air supply . . ., allowing the use of simpler semi-closed life support systems where losses could be continuously made up from freshly produced air supplies."[34] In the speculative future that Meyer and McKay envision, and that has captured the imagination of billionaires like Elon Musk, ISRU might be the first step in jump-starting the same evolutionary processes that took place on Precambrian Earth—in exponentially accelerated fashion—on Mars.[35]

Unconstrained by laboratory space or budgets, thought experiments about terraforming Mars drew implicitly and explicitly on science fiction and produced a range of sometimes fascinating, sometimes bizarre ideas about how to re-engineer a planetary environment. Several scientists suggested that introducing chlorofluorocarbons into Mars's atmosphere (the same pollutants that comprise a key portion of the ozone layer on Earth) could melt the polar caps, warm the planet, and promote the outgassing of carbon dioxide trapped in rocks and the regolith. This would thicken the atmosphere and create a positive feedback loop. Picking up on ideas straight out of the pulps, a few researchers suggested that we could "free" the water and ice that exist below the Martian surface and in the polar caps by detonating thermonuclear explosions. Other scientists theorized that placing giant mirrors in stationary orbits near Mars could increase insolation and warm the surface; and still others (shades of Asimov's "The Martian Way") suggested crashing ice-rich asteroids into the planet's atmosphere, instantly thickening it and providing water for plants to survive. Many of these thought experiments draw on a novel that is cited almost reverently in the scientific literature: *The Greening of Mars*, coauthored by two prominent scientists, James Lovelock, the originator of the Gaia hypothesis, and Michael Allaby. In their novel, Lovelock and Allaby envision ICBM missiles with payloads of CFCs sent to Mars to create a runaway greenhouse effect and a carbon dioxide–rich atmosphere that sustains wide varieties of plant life.[36] In imagining how to convert the nightmarish byproducts of industrial civilization to benevolent uses, the novel offers a parable of ecological restitution on a planetary scale: the authors' terraformed Mars exports the Gaia hypothesis to the red planet, universalizing the balances and feedback loops of Earth's self-sustaining biosphere.[37]

Even as some scientists continue to dream about harnessing solar mirrors and setting off nuclear explosions to terraform Mars, their rhetoric invokes antithetical ideas about humankind's relationship to terrestrial nature: on the one hand, an ecology that exists in a homeostatic balance, and, on the other, a world of natural resources that can be exploited for profit and pleasure. For the more ecologically minded, terraforming Mars does not seem like imposing humankind's will on an alien environment but a heroic project to re-create conditions that existed four billion years ago on a warmer and wetter Mars.[38] As McKay puts it, "Mars lived fast, died young, and left a beautiful body—the Sylvia Plath approach to planetary science. We could play Ted and just ignore it, or we could do something better and bring it back to life."[39] This literary allusion turns planetary engineering into a resurrection fantasy, and McKay suggests restoring Mars to its (hypothesized) biological, geochemical, and hydrological cycles of four billion years ago, with Martian microorganisms interacting with "restored" versions of its ancient atmospheric and surface environments. In Frederick Turner's 10,000-line epic poem, *Genesis*, ecopoeisis on Mars is cast in an allusive language that blends epic conventions and Gaian ecology. Before terraforming, humankind encounters Mars in the twenty-first century as the abode of "a stunted and abortive chemistry,/ A backward travesty of life." Terraformed by both dedicated science and mystical incantation, Mars becomes a self-sustaining biosphere, "an arch-economy/ Dynamically balanced by the pull/ Of matched antagonists, controlled and led/ By a fine dance of feedbacks, asymptotic,/ Cyclical, damping, even catastrophic."[40] In the poem, the myth of biogenic resurrection makes ecopoeisis on Mars the fulfillment of our faith in the manifest destiny of human technoscience and terrestrial biota on another world: planetary engineering creates a self-regulating biosphere in which humanity and lower forms of life—"beetles and bacteria/ And molds and saprophytes"—"can start anew."[41] This myth of ecopoeisis as resurrection, though, is as much dream vision as scientific speculation: terraformed Mars gives scientific and poetic shape to wishful dreams of a prelapsarian ecology on Earth.

If terraforming, for some, projects the ethos of Lovelock's Gaia hypothesis onto Mars, for others the planet becomes the imaginary space of a new frontier, the ultimate goal of a space-age manifest destiny. In promoting his Mars Direct scenario (discussed in *Dying Planet*, chapter 8), Robert Zubrin, the long-time president of the Mars Society, forges explicit connections between the frontier thesis of Frederick Jackson Turner and the rationale for an American-led, all-out effort to colonize the red planet. "Without a frontier to grow in," Zubrin asserts, "not only American society, but the entire global civilization based upon Western enlightenment values of humanism, reason, science and progress will ultimately die."[42] This romantic vision of the American frontier—as Robinson implies throughout the Mars trilogy—is based on a dubious understanding of American history that shunts aside the humanitarian and ecological consequences of colonization. Projected into the future, this romanticized history of the North American frontier turns the clever engineering strategies behind Mars Direct—using the Martian atmosphere to manufacture water and fuel—into a vision of freedom and prosperity founded on the prospect of exploiting the planet's resources.

Zubrin's libertarian rhetoric depends on the economic dream of the infinite exploitability of resources: "Only in a universe of unlimited resources," he asserts, "can all men be brothers" because capitalist and democratic values were "born in expansion, grew in expansion, and can only exist in a dynamic expansion."[43] In this regard, his argument reinforces the belief that humanity's only hope is to repeat on Mars, and then presumably in the asteroid belt, the same practices that have devastated the Earth's environment. In his mind, to terraform Mars—into both a biosphere and a mining colony—will reinvigorate our civilization and become, as Turner puts it, "a project that will allow us to pursue beauty and truth on a grand scale."[44] Terraforming, in brief, projects onto Mars visions of prosperity and truth that turn an irradiated, frigid, and oxygen-poor planet into humanity's last best hope for survival through "dynamic expansion."

If Zubrin projects the idealized past of American manifest destiny into the future, the Mars trilogy challenges the idea that terraforming an alien world is, in any sense, akin to terrestrial new frontiers. Eco-economics counters colonialist fantasies of the mastery of nature, and Robinson's terraforming novels are not a blueprint for the future but a way to think about the interanimating logics of economics, labor, ecology, politics, and culture as they currently exist on Earth. At a crisis point in *Red Mars*, Frank Chalmers, the co-director of the mission to Mars and an inveterate politician, explains to the idealistic John Boone the logic behind interplanetary colonization:

> Russia and our United States of America were desperate.... Decrepit, outmoded industrial dinosaurs, that's what we were, about to get eaten up by Japan and Europe and all the little tigers popping up in Asia. And we had all this space experience going to waste, and a couple of huge and unnecessary aerospace industries, and so we pooled them and came here on the chance that we'd find something worthwhile, and it paid off! ... And now even though we got a head start up here, there are a lot of new tigers down there who are better at things than we are, and they all want a piece of the action. There's a lot of countries down there with no room and no resources, ten billion people standing in their own shit. (*RM*, 352–53)

In Frank's mind, terraforming Mars is a gamble, born of desperation, overpopulation, and the exhaustion of Earth's natural resources. His cynicism echoes throughout *Red Mars* as a counterpoint to both debates about eco-poeisis and revolutionary struggles to determine who controls Mars and its resources. In one sense, the utopian project of *Green Mars* and *Blue Mars* is to transcend Frank's brand of cynicism, to render it, as far as possible, a historical artifact. Taken as a three-part epic, the trilogy replaces the politics of desperation and exploitative, corporatist economics with the hard-won forms of cooperation that eco-economics fosters. In another sense, Mars, as it undergoes its sea-change from red to green to blue, offers its citizens (and the novels' readers) opportunities to reconsider the hyper-individualistic and opportunistic values of the frontier in favor of a tektology that overcomes the fear that history will continue as "a series of human wave assaults on misery, failing time after time" (*GM*, 516). In later novels like *2312* and *Galileo's Dream* Robinson revisits the expansion of humankind into the solar system during the centuries that follow the terraforming of Mars to emphasize that utopia is a process, not a be-all and end-all. The utopian drive in the trilogy does not mean that humanity has triumphed over its problems but that it has found ways to push forward into an interplanetary history.

THE MARTIAN LANDSCAPE

It's a rough road to utopia. The longevity treatment developed by Vlad and his cohorts allows some characters, middle-aged in 2027 when *Red Mars* begins, to survive into the twenty-third century. They debate—decade after decade as the planet changes around them—competing views of terraforming Mars and, consequently, competing views of politics, economics, and social organization. During the course of two centuries, the conflicts over the implications of terraforming explode in revolutionary upheaval, anarchy, civil war, and corporatist repression. Given its breadth, sophisticated political analysis, and attention to the psychological changes that transform his major characters over centuries, the trilogy makes Robinson seem more akin to Anthony Trollope than to, say, Ben Bova.[45] The hero of his novels, nonetheless, remains Mars itself, particularly if we are alert to the ways in which humans—immigrants and then native "Martians"—shape and are shaped by the planet's outgassing regolith, thickening atmosphere, proliferating plant and animal life, and expanding oceans. The evolving biosphere is not a backdrop for a tale of social evolution but an integral part of the complex workings of eco-economics on a terraformed world.

The political, ecological, and philosophical conflicts in all three novels pit the opponents of terraforming, the Reds, against the champions of ecopoeisis, the Greens. In one sense, these struggles project into the future the philosophical questions already being asked by scientists. "On earth," McKay notes, "the notion of life and the notion of nature are inseparable. But on Mars and in the rest of the solar system, life and nature are two different things. Mars appears to be a dead planet, yet it is undeniably a beautiful, valuable planet."[46] The extent to which "life" and "nature" can—or should—be separated lies at the heart of the conflicts between the Reds and Greens in the trilogy.

In *Red Mars*, the key advocates of Red and Green philosophies—the geologist, Ann Clayborne, and the scientific polymath, Sax Russell—voice their positions while the course and consequences of terraforming remain uncertain. Terraforming a world is "too big," as Sax says, with "too many factors, many of them unknown" to "model adequately" (*RM*, 171); nonetheless, he believes that transforming Mars into a habitable environment is essential to both their mission and future colonization. In an effort to halt the first efforts to re-engineer the planet, Ann sends private messages to Earth, is caught red-handed, and then must face her peers, most of them terraforming enthusiasts. Her "tirade" against terraforming casts them as careless children:

> Here you sit in your little holes running your little experiments, making things like kids with a chemistry set in the basement, while the whole time an entire world sits outside your door. A world where the landforms are a hundred times larger than their counterparts on Earth, and a thousand times older, with evidence concerning the beginning of the solar system scattered all over, as well as the whole history of a planet, scarcely changed in the last billion years. And you're going to wreck it all. . . . You want to do that [the "mass alteration of the environment"] because you think you can. You want to try it out and see—as if this were some big playground sandbox for you to build castles in. A big Mars jar! You find your justifications where you can, but it's bad faith, and it's not science. (176–77)

Ann zeroes in on the moral obligations of humankind to a (new) environment, a beautiful and valuable nature without life. In her mind, the Martian landscape itself challenges anthropocentric and biogenic justifications for terraforming;

creating the conditions for life is a form of contamination or destruction because the surface of the planet in its pristine state is inherently valuable as a "record" of planetary and solar system history that dwarfs human technologies, intentions, and desires. If Red Mars is "a beautiful pure landscape," however, then that purity, like its scientific value, can be appreciated only by human consciousness, and, in responding to Ann, Sax argues that we can imagine beauty and foster scientific knowledge without giving in to a selfish anthropocentrism. "'The beauty of Mars exists in the human mind,' [Sax] said in that dry factual tone, and everyone stared at him amazed. 'Without the human presence it is just a collection of atoms, no different than any other random speck of matter in the universe. It's we who understand it, and we who give it meaning'" (177). Sax's response suggests both the attractions and limitations of his by-the-book view of science and the universe—and his worldview (or Marsview) evolves dramatically in Green Mars and Blue Mars. If Ann's defense of a pristine Mars challenges humankind's technoscientific hubris, Sax makes knowledge the ultimate rationale for terraforming Mars. His response to Ann becomes a kind of philosophical one-upmanship: it is human intervention that produces "meaning." Even her celebration of "pure" observation and a scientific ideal of nonintervention depend on what he calls "the human presence." Yet Sax's insistence on anthropocentric meaning in an otherwise meaningless universe ironically reveals the accuracy of Ann's criticism: the basis of terraforming is an unbridled faith in human significance, a will to play (and play God) with the universe at the expense of what she considers a disinterested commitment to science. For Sax—and for Robinson's other scientist-heroes: Heather in Shaman, Frank Vanderwal in the Science in the Capital trilogy, Galileo, and Devi in Aurora—science has its limitations, but the mind remains capable of developing experimental programs and then using the results to generate rather than simply recognize a preexistent meaning in the cosmos.

These Red and Green philosophical positions—reiterated, modified, and contested during the course of the trilogy—mutate in response to the characters' experiences of terraforming. The conceptual, political, and spiritual arc of the trilogy moves the Reds and Greens toward reconciliation; antagonists throughout the three novels, Ann and Sax become romantically linked at the end of Blue Mars, a measure of the operations of viriditas on both. The alchemical sublime for the emergence of a blue Mars on which humans can walk, glide, and sail is the philosophy of Hiroko Ai, "the Japanese prodigy of biosphere design" (*RM*, 32), who articulates and embodies the holistic imperatives of a Martian ecophilosophy that anticipates the interactions of Buddhism and science in the Science in the Capital trilogy. As the First Hundred branch out from their scientific station at Underhill and other settlers arrive from Earth, Hiroko and her followers leave for the southern hemisphere to further the ecopoeisis of Mars in a nascent utopian community that resists and transcends the anti-ecological, oligarchic efforts of transnational corporations to treat the planet as a vast mining camp. The isolation of Hiroko's "Lost Colony" allows its members to survive the civil war of 2061, when corporate forces brutally quash attempts to establish an independent Mars, killing thousands, including many of the First Hundred.

Green Mars, which spans the decades after the war, could be seen as Hiroko's book because it is the moral force of her lived philosophy of *viriditas* that brings together the scattered groups of the underground in a loose confederation. The survivors of the First Hundred, their descendants, and allies among new immigrants from Earth eventually draw on the promise of her utopian community to provide the moral authority for their collective efforts to achieve Martian independence. In the process, politics itself is transformed. At the beginning of this novel, Hiroko and her followers, including a generation of genetically engineered "ectogenes," have created a utopian community, Zygote, in an ice dome under the south pole. As its spiritual leader, she gives voice to a philosophy that seeks to unify microcosm and macrocosm and prepares members of the underground for their eventual reemergence as a political as well as moral force:

> Look at the pattern this seashell makes. The dappled whorl, curving inward to infinity. That's the shape of the universe itself. There's a constant pressure, pushing toward pattern. A tendency in matter to evolve into ever more complex forms. It's a kind of pattern gravity, a holy greening power we call *viriditas*, and it is the driving force in the cosmos. Life, you see. . . . And because we are alive, the universe must be said to be alive. We are its consciousness as well as our own. We rise out of the cosmos and we see its mesh of patterns, and it strikes us as beautiful. And that feeling is the most important thing in all the universe—its culmination, like the color of the flower at first bloom on a wet morning. It's a holy feeling, and our task in this world is to do everything we can to foster it. (*GM*, 19)

Hiroko's celebration of viriditas inscribes the principles of a scientific will-to-meaning (the artificial-intelligence pun in her name: Ai) on sensory experience. The greening power she invokes gestures toward a union of spirit and matter, a synthesis of organic complexity and the spiritual growth that attends the processes of genetically fostering ecopoeisis as the "supreme act of love" (19). As life forms spread across Mars, this moral and aesthetic imperative to create beauty complements the political efforts of the underground to move stochastically toward a rough-hewn, evolving eco-economics. Viriditas, then, is not a thought experiment imposed on Mars but the embodied experience of greening a tektology to live on a greening planet.

Throughout the trilogy there are anticipations of the eventual reconciliation of Red and Green, of the alien landscape and the unforeseeable consequences of terraforming. Such anticipations, though, are scripted upon bodies and organisms, inscribed genetically rather than embedded thematically. This is the process of "areoformation": "an endeavor driven at a level below intention." Conscious political intentions and philosophical positions are acted on and sublimated by the landscape itself, fostering complex processes of ideational as well as genetic evolution. The opening of *Green Mars* reads: "The point is not to make another Earth. . . . The point is to make something new and strange, something Martian. . . . All the genetic templates for [the] new biota are Terran; the minds designing them are Terran; but the terrain is Martian. And terrain is a powerful genetic engineer, determining what flourishes and what doesn't, pushing along progressive differentiation, and thus the evolution of new species" (13). In Robinson's descriptions of the landscape, Mars is sensed and felt as much as seen. The planet acts from the start on the colonists, beginning a process of conceptual and evolutionary change even before the effects of terraforming—greater warmth, engineered life forms, and a thickened and hydrated atmosphere—take hold.

On an early expedition to the north pole, Nadia, a Russian engineer and later the first president of an independent Mars, experiences the planet's alien beauty. Robinson's description extends the strategies of aesthetic and psychological inquiry that characterized Roger's epiphany in "Fossil Canyon":

The sun touched the horizon, and the dune crests faded to shadow. The little button sun sank under the black line to the west. Now the sky was a maroon dome, the high clouds the pink of moss campion. Stars were popping out everywhere, and the maroon sky shifted to a vivid dark violet, an electric color that was picked up by the dune crests, so that it seemed crescents of liquid twilight lay across the black plain. Suddenly Nadia felt a breeze swirl through her nervous system, running up her spine and out into her skin; her cheeks tingled, and she could feel her spinal cord thrum. Beauty could make you shiver! It was a shock to feel such a physical response to beauty, a thrill like some kind of sex. And this beauty was so strange, so alien. . . . [S]he had been enjoying her life as if it were a Siberia made right, so that really she had been living in a huge analogy, understanding everything in terms of her past. But now she stood under a tall violet sky on the surface of a petrified black ocean, all new, all strange; it was absolutely impossible to compare it to anything she had seen before. (*RM*, 141–42)

Robinson's prose re-creates the imagined sensory overload of experiencing the planet's unearthly colors, massive land formations, and weak gravity so that beauty becomes both physical and geophysical, the product of the sublime entanglement of human physiology and Martian landforms. Nadia's response to the alien beauty of violet skies and frozen silicate oceans is emblematic of the changes that Mars works on its colonists. The terrain suggests the inadequacy of frontier metaphors and economic rationalizations to describe areoformation, the changes wrought by the planet on humans as well as by humans on the planet. The impossibility of fitting Mars into paradigms imported from Earth forces characters to move beyond historical analogies and, consequently, to take moral responsibility for the complex changes—socioeconomic as well as biospheric—initiated by terraforming. This responsibility is what ultimately distinguishes viriditas from both corporatist models of terraformation as an investment strategy and the passive worship of a romanticized nature. Areoformation, another name for this responsibility, resists the acts of simplification and demonization that construct Mars—or the Earth—as a storehouse of materials and energies waiting to be extracted, priced, and marketed. In this light, the ebb and flow between Red and Green areophanies reveals the paradox that there is value in both the pristine terrain of Mars and in life spreading across and irrevocably altering the planet. If viriditas in the abstract tends toward a kind of eco-mysticism, it is constrained as practice by the land itself, by what Sax refers to repeatedly as the "thisness" of biospheric alchemy, of life evolving on and transforming the planet.

RETHINKING HISTORY, RETHINKING ECONOMICS

In *Red Mars*, *Green Mars*, and *Blue Mars*, a number of characters sift through the history of human societies on Earth in an effort to help them make sense of their experiences on a new world. History itself becomes an obsession for many of them, and, in this respect, the novels extend the thematic concerns of Robinson's earlier fiction and anticipate the rewriting of Earth's history in *Years of Rice and Salt* and the solar system's in *2312*. On the initial voyage to Mars, John Boone and Phyllis Boyle, a true believer, debate the theological implications of history (*RM*, 52–54). Later in the novel, when he is traveling across Mars seeking a consensus on what form a new Martian society might take, John describes history as "what happened when you weren't looking—an unknowable infinity of events . . . a nightmare, a compendium of examples to be avoided" (283–84). Decades later, Sax searches for a "science of history" to explain the illogic behind social stratification, but he eventually gives up his inquiries, concluding that history is "nonrepeatable and contingent" (*GM*, 205–6). In the 2170s, Charlotte Dorsa Brevia, brought up in an autonomous matriarchal commune, publishes a "metahistory," a "kind of master narrative," to explain the emergence of a "democratic Martian society" from the wreckage of the "dominance hierarchies" characteristic of both feudalism and capitalism (*BM*, 393, 392). Her analysis of history tracks "a fundamental shift in systems" from the feudal-capitalist coercion of labor and monopolizing of profits to a "cooperative democratic economy" in which "everyone saw the stakes were high; everyone felt responsible for their collective fate; and everyone benefited from the frenetic burst of coordinated construction that was going on everywhere in the solar system" (*BM*, 393). Although her description of a "cooperative democratic economy" (like Zubrin's arguments for funding Mars Direct) requires more energy and resources to colonize the solar system, Robinson critiques boilerplate accounts of history-as-progress for ignoring the complex effects of human needs, desires, and conflicts. On Mars, utopia is a survival strategy—the only way to step back from the spiraling cycles of corrosive competition for resources and antidemocratic political and economic systems. The abstract systems and disembodied beliefs that underwrite feudalism and capitalism, Charlotte's "metahistory" suggests, feed off an anthropocentric faith in the superiority of ideas to lived experience. Such models invite disillusionment when they lead inevitably to violence, stagnation, and environmental degradation, leaving "ten billion people standing in their own shit." On Blue Mars, in contrast, a utopian history-in-the-making turns viriditas into an ethics and politics of becoming.

Robinson's future history in the trilogy begins with an act of near-biblical betrayal: Frank Chalmers suborns the murder of his erstwhile friend and romantic rival, John Boone, by misrepresenting John's desire for a democratic Mars as a threat to the beliefs and practices of a radical Arab faction. John, the first man to land on Mars, is an idealist, and his efforts to forge "a scientific system [of social organization] designed for Mars, designed to [the settlers'] specifications, fair and just and rational and all those good things" make him the point man for the as yet unfocussed attempts in Red Mars to "point the way to a new Mars" (283). Frank's motives for the murder remain, to some extent, unclear even to him. Frank fears being cut out of the negotiations with Earth to revise the treaty that governs interplanetary relations; he finds John's plans for Mars unrealistic, insufficiently attuned to "the ethnic hatreds, the religious manias" (16) that characterize an expanding, multiethnic Martian society; and he is jealous of John's continuing relationship with his former lover, Maya Toitovna, the leader of the Russian contingent of the First Hundred. Frank does not want authoritarian power but the authority to negotiate for Mars in its unending squabbles with Earth. His resorting to murder—"diplomacy by other means" (17)—testifies to the profound problems of trying to impose earthly values and assumptions on Mars. Frank becomes a crisis manager without a vision, "empty, and cold in the chest" (400), bickering with Maya and endlessly placating contending factions on Earth and Mars. In contrast to John's idealism, his go-to strategy for trying to unify Mars is to keep playing one group off against another, hoping to forestall outright conflicts. He dies at the end of Red Mars without having confessed to John's murder, but—in one of his few uncalculated, unselfish acts—saves Maya, Ann, Sax, and other refugees from the violence of 2061 during the massive floods triggered by the revolutionaries' sabotage of subsurface aquifers. Frank's death, then, coincides with the catastrophic reconfiguring of the landscape, the floods that alter "every single feature of the primal Mars," signaling irrevocably that "Red Mars was gone" (550). As he is swept away by the flood, the conventional notions that Martian politics can be micromanaged by Terran realpolitik—expediency, arm-twisting, and violence—are swept away as well.

The survivors of 2061 who continue the struggle toward eco-economics, toward a Martian tektology, fall not only into history but into theory—that is, into meta-explanations of the ongoing processes of areoformation. In *Green Mars*, Sax emerges as the hero of this quest to understand the complex transformations occurring on Mars. Part 4 of the novel, by far the longest, is titled "The Scientist as Hero" and tracks Sax's progress from the anthropocentric views of terraforming he voiced in *Red Mars* to his efforts to promote the greening of the planet and its inhabitants. During the course of this novel, Sax is given a new face and new identity so that he can work above ground as a plant geneticist. In this disguise, he is seduced by Phyllis, who represents the unholy alliance of Christian apologetics and capitalist ruthlessness. When she discovers who he is, she has him tortured and mind-probed to reveal what he knows about the anti-corporatist underground. After his eventual rescue by Maya and others, Sax struggles during a long rehabilitation to overcome the effects of a torture-induced stroke and to relearn the intricacies of putting thoughts into words. His efforts to regain his speech metaphorically underscore his emergence as a symbol and practitioner of a science committed to the imperatives of viriditas and eco-economics. During his rehabilitation, Sax engages in extensive conversations with Michel Duval, the psychologist sent with the First Hundred, who had saved himself from despair by joining Hiroko's group. For Michel, the scientist's job is

> to explore everything. No matter the difficulties! To stay open, to accept ambiguity. To attempt to fuse with the object of knowledge. To admit that there are values shot through the whole enterprise. To love it. To work toward discovering the values by which we should live. To work to enact those values in the world. To explore—and more than that—to create! (*GM*, 373)

Sax's response, "I'll have to think about that," testifies to his professional dispassion even as he puts many of Michel's injunctions into practice. In the second half of *Green Mars* and in *Blue Mars*, Sax becomes a key figure in the development of a democratic Martian society, whether destroying the Martian moon Deimos so that it cannot be used as a base to attack the rebels during the second revolution against metanational authority, seeking to reconcile Ann and other Reds to the effects of terraforming, or developing an antidote for the memory losses that increasingly plague the aged survivors of two centuries of Martian history. If science, for Sax, remains committed to exploration and discovery, it also becomes, in his mind, a utopian politics that redefines the relationship between objective knowledge and moral commitment. In this respect, he becomes a figure of the archetypal scientist, a Frank Vanderwal or Galileo, on Mars. Utopian science *creates* a future rather than simply trying to predict it.

This reimagining of science informs and is informed by a rethinking of both conventional and revolutionary politics.[47] Even as it ensures that the "whole enterprise" of settling Mars is "shot through" with egalitarian values, science provides a way to imagine recasting politics so that decisions about immigration from Earth, resource management, and governance reflect its commitments to eco-economics. Few science-fiction novels (at least before Robinson's Science in the Capital trilogy) devote as much attention as *Green Mars* and *Blue Mars* to the complexities of political debate and compromise, and this is one reason the novels serve a heuristic function for critics concerned with environmental crisis management on Earth. In *Green Mars*, the underground gathers at Dorsa Brevia to hash out the principles that become the basis for Martian independence; in *Blue Mars*, Reds, Greens, anarchistic collectives, and a range of ethnic and religious communities struggle to write a constitution based on the fundamental values of eco-economics.[48] These political meetings are foreshadowed, in some respects, by the scientific conference on the progress of terraforming, which Sax attends in his new identity as Stephen Lindholm, in *Green Mars*. Initially eager to catch up on developments that have occurred during his years in the underground, Sax becomes increasingly dismayed by the politicization of science as different speakers plug the latest schemes of the corporations that fund their research: a "degraded dark zone invade[s] the heretofore neutral terrain of [the] conference" (199). This blasted ideal of disinterested scientific knowledge, however, reemerges as the animating force behind the efforts of Maya, Nadia, Sax, and others to broker the constitution that turns utopian striving into political reality in *Blue Mars*.

What finally succeeds at the constitutional conference is the process of compromise itself, a utopia by committee. The realities of governing by eco-economic principles are fraught with conflict, but a free Mars evolves to meet crisis after crisis in the years following independence. Such agreements, though, are unthinkable without terraforming: in 2061 the revolution fails because the rebels, in their domed structures, are easy prey to devastating attacks from space, as Hjalmar Nederland realizes in *Icehenge*. At the end of *Green Mars*, Reds destroy the dikes that hold back one of Mars's new oceans and send a flood racing toward the rebel stronghold of Burroughs. But on a rapidly terraforming planet, the entire population is able to escape by using masks to filter the carbon dioxide remaining in the atmosphere and walk seventy kilometers to safety in the cold but thickened and oxygen-rich atmosphere. In the course of the three novels, the idealists, dreamers, and politicians are killed off: John, Frank, the aptly named Arkady Bogdanov (Nadia's anarchist lover), and Phyllis. Hiroko disappears in a transnational attack at the end of *Green Mars*. The scientists—Vlad, Sax, Nadia, and their allies—press on. As is often the case in Robinson's novels, it is the nomads who tend to prosper, including the stowaway, Coyote, who survives for two centuries as trickster, jack-of-all-trades, roving ambassador to underground settlements, revolutionary, and party-goer. His lifestyle embodies what utopia comes to mean.

The struggle for Mars in the trilogy is defined by a tektology—an eco-economics—that is forged in revolutions, conflicts, and conferences and that survives floods, wars, and planetary engineering. This effort to develop a means to live in concert with the realities of areoformation is, to say the least, hard-won on a planet struggling against the gravitational inertia of centuries of terrestrial history. At the constitutional convention in *Blue Mars*, Vlad defends eco-economics as "more democratic, more just" (119) than efforts by some of the younger generation to institute on Mars the verities of capitalist acquisition and ownership:

> If democracy and self-rule are fundamentals, then why should people give up these rights when they enter the workplace? In politics we fight like tigers for freedom, for the right to elect our leaders, for freedom of movement, choice of residence, choice of what work to pursue—control of our lives, in short. And then we wake up in the morning and go to work, and all those rights disappear. We no longer insist on them. And so for most of the day we return to feudalism. That is what capitalism is—a version of feudalism in which capital replaces land, and business leaders replace kings. But the hierarchy remains. . . . There is no reason why a tiny nobility should own the capital, and everyone else therefore be in service to them. There is no reason they should give us a living wage and take all the rest that we produce. No! The system called capitalist democracy was

not really democratic at all. . . . History has shown us which values were real in that system. (*BM*, 116–17)

Eco-economics rewrites the rules governing investment, capital, and labor. For economists, the conflation of feudalism and capitalism may seem ahistorical, but Robinson insists on this identification at several points in the trilogy (*GM*, 85; *BM*, 392–93). In a telling passage, the narrator describes the effects of Vlad's speech in the rhetoric of prophetic fury: "One of the ancient radicals had gotten mad and risen up to smite one of the neoconservative young power mongers" (*BM*, 120). Vlad emphasizes that ownership has been the guiding force of economic history—ownership defined as the unchecked and scientifically unsound privilege to treat common resources as private property. In contrast, the Dorsa Brevia accord recognizes "an economics based on ecological science." "The goal of Martian economics," the document continues, "is not 'sustainable development' but a sustainable prosperity for its entire biosphere" (*GM*, 358). To charges that he is a utopian dreamer or the avatar of twentieth-century socialism returned, Vlad reiterates the ecocentric principles of the Dorsa Brevia agreement: "The land, air, and water of Mars belong to no one . . . we are the stewards of it for all future generations" (*BM*, 119). This idea of a future-oriented stewardship challenges capitalist logic by refusing to commodify the resources that terraforming has produced and by insisting that the control of capital remains in the hands of those who produce it. As Vlad puts it, "in our system workers will hire capital rather than the other way around" (119). The ideal of a self-regulating biosphere advanced by Lovelock and Allaby in *The Greening of Mars* is extrapolated in Robinson's eco-economics to the realm of a utopian sociopolitical organization. On Blue Mars, people not only try to live in harmony with a newly created biosphere but also participate in an open, evolving system of elaborate feedback loops, checks and balances, and safeguards to ensure that there are no threatening accumulations of capital by a "tiny nobility." This prospect, for Robinson, is as dangerous as the deadly buildup of atmospheric pollutants.

TERRAFORMING AND ITS LIMIT CONDITIONS

In all three novels, major characters—John, Frank, and Maya in *Red Mars*; Sax, Maya, Nadia, and Nirgal (one of Hiroko's sons) in *Green Mars*; and

Nirgal, Sax, Maya, Ann, Jackie (John's daughter), and Zo (Jackie's daughter) in *Blue Mars*—wander across Mars, working on various projects, meeting new settlers and old friends, and taking stock of the endless changes being wrought on the planet and its inhabitants. In some respects this nomadic existence seems an escape from the bureaucracy, interference, and tyranny of metanational capitalism; in others, it testifies to the redefinition of notions of identity that the terraformed landscape of Mars fosters.[49] In his travels John comes to recognize that he was "probably wrong" to assume that "if he only saw more of the planet, visited one more settlement, talked to one more person, that he would somehow . . . get it—and that this holistic understanding would then flow back from him to everybody else." John's efforts to become the "articulator of all [the settlers'] hopes and desires" (*RM*, 284), fail, in part, because he inadvertently divorces social, ethnic, economic, and psychological identities from the processes of areoformation, from the landscape itself. As John comes to recognize, Red Mars is already being transformed and transforming its inhabitants: character is interpenetrated by a sense of place, of areography, as well as by historical experiences and psychic traumas.

More than a century later, Nirgal, who (rather than his sometime lover, Jackie Boone) inherits John's role as the ethical consciousness of his generation, finds himself rootless in the aftermath of independence. His disorientation marks both his recognition of and his resistance to the mutual inflections of identity, vocation, and place:

> All his life he had wandered Mars talking to people about a free Mars, about inhabitation rather than colonization, about becoming indigenous to the land. Now that task was ended. . . . It was hard to give up being a revolutionary. Nothing seemed to follow from it, either logically or emotionally. . . . On the one hand he wanted to stay a wanderer, to fly and walk and sail all over the world, a nomad forever, wandering ceaselessly until he knew Mars better than anyone else. Ah yes; it was a familiar euphoria. On the other hand, it *was* familiar, he had done that all his life. It would be the form of his previous life, without the content. And he knew already the loneliness of that life, the rootlessness that made him feel so detached. . . . Coming from everywhere he came from nowhere. He had no home. And so now he wanted that home, as much as freedom or more. (*BM* 301)

Nirgal's efforts to turn farmer, however, are devastated by a dust storm, and he returns to a nomadic existence, for a time joining a tribe of hunter-gatherers, future primitives who roam Mars and live off the terraformed land. He finds that his "home"—Mars itself—is constantly undergoing alchemical transmutations: ancient craters fill with water and become seas; the population expands into previously pristine areas; the atmosphere thickens enough so that, with some genetic adjustments, humans can breathe the air without masks; and the sky evolves to various shades of an oxygen-rich reddish-blue. On blue Mars, "home," like one's sense of self, is areoformed, and Nirgal's rootlessness comes to seem the natural condition for settlers whose lives extend to centuries and whose efforts to sustain a new biosphere define where they are and who they are becoming. As an ectogenic *homo martialis*, Nirgal does not practice eco-economics so much as he embodies its aerophonic energies. The generation of Martian natives he represents marks the end of the classically conceived *homo economicus*—that phantom of endless self-aggrandizement—who must be banished for any ecotopian tektology to thrive.

By the end of *Blue Mars*, Ann and Sax are lovers, the opposition of Reds and Greens subsumed by aerophonic blue. Mars has avoided a third inter-planetary war and offered itself as a model for an Earth struggling through crises of overpopulation (the result of the longevity treatment) and ecological devastation caused by the flooding of coastal regions when the Ross Ice Shelf in Antarctica is melted by volcanic eruptions. The trilogy ends on a Martian beach with children eating ice cream and Ann willing herself to survive a bout of arrhythmia. The technologies of terraforming offer, ultimately, a vision of small-town life, or such a life experienced in an ecologically pristine equivalent of Santa Barbara, an El Modena of the mind: scenic beauty, good restaurants. Robinson returns his readers to the doubled desires of the technologies of terraforming—the utopian possibility of a future primitive beyond the ecological degradation and economic injustices of the late twentieth century. With Mars terraformed, planetary engineering gives way to a self-regulating biosphere; the true ecopoeisis becomes the creation of new forms of social as well as biological life. Robinson's seventeen-hundred-page thought experiment, what he has described as a "Victorian triple-decker" (2013), finally presents itself as a utopian odyssey, a falling into ecotopian theory. The Mars trilogy, for many of its readers, is both a utopian policy statement and a hard-won course charted to an imagined holism.

And yet terraforming remains a sequence of dynamic and unpredictable interactions between human intentions and irreducibly complex environmental changes, adaptations, and reconfigurations. Although the First Hundred imagine Mars as "a blank red slate" on which, according to Arkady, they can "transform . . . ourselves and our social reality" (177), the planet ultimately proves recalcitrant. In the last prose story in *The Martians*, "A Martian Romance," Robinson returns to the romance of Eileen Monday and Roger Clayborne on a Mars where terraforming has begun to fail: the planet is locked in an ice age that may require a reengineering of the planetary environment. Blue Mars has given way to a deep freeze that redefines the limits and possibilities of human inhabitation of the planet. "Winterkill is winterkill," says Eileen, "but this is ridiculous. The whole world is dying" (349). Their ice-boat trip across the frozen oceans of the north leads them back to the problems posed by terraforming that had sparked debates between the Reds and Greens throughout the trilogy. Hans Boethe, an areologist who had ascended Olympus Mons with them centuries earlier, offers a litany of ways that the Martian ice age might be reversed:

> Bombs below the regolith. . . . A flying [orbital] lens to focus some of the mirrors' light, heat the surface with focused sunlight. Then bring in some nitrogen from Titan. Direct a few comets to unpopulated areas, or aerobrake them so that they burn up in the atmosphere. That would thicken things up fast. And more halocarbon factories. (352)

These "industrial" solutions are countered by Roger, who reinvokes modes of "ecopoeisis" as offering "less violence to the landscape" (352). This debate about re-terraforming Mars is not resolved, and "it begins to seem as if they are on an all-ice world, like Calisto or Europa" (353)—or in Antarctica, the setting for Robinson's 1997 novel. The deep freeze on Mars offers both a coda to the trilogy and a meditation about the limitations of humankind's ability to transform nature into habitat. Even at the end of *The Gold Coast*, Robinson counters the dystopian vision of a landscape of triple-tiered highways and endemic pollution with a climb into the Sierra Nevada that presents Jim McPherson the potential for both escape and renewal. Throughout his fiction, mountain environments represent the possibility of a human relationship with the Earth that resists greed and ecological degradation. The view from the mountains provides the glimmer of a utopian—or at least a different—future from the one force-fed us by late capitalism. The reversal of terraforming in "A Martian Romance," however, is not experienced by the younger characters as a tragedy. In contrast to "the despair of the [environmental] crash" perceived by the older generation and the prospect that "warm[ing] things up again . . . could take thousands of years," the young Jean-Claude "shrugs": "It's the work that matters, not the end of the work." The story ends with his affirmation that even if "everything alive now will die, [and even if] the planet will stay frozen for thousands of years, . . . there *will be* life on Mars" (360). This is not the affirmation of a red or green philosophy so much as it is a meditation on the bio-expansionism that is, after all, one of the generic bases of science fiction.

Rather than the theological "destiny of man" that Walter A. Miller evokes in his 1950 vision of terraforming Mars, human love is not directed toward a transcendence of suffering but refigured as an ethical commitment to the dynamic relationship between life and environment, a relationship that is transforming humans as humans transform the land.[50] In this regard, while love, friendship, and dialogue are crucial to Robinson's achievement in the Mars trilogy, such experience is never divorced from the politics and ethics of being "visitors on this planet" (*Martians*, 385), whether Earth or Mars. Love is finally defined by human efforts "to do something good, something useful," by the complex relationships between "red rock red dust the bare / mineral here of now / and we the animals standing in it" (385). The ultimate challenge posed by planetary transformation remains as much ethical as scientific.

As "A Martian Romance" suggests, terraforming—living on planets real and imagined—is an ongoing and collective endeavor. In Robinson's subsequent solar system novels, terraformed Mars remains offstage as the action shifts in *Galileo's Dream* and *2312* both out to the moons of Saturn and Jupiter and back to a future Earth dealing with its own crises of too much or too little planetary engineering. The Mars trilogy represents one version of a struggle toward a utopian future, and in the novels that Robinson has written in the two decades since *Blue Mars*—*The Years of Rice and Salt*, the Science in the Capital trilogy, *Galileo's Dream*, *2312*, and *New York 2140*—different struggles, different paths emerge as his heroes and heroines press forward.

CHAPTER 4

"HOW TO GO FORWARD":
CATASTROPHE AND COMEDY
IN THE SCIENCE IN THE CAPITAL TRILOGY

In 2015, inspired by Peter Matthiessen's *Shadow Country* (2008)—a one-volume version of his trilogy, *Killing Mr. Watson* (1990), *Lost Man's River* (1997), and *Bone by Bone* (1999)—Robinson shortened his influential trilogy about climate change, *Forty Signs of Rain* (2004), *Fifty Degrees Below* (2005), and *Sixty Days and Counting* (2007), into a single novel, *Green Earth*.[1] This compressed and tightened novel, Robinson suggests, "has a better flow" (xiii) than the original volumes, in part because *Green Earth* cuts a lot of the scientific discussion about global warming that has become more widely known since 2004. While it would be fun for future scholars to track Robinson's edits and discuss his reshaping of the novel, I want to concentrate in this chapter on the original trilogy, an extremely influential contribution to the emerging genre of climate fiction or "cli-fi."[2] While the role of literature in combatting global warming has attracted increasing attention by novelists, notably Amitav Ghosh, as well as numerous critics, Robinson's Science in the Capital trilogy and his subsequent comments on it remain central to questions of the politics of novel writing, the role of fiction in political and scientific debate, and the specter of environmental catastrophe.[3]

In his introduction to *Green Earth*, Robinson suggests that since its initial publication his trilogy has become "a peculiar mix of historical fiction, contemporary fiction, and science fiction, in the sense that some of it has already happened, some is happening now, and some of it will happen soon" (xiv). As this comment suggests, questions about genre in *Forty Signs*, *Fifty Degrees*, and *Sixty Days* are also questions about embodied and future histories. The Science in the Capital trilogy creates for its characters and readers a kind of liminal state, as though we were still half-dreaming and half-waking from the histories that we remember (the hopes represented by Obama's election in 2008), the times that we fear (the Trumpian nightmares through which we are now living), and the prospect of environmental devastation that already haunts our everyday existence.[4] These histories—remembered, experienced, and projected into the future—suggest why Robinson's trilogy transcends Ghosh's critique of the shortcomings of realist fiction to confront the consequences of climate change. As a touchstone for a literature-in-the-making of climate change, *Forty*, *Fifty*, and *Sixty* redefine what twenty-first-century readers consider "real." It is worth quoting again what Robinson says in his preface to *Green Earth*: "If you want to write a novel about our world now, you'd better write science fiction, or you will be doing some kind of inadvertent nostalgia piece; you will lack depth, miss the point, and remain confused" (xii). In a trilogy in which Robinson delights in "describing Washington D.C. as if it were orbiting Aldebaran" (xii), even the passages he later condensed or cut for *Green Earth* gesture toward a utopian clarity emerging from the stasis, confusion, and disorientation of a realism that we can no longer afford.

Although climate-change fiction has become a burgeoning genre in its own right, novels set on a radically warmer or colder Earth have been a staple of science fiction for some time. Adam Trexler's invaluable study *Anthropocene Fictions* charts the upsurge in late-twentieth- and twentieth-first-century novels that have taken as their premise the struggles of humanity to cope with climatic instability or disaster.[5] While speculations about environmental disaster have been around for more than a century, Earth since World War II has been ravaged in numerous sf classics by nuclear warfare, radiation, disease, or radical alterations in the climate. In J. G. Ballard's *The Drowned World* (1962), solar storms have melted the polar ice caps, warming the earth to primordial temperatures and forcing the remnants of civilization to flee northward to the shores of the Arctic Sea, as the great cities of Europe lie drowned. Under this non-anthropogenic global warming, the world slithers back into primeval violence.[6] More recently, however, as in the Science in the Capital trilogy, Anthropocene fictions force humans to confront the consequences of two centuries of fossil-fueled industrialization. In Jim Shepherd's "The Netherlands Lives with Water" (2009), Rotterdam is the focal point for a climate-induced cataclysmic flood; in Stephen Markley's "On the Phase Transition of Methane Hydrates," a climate researcher receives an anonymous, threatening letter in an envelope filled with white powder.[7] With their close attention to the science of climate change, both writers imply that computer modeling and the speculative projections of risk assessment are reshaping fiction itself. In the genre of cli-fi, however, the Science in the Capital trilogy, its condensed version in *Green Earth*, and *New York 2140* stand out as landmark interventions in turning the "minor literary problem" of utopia into a "necessary survival strategy" for an overheated planet.[8]

THE DROWNED CITY

At the end of *Forty Signs of Rain*, Washington, D.C., is hit by a perfect storm: during a record high tide, a tropical-storm surge races up the Potomac, and ten inches of rain in the Chesapeake watershed rush downriver. The city floods. In an uncanny foreshadowing of the disasters that struck Aceh in 2004 and New Orleans in 2005, the drowned city becomes a landscape of widespread devastation as well as the site of acts of heroism, altruism, and utopian possibility. As "images from the [flooded] Mall dominated the media," television viewers around the nation also see "TV helicopters often interrupt[ing] their overviews to pluck people from rooftops. Rescues by boat were occurring all though the Southwest district and up the Anacostia Basin" (352). Published a year before Katrina, eight years before super storm Sandy, and more than a decade before Irma and Harvey, *Forty Signs* anticipates the sequence of natural disasters and political failures that plagued New Orleans, the New York metropolitan area, Houston, and Puerto Rico during and after these storms; its sequels, *Fifty Degrees Below* and *Sixty Days and Counting*, imagine how utopian strategies might emerge from the ecological, political, and socioeconomic crises triggered by global warming. In subjecting Washington to a climatological quasi-apocalypse, Robinson extends his exploration of human adaptation to extreme climates that figured prominently in the Mars trilogy and his stand-alone novel, *Antarctica* (1999). In this regard, the Science in the Capital trilogy is less a future history or (from the vantage point of 2019) an alternative history than a visionary reassessment of the assumptions and values that define contemporary science.

As we saw in chapter 1, in "Rethinking History," "The Lucky Strike," and *The Years of Rice and Salt* Robinson adapts the genre of alternative history to change the ways we think about the historical narratives and eco-cultural contexts that shape personal and political identities. The Science in the Capital trilogy explores the complex relationships between technoscience and lived experience, between knowledge and socioecological commitment, in ways that recall and reenergize an American transcendentalist vision of a utopia always on the horizon. Rather than making global warming a backdrop for studies of climate and character (as in Ian McEwan's *Solar* [2010]) or the setup for a satiric dystopia (as in Will Self's *The Book of Dave* [2006]), Robinson asks us to take seriously the potential of science—from genetic engineering to paleoclimatology—to foster new, expansive visions of humankind's co-implication in the natural world.[9] If novels like McEwan's paradoxically tend to edge the sciences of climate-change mitigation toward the wings, the Science in the Capital trilogy challenges its readers to recognize that anthropogenic climate change profoundly unsettles traditional understandings of ecology founded on metaphors of balance, harmony, and appreciation. In this regard, the novels read, as Robinson says, as "a domestic comedy about global catastrophe":[10] they imagine a history that should be, or might have been, rather than reflect a past that cannot be escaped.

As Robinson acknowledges in his introduction to *Green Earth*, the original trilogy is a long, utopian novel based on the transformative potential of what he calls "science's ongoing project of self-improvement," its "powerful and utopian set of mental habits" (*Amazon Shorts [AS]*, 7). The title for the trilogy,

Science in the Capital, is taken from chapter 2 of *Antarctica*, and, in some respects, Robinson's approach to this "domestic comedy" takes up where the earlier novel left off: the characters in *Antarctica* inhabit a near-future that uses the scientific investigation of the polar region as a test case for creating a utopian science for the twenty-first century. Broadcasting from Antarctica back to audiences in China, the journalist/poet Ta-shu reminds his listeners that "the Earth is the imagination's home and body" (203). In turn, this recognition animates the underlying belief in both *Antarctica* and the trilogy: the project of a utopian eco-economics in the twenty-first century is to encourage humankind to strive to create "the home that has never yet existed" (383).[11] In the earlier novel, this search for "home" takes different characters down different, if related, paths: the worker at McMurdo Station known only as X reads "backwards in the history of philosophy, trying to track his analysis to its source. Everything that impressed him turned out to be based on something that had come earlier"; after reading Nietzsche and Marx, he finds himself skipping "back to Heraclitus" (48). Ta-shu envisions in the coming century "a returned clarity, as fewer of us get along ever more cleverly, our technologies and our social systems all meshed with each other and with this sacred Earth, in the growing clarity of a dynamic and ever-evolving permaculture" (376). The tour guide Val turns from guiding rich folks on adventure treks across Antarctica to joining a collective of utopian "indigenes" who have gone native on the continent, living as simply and as ecologically unobtrusively as they can on the frozen land. In all these respects, Antarctica serves as a laboratory for humanity to recognize the significance of the eighth and final principle of a renewed treaty to protect the continent: "What is true in Antarctica is true everywhere else" (397). In moving from *Antarctica* as a novel about contemporary ecological crises to the Science in the Capital trilogy, Robinson explores the ways that "everywhere else"—the centers of political power and population along the East and West Coasts of the United States—might respond to catastrophic climate change.

The interweaving stories of his major characters in the trilogy dramatize the individual and collective commitments essential to fostering radical change. They offer as well a mosaic of possibilities on how contemporary science—from climatology to bioinformatics to neuroscience—dovetails with Buddhist practices and philosophy. The possibility of altering how we live, as I have suggested, has been a driving force in Robinson's fiction since his Orange County trilogy, and the Science in the Capital novels reimagine what *Pacific Edge* gestures toward: the transformative politics and science that Tom Barnard, trying to envision utopia in a fictional 2012, can glimpse only through a glass darkly. Robinson's utopian "survival strategy," therefore, depends on getting his readers to reexamine what science does, how it operates on a day-to-day basis, and how its dedication to self-improvement requires a self-conscious understanding of its cultural, ecological, and socioeconomic entanglements. In the Science in the Capital trilogy, the sciences devoted to climate-change mitigation must remain open to (and enriched by) a Buddhist way of becoming that celebrates living in a dynamic world rather than trying to invent new ways to exploit its resources.

At the same time, Robinson's cast of characters—the environmentalist senator, Phil Chase, who is running for president; his aide, Charlie Quibler; the head of the National Science Foundation, Diane Chang; her powerful colleague, Anna Quibler; and the scientist as troubled hero, Frank Vanderwal—tend to see themselves as part of an ongoing project of national as well as spiritual renewal. As they fight through political crises and struggle against nefarious intelligence operatives, they try to breathe new life into a transcendentalist vision of a natural world and an American history restored to a utopian course. As the eco-cultural touchstones of American nature-writing, Ralph Waldo Emerson and Henry David Thoreau make frequent and strategic appearances in the trilogy; their works help to structure characters' efforts to reclaim the entwined legacies of political action and environmental stewardship. In different ways, Frank, Charlie, Phil, Diane, and Anna grasp intuitively transcendentalism's profound affinities with the values embodied by the Buddhism of the displaced Tibetans, the Khembalis, who move to Washington, D.C., as their small island in the Sundarbans (in the vast delta straddling the border of West Bengal and Bangladesh) is engulfed by rising seas. As counterweights to the political intrigue, hyper-surveillance, and bureaucratic infighting that often demand the other characters' attention, the Khembalis serve as a chorus for the efforts of Frank, Charlie, Anna, Diane, and Phil as they struggle to resacralize humankind's relationship to a natural world irrevocably altered from the one known by Emerson and Thoreau. It is only through a collective rethinking of history, science, and nature that a new civilization can begin to emerge. As Charlie puts it as he contemplates the fate of a watered-down, alternative energy bill mired in Congress, "people had lived cocooned in oil for a few generations, but beyond that the world remained the same, waiting for them to re-emerge into it" (*Fifty*, 209). At stake in Robinson's trilogy are the psychological, political, and ecological conditions of that reemergence. The centuries-long project of terraforming Mars that Robinson explored in his earlier trilogy is telescoped into a few political seasons as the characters try to overcome the lassitude and corruption endemic on twenty-first-century Earth.

SCIENCE, UTOPIA, BUREAUCRACY

In contrast to a long tradition of anticapitalist, antigovernment sf thrillers, like Neal Stephenson's *Zodiac* (1988), the Science in the Capital trilogy treats science as an integral part of an ethical and spiritual, rather than a purely instrumental, solution to environmental crisis. No fiction writer today exhibits a better sense than Robinson of the rhythms, nuances, and complexities of scientific discussion, and his commitment to the utopian possibilities of change focuses on humankind's recognition of its planetary responsibilities—an eco-economics for twenty-first-century Earth rather than terraformed Mars. In the years during and after the publication of the three novels in the Science in the Capital trilogy, Robinson became a frequent commentator on the fate of the Earth in an age of global warming and has been forthright in describing his "tremendous admiration for science as a way of thought (a kind of Buddhism already) and a form of social organization, a utopian political system" (*AS*, 16). Science in action becomes an alternative to the self-interest, hyper-individualism, and competition that dominate the antagonistic politics of late capitalism. "The simple truth," as he writes in *Antarctica*, is "that science was a matter of making alliances to help you show what you wanted to show, and to make clear also that what you were showing was important" (196). This description of modern science in almost Latourian terms underscores why Robinson is widely cited by scholars in science studies.[12] The planetologist (and sf novelist) William Hartmann argues that science "works . . . by appeal to evidence. . . . All the data are spread out, and the best estimate of truth emerges from it, not from the rhetoric of the person who makes the best case."[13] In emphasizing the workings of an "ideal science" in which the data speaks for itself, Hartmann suggests one way to understand the discussions at the National Science Foundation that figure prominently in Robinson's trilogy. In contrast to the heated debates between the Reds and Greens in the Mars trilogy, the scientific consensus about anthropogenic climate change in *Forty Signs*, *Fifty Degrees*, and *Sixty Days* exemplifies science's commitment to its "ongoing project of self-improvement." In *Antarctica* the community of polar scientists tries to bring the consequences of global warming to the attention of politicians in Washington, and Phil Chase, although sympathetic, makes cameo appearances only as a disembodied voice on the other end of a satellite phone. As Chase moves to the center of Washington politics in the trilogy, scientific procedures—collecting data, testing hypotheses, and rewarding successful pilot projects—offer a utopian model of how politics *should* work to further humanity's "self-improvement."

At Robinson's fictional NSF, oceanographers, atmospheric scientists, specialists in bioinformatics, mathematicians, sociobiologists, and physicians confront problems of a staggering complexity after the Gulf Stream stalls, reproducing the scenario that led to the last Ice Age in North America and Europe.[14] One of the few novelists to take seriously, rather than treat satirically, the bureaucratic processes in and through which we live, Robinson describes at length meetings at the NSF devoted to deciding what grants to fund and what projects to prioritize. Even on committees given to infighting, conflicts of interest, and horse-trading for votes, science moves asymptotically toward a strategic and hard-won utopianism—a utopianism all the more compelling because no space colonies beckon and no off-world resources or technologies (as in *2312*) arrive to help revolutionize Earth. In large measure, the comic arc of the trilogy depends on Frank and his fellow scientists keeping this "necessary survival strategy" in mind as they find themselves pitted against the head-in-the-sand politics of a fictionalized George W. Bush presidency and bureaucratic turf wars with other agencies.

As an NSF section chief, Anna Quibler deals with these complex, multidisciplinary efforts, as well as her hectic life as a wife and mother, by turning the scientific method itself into a strategy for coping with "the hysterical operatics of 'history'": "Take a problem, break it down into parts (analyze) quantify whatever parts you could, see if what you learned suggested anything about causes and effects; then see if this suggested anything about long-term plans, and tangible things to do. She did not believe in revolution of any kind, and only trusted the mass application of the scientific method to get any real-world results" (*Fifty*, 354). This kind of instrumentality is often the object of satire or, on the part of many humanists, disdain. In McEwan's *Solar* this kind of commitment is swallowed up (figuratively and literally) by the hero's bodily appetites. But in Robinson's trilogy Anna's trust in "the mass application of the scientific method" offers an alternative to "revolution" as a response to a corrupt political system and a world headed for climatological disaster. By focusing on the efforts of a core group of scientists, Robinson redefines the horizon of utopian speculation, shifting from the socioeconomic focus of Marxian theory to an ethical calculus of socioecological justice and sustainability. The eco-economics that he describes in the Mars trilogy is brought down to earth in *Fifty Degrees* and *Sixty Days*; the kind of strategic utopianism implicit in Anna's belief in the scientific method is not a function of a "messianic time"—that is, a time that marks the end of a corrupt or dystopian regime—but of what Robinson calls "a progressive course [of history] in which things become more just and sustainable over the generations."[15] In the trilogy, fostering a sustainable network of institutions and practices is essential to imagining a sustainable planet.

A scaling up of Anna's insights into an eco-cultural utopianism depends on developing alternatives to the corporatist assumptions and values of an exploitative, fossil-fueled economics. As Frank comes to realize early in the trilogy,

> science didn't work like capitalism. That was the rub, that was one of the rubs in the general dysfunction of the world. Capitalism ruled, but money was too simplistic and inadequate a measure of the wealth that science generated. In science, one built up over the course of a career a fund of "scientific credit," by giving work to the system in a way that could seem altruistic. People remembered what you gave, and later on there were various forms of return on the gift—jobs, labs. In that sense a good investment for the individual, but in the form of a gift to the group. . . . That was one of the things science was—a place that one entered by agreeing to hold to the strategies of cooperation, to maximize the total return. (*Forty*, 124)

Frank's recognition resolves the debate about institutionalized science that Robinson had foregrounded in *Antarctica*: while X despairs that scientists, on "their island utopia," are "not doing anything to save the world" because "they're just part of the capitalist machinery," Carlos (himself a scientist) recognizes that while "science itself is part of the battlefield and can be corrupted," it remains, organizationally and structurally, "a utopian politics and worldview already" (A, 221–22). For Frank, science is altruistic because its cooperative strategies incorporate, reward, and transcend individual accomplishments. Consequently, it offers a challenge to the monetized values of late capitalism by rejecting asymmetric economies of debt and obligation in favor of an ethics of mutual co-implication and responsibility. In turn, scientific cooperation depends on a self-reflexive questioning of received knowledge and an ongoing quest for the most comprehensive and reliable data. In another sense, though, the utopian tendencies of scientific practice might be seen as a kind of science fiction—a way of seeing the world that fosters, as Robinson suggests, a comic solution to the ultimate dilemma of *homo bureaucratus*: as Anna exclaims in exasperation, "We know, but we can't act" (*Fifty*, 253). While this frustration echoes throughout the first two installments of the trilogy, until the election of Phil Chase as president at the end of *Fifty Degrees,* Robinson rejects the pervasive cynicism—or "cynical reason"—that often seems the default condition and ethical horizon of contemporary existence.[16] This is not, then, a science that exists today (as anyone who has applied for an NSF grant knows) but a science that is to come; it exists only in the quasi-utopian spaces (the NSF, the University of California, San Diego) that Robinson insulates in his narrative from budget crises, a narrow vocational utilitarianism, and corporatist profit-seeking.[17] To become a lever to move the political world, a utopian science must overcome proprietary strangleholds on energy generation and food production and transform bureaucratic inertia into ways "to maximize [its] total [socioecological] return."

Early in the trilogy, Frank drafts, delivers, and then tries to steal back a letter to Diane that criticizes the NSF's hands-off, disinterested approach to science policy at a time when "humanity is exceeding the planet's carrying capacity for our species, badly damaging the biosphere" (*Forty*, 193). His near-jeremiad voices an uncompromising push for justice—social, economic, and ecological—that echoes throughout the trilogy. As he writes to Diane, "[W]e have the technological means to feed everyone, house everyone, clothe everyone, doctor everyone, educate everyone—the ability to end suffering and want as well as ecological collapse is *right here at hand,* and yet NSF continues to dole out its little grants, fiddling while Rome burns!!!" (*Forty,* 194). While this moral outrage at bureaucratic inertia allows Frank to vent his frustrations, political revolution, for Robinson, is never enough. He and his fellow scientists and their allies need to learn, in a couple of years, what humanity as a whole struggles toward during the centuries of *Years of Rice and Salt.* By second-guessing his way back into the system, Frank becomes an agent for conceptual and institutional change when he accepts Diane's offer to remain at the NSF, leading a proactive arm of the agency devoted to promoting efforts to mitigate the effects of global warming. Rather than promoting a Marxian view of revolution, the trilogy fictionalizes the ways in which contemporary scientists and their allies might fight their way through to a more just, equitable, and sustainable society.[18]

In his commitment to eco-political change, if not in his turbulent personal life, Frank brings back to Earth the scientist-as-hero of the Mars trilogy, Sax Russell. At the beginning of *Red Mars* Sax advocates an aggressive program of terraforming the red planet, even though he concedes that the process is "too big," too beset by "too many factors, many of them unknown," to "model adequately" (*RM,* 171). Yet, as we have seen, his views gradually evolve over the course of the Mars trilogy to reflect his commitment to social change and ecological transformation precisely *because* the planet is too complex to understand fully. Like Sax, who also suffers a traumatic brain injury, Frank plays a transformational role in the emergence of a utopian society in the making. Yet in his bouts of indecision and frenetic activity, he also becomes an avatar of the psychospiritual conflicts that midwife utopian change. He embodies the tensions—between mind and body, love and work, exasperation and activism, and insecurity and commitment—that define, however paradoxically, the means and the obstacles to a future eco-cultural transformation.

In a crucial scene near the end of *Forty Signs,* Frank attends a lecture, or really an extended meditation, on the complementarity of science and Buddhism by Rudra Cakrin, a spiritual leader of the displaced Khembalis. Rudra describes science and Buddhism as "parallel studies"—the former devoted to "natural observations," the latter to "human observations, to find out—how to become. Behave. What to do. How to go forward" (*Forty,* 242). The question of "how to become . . . how to go forward" shocks Frank into recognizing that a life devoted to science must transcend institutionalized rewards and the possibility of monetizing discoveries to promote a profoundly ethical relation to others and to the planet as a whole. A utopian science must redefine progress in terms beyond efficiency and material gratification, beyond the false promises of what Rudra calls "an excess of reason" (244). In *Years of Rice and Salt*, that "excess" is the history of repression, violence, and struggle that must be endured rather than transcended. In the Science in the Capital trilogy, as in *Galileo's Dream*, it is "science" itself that must move beyond its own birth-fictions of "reason."

Frank's crisis of faith reinforces his appreciation for the collaborative, interpersonal, and inter-agential, workings of science.[19] A utopian science rejects "an excess of reason" in order to reassert its collective and cumulative enterprise—"a cosmic history read out of signs so subtle and mathematical that only the effort of a huge transtemporal group of powerful minds could ever have teased it out" (*Forty*, 248). This "cosmic history" recalls Robinson's Mars trilogy and looks forward to *Galileo's Dream*, even as it extends across time and space Anna's faith in the scientific method. In imagining science as a "transtemporal" mode of utopian politics, Robinson emphasizes the mathematical complexity of climatological models because these sophisticated simulations represent a kind of projective thinking akin to science fiction: "Knowledge of the existence of the future," as Frank puts it, "awareness of the future as part of the calculations made in daily life" (*Forty*, 248). For Frank and his colleagues, the future becomes a dynamic and infinitely complex set of possibilities that shape and are shaped by the "calculations [of] daily life," from each individual's carbon footprint to planetary engineering. This "knowledge of the future" becomes an ethical imperative in daily existence and gives science a way to imagine existence beyond the "hysterical operatics of 'history.'" This obligation to the future, Frank realizes, "was what science was. This was what life was" (*Forty*, 248). In *Sixty Days* a fictional interview with the Dalai Lama reinforces the productive symbiosis between science and Buddhism: "Buddhism as the Dalai Lama's science; science as the scientist's Buddhism" (*Sixty*, 234). Utopian science offers an alternative to the "excess of reason" that deforms our "obligation to the future" into crude measures of profit and loss and the corrosive cynicism that attends them.

Although Frank realizes that science and Buddhism share a "rage to live, an urge to goodness" (*Forty*, 249), he is also very much an American hero fascinated by the legacies of transcendentalism.[20] In many respects, the Science in the Capital trilogy turns "global catastrophe" into an American "domestic comedy": Washington, D.C., remains the center of power; the Khembalis resettle in the suburbs as the last best hope for their community; the NSF becomes the engine for global efforts to deal with the climatological crisis; and United States aircraft carriers hook into China's power grid in order to keep electricity flowing during that nation's crash conversion from coal-burning power plants to wind and solar energy generation. The American landscape—from La Jolla, California, to Mount Desert Island in Maine—defines the planet-wide tragedy of environmental degradation and the utopian promise of ecological renewal. In *Sixty Days*, Frank and Diane visit a Frederic Church exhibit at the National Gallery; the artist's "almost photorealist technique in the service of a Transcendentalist eye" leaves them stunned because his paintings capture for them "the visionary, sacred landscape of Emerson and Thoreau" (168). This "visionary, sacred landscape" holds open the possibility that the characters can "go forward" and reinvigorate a beleaguered heritage of democracy, social justice, and community in a future beyond the frantic consumption of fossil fuels. As Phil Chase charts a new course for a sustainable future, some characters are caught up in visions of a golden age of landscape restoration: "The emptying high plains—you could repopulate a region where too few people meant the end of town after town. Landscape restoration—habitat—buffalo biome—wolves and bears. Grizzly bears. Cost, about fifty billion dollars. These are such bargains! The OMB guy kept exclaiming" (238). This kind of enthusiasm underlies Robinson's critical utopia because it gives voice to a tradition of visionary speculation about the natural world. The sciences of carbon neutrality and biome restoration, in an important sense, are markers of transcendentalism's utopian legacy.

Recovering from surgery to repair a subdural hematoma that he fears has affected his decision making, Frank immerses himself in Thoreau's journals and *Walden* with a passion that extends beyond philosophical interest: "*Walden* was a kind of glorious distillate of [Thoreau's] journal, and this book grew and grew in the American consciousness, became a living monument and a challenge to each generation in turn. Could America live up to *Walden*? Could America live up to Emerson? It was still an open question" (310). Robinson's emphasis on "liv[ing] up *to Walden*" reveals the extent to which Frank and many of his colleagues experience this "living monument" viscerally: rock climbing, kayaking rapids, and hiking through a closed Rock Creek Park that the flood has thrown back into a pre-urban quasi-wilderness. The "open question"—for Robinson's readers as well as his characters—is whether this Thoreauvian legacy can make a political difference in a multicultural, politically divided nation in the twenty-first century. In reading Thoreau and Emerson, Frank is struck by the realization "that America's first great thinkers had been raving nature mystics. . . . The land had spoken through them. They had lived outdoors in the great stony forest of New England, with its Himalayan weather" (239).[21] Although Frank returns several times to La Jolla during the course of the three novels, a significant part of the action in *Sixty Days and Counting* is set in this "great stony forest." Throughout the trilogy, Frank, Charlie, and other characters strive to recapture America's past and mold its future by seeking to return to and reexperience "the land" that in the nineteenth century had shaped Emerson and Thoreau's imagination. Frank and Caroline trace lost trails on Mount Desert Island in Maine, where Church painted some of his landscapes; Frank returns periodically to California, checks in at UCSD, and climbs the Sierra Nevada with Charlie. Emerson and Thoreau become the conduits for the characters (and Robinson's readers) to distinguish "the land"—an infinitely complex Nature—from its fragmentation in modern economics and politics that treat the natural world as a storehouse of resources to exploit.

Without disowning the transcendentalist view that the task of the poet, philosopher, and scientist is to re-enchant the universe, Robinson calls attention to the "cognitive estrangement" that reading Emerson and Thoreau can produce.[22] In contrast to mainstream nature writers like Annie Dillard and Barry Lopez, who tend to project themselves back into a nineteenth-century mindset by making a "return" to Nature somehow intrinsically redemptive, Robinson recasts the transcendentalist legacy of Emerson and Thoreau as a mode of science fiction.[23] In *The Wild Shore* Robinson had reimagined the postapocalyptic return to nature of George Stewart's *The Earth Abides* (1947) and Kate Wilhelm's *Where Late the Sweet Birds Sang* (1976). Twenty years later, the idea of a return to a "natural" existence—a rewilding of the environment—involves weaving together the legacy of these "nature mystics" and cutting-edge science. By reading the transcendentalists, Frank is able to overcome much of the dour disillusionment and cynicism fostered by twenty-first-century capitalism. Emerson and Thoreau become his spirit guides in navigating a visionary landscape—offering a glimpse of what a utopian, post–fossil-fueled world might be. Church's "almost photorealist technique," then, becomes the imaginative ground for envisioning a climatologically and socioeconomically sustainable future—a future that is both familiar and intriguingly other. For Robinson, it is only through the refracting lenses of science fiction that we can imagine a (re)emergent world that has been waiting for a civilization no longer "cocooned in oil."

The narrative challenge that Robinson faces in the trilogy, then, is bringing climatological time within the realms of subjective experience.[24] To the extent that the transcendentalist vision of Nature (what Emerson called "the circumstance which dwarfs every other circumstance") offers the promise of an unalienated universalism, it gestures toward geological and paleontological timescales that, in the nineteenth century, were only beginning to be understood.[25] The dialectic of inward enlightenment and outward vision—of momentary time that expands organically to intimations of the infinite—depends on an experiential Nature that can be felt and touched. In "Nature," Emerson invokes the "halcyons . . . [of] that pure October weather" in New England in order to ground his belief that "Nature is the incarnation of a thought, and turns to a thought again, as ice becomes water and gas." On these days, he continues, "the world reaches its perfection, when the air, the heavenly bodies, and the earth, make a harmony, . . . when, in these bleak upper sides of the planet, nothing is to desire that we have heard of in the happiest latitudes, and we bask in the shining hours of Florida and Cuba[.] . . . The day, immeasurably long, sleeps over the broad hills and warm wide fields."[26] Yet this vision of natural "perfection," as Robinson reminds us throughout the trilogy, is climatologically specific. "Ice [becoming] water and gas" assumes unintended ironies in an era of global warming and retreating glaciers. In describing the universe as a web of complex, proliferating, and dynamic energies, Emerson's distillation of "longevity" into the "sunny hours" of "pure October weather" becomes a kind of primeval negation of blinkered, industrial-era efforts to reduce to mechanics a "power which does not respect quantity, which makes the whole and the particle its equal channel." This implicit challenge to rigid quantification does not extend to the sciences of complexity that have developed sophisticated strategies to study the relationships between "the whole" and "the particle." The climatological forces that shaped the fields and coastlines of Emerson's New England lie beyond his and his readers' experience: and the "shining hours" of the Caribbean presuppose a climatologically stable "Nature," a world in which Miami has not been inundated by rising sea levels, as it is in *2312*, or New York has not become a "super Venice," as it is in *New York 2140*. Emerson's vision of a world alive with dynamic and proliferating energies is extended in Robinson's trilogy to the experience of temporal and topographical dislocations. The prospect of "global catastrophe," in this respect, can be rendered only by the kinds of imaginative analogies that Robinson uses in striking fashion in *Forty Signs*, *Fifty Degrees*, and *Sixty Days*: the cliffs of La Jolla crumbling into the ocean, Washington frozen into a Siberian outpost; New England's "Himalayan weather." These alien landscapes of near-future catastrophe seem as provocative and mesmerizing as his Martian vistas.

At the scientific climax of *Fifty Degrees*, a consortium of European reinsurance giants fund a massive effort to restart the stalled Gulf Stream by re-salinating the North Atlantic, after the melting of the Laurentian ice sheet has sent massive floods of fresh water pouring into the ocean off Newfoundland. The timescales of paleoclimatology may dwarf and beggar the human imagination, yet the verisimilitude of Robinson's descriptions depend on a dynamic overlay of subjective and planetary time. Drawing on the work of paleoclimatologists on thermohaline convection patterns, Robinson dramatizes the ways in which abrupt climate change was triggered in the past.[27]

The last great ice age to cover the northern hemisphere, the Younger Dryas, began abruptly eleven thousand years ago; ice core samples reveal that climate patterns in Europe and North America shifted within a few years, triggered by the stalling of the Gulf Stream. Prior to this event, North America had been warming gradually, and enormous pools of melted ice-water formed on top of the Canadian ice cap, held back by immense ice dams.[28] As temperatures climbed above freezing, these freshwater lakes periodically broke through the weakening ice dams and rushed down into the oceans in cataclysmic outburst floods. When the ice sheet covering the Canadian arctic melted during a prolonged period of above-normal temperatures, ice dams gave way, releasing, in a matter of weeks, a volume of water as large as that contained in all of the Great Lakes into the Atlantic. This fresh water sat as a cap on the warmer water of the Gulf Stream, inhibiting a crucial part of the system of ocean circulation. The Gulf Stream is part of a much larger system of ocean currents, and it carries warm water on the surface of the Atlantic much farther north than it would otherwise travel. Once the water cools enough (off the coasts of Iceland, Greenland, and Scotland), it sinks to the seafloor and runs south. These areas of downwelling can occur *only* if the water is salty enough because water density is a function of both heat and salinity: hence, the term thermohaline convection. Downwelling drives the process called deep-water formation that occurs in only a few areas in the waters of the polar regions: colder waters are forced by downwelling into deep ocean currents that run south and provide much of the energy to drive the entire complex system of oceanic circulation. When the freshwater from Arctic floods rushed into the north Atlantic eleven thousand years ago, it disrupted the massive heat transfer necessary to continue the cycle of downwelling. Temperatures in Europe and the eastern half of North America consequently dropped by fifteen to thirty degrees Fahrenheit, triggering the most recent ice age.

The stalling of the Gulf Stream in the trilogy turns an act of imaginative, paleoclimatological recovery into a science-fiction vision of the future: a cold, dying planet that has to be terraformed back to a natural world that Emerson might recognize. Although Robinson terms the $100 billion effort to resalinate the North Atlantic in *Fifty Degrees*, using a fleet of one thousand previously mothballed, single-hulled oil tankers filled with 500 million metric tons of salt, "the first major act of planetary engineering ever attempted" (*Fifty*, 379), his emphasis is less on world (re)building than it is on a science freeing itself from "an excess of reason" and figuring out a "way to go forward." If nature writing is reimagined as science fiction, the novelist's challenge becomes to render convincingly the overlay of climatological and subjective or experiential time. In this regard, the journey toward utopia takes place within the individual's consciousness and propels "forward" his or her body. What Peter Middleton calls the "immersive simulations" of novels about global warming are focused, in large measure, on Frank Vanderwal, who, for much of the trilogy, remains caught between mind and body, thought and physical exertion, and anxiety and love.[29]

THE SCIENTIST GONE FERAL

For much of the last two novels of the trilogy, Frank experiences the "global catastrophe" of the stalled Gulf Stream as a nomad. Because the lease on his apartment expired before the flood, he has no fixed address in its Katrina-like aftermath: rents in and around the District have skyrocketed, buildings stand abandoned to squatters in the worst-hit areas of Washington, and bitter cold reduces him for a few nights to sleeping in his van. He soon decides he is better off going feral and escaping, after work, from the condomundo-like cubicles that define modern existence. He builds a treehouse in the semi-wilderness of the closed Rock Creek Park, equipped with the cutting-edge gadgets and high-tech fabrics favored by twenty-first-century adventurers. After long working hours at the NSF, Frank, at night, becomes an avatar of the paleolithic postmodernist by adapting to the oddly pristine landscape of the flood-ravaged park. He hangs out with homeless men who congregate around one of the firepits and plays frisbee golf with a group of fregans who have chosen to live off the grid in abandoned houses and forage food from restaurant dumpsters. He tracks animals from the Washington Zoo (turned loose as the flood hit at the end of *Forty Signs of Rain*) that have gone feral in Rock Creek Park, and he imitates the vocalizations of gibbons and siamangs that lead their own fregan-like existence. As a sociobiologist, Frank recognizes that he has turned instinctively to the strategies and technologies of acclimatization of our species' nomadic past:[30]

> He was the Paleolithic in the park. A recent article in *The Journal of Sociobiology* had reminded him of the man in the ice, a man who had died crossing a Tyrolean pass some five thousand years before. He had lain there frozen in a glacier until [he had been] discovered in 1991. All his personal possessions had been preserved along with his body. . . . Reading the inventory of his possessions, Frank had noticed how many correlations there were between his own gear and the man in the ice. Probably both kits were pretty much what people had carried in the cold for the last fifty thousand years. (*Fifty*, 231–32)

Frank then lists these correlations: sewn furs / his down jacket; a paleolithic small tool of bones / his Swiss Army knife; a copper-headed axe / his mountaineering ice axe; a "backpack made of wood and fur" / his nylon backpack; a birch-bark container to carry embers, and a stone bowl and flints / his cigarette lighter; and birch fungus that might have been a medicine / his aspirin. "All [things] down the list," Frank realizes, "familiar stuff. . . . He was the Alpine man!" (232). Rather than burning wood or fossil fuels, Frank returns to age-old survival strategies: camouflaging his treehouse; pulling up his ladder with a winch; keeping his body warm in a high-tech sleeping bag instead of trying to heat a large living space. Fascinated by his nomadic existence, Frank asks and embodies the question of whether a species whose brain evolved on the savannah running down game and crafting Acheulian hand axes can remain sane in the closed boxes of *homo urbanus*: elevators, office cubicles, cars, hotel rooms, and apartments.[31] He becomes, in one sense, the distant offspring of Loon and his tribe in *Shaman*.

Frank's daily existence—sleeping in his treehouse until dawn, then exercising and showering at his health club, working all day, eating dinner at restaurants, and spending his evenings with the new nomads in the park—provokes questions that even Frank, the editor of the *Journal of Sociobiology*, cannot answer. Are tracking animals and interpreting data from weather satellites different cognitive functions? How can we analyze the complex relationships between conscious thought and unconscious bodily responses? Is our evolutionary fate written in our genes? For the feral scientist, these questions pose ethical as well as scientific dilemmas because living as a nomad recalibrates what we think of as commonsense views of the relationships among body, thought, and topography. Running through the deserted park, Frank almost trips, catches himself, and continues on, marveling at the coordination of brain and muscles:

> How had he done that? No warning, instant reaction, how had there been time? In thousandths of a second his body had sensed the absence of ground, stiffened the appropriate muscles by the appropriate amount, and launched into an improvised solution. . . . So just how fast *was* the brain? It appeared to be almost inconceivably fast, and in those split seconds, extremely creative and decisive. . . . Indeed, running steeplechase and watching what his body did, especially after unforeseen problems were solved, Frank had to conclude that he was the inadvertent jailer of a mute genius. . . . Eleven million bits of data per second were taken in at the sensory endings of the nervous system, he read. In each second all incoming data were scanned, categorized, judged for danger, prioritized, and reacted to, this going on continuously, second after second. . . . Parallel processing of different activities in the parcellated mind, at different speeds. (95–96)

While our conscious minds remain caught up in "an excess of reason," our "unconscious" brain remains "creative and decisive," working at incredible speeds to react to dangers and unforeseeable circumstances. Frank's life in the woods, particularly in *Fifty Degrees*, suggests to him that a brain devoted to massive parallel processing in an always changing environment evolved in tandem with nomadic survival strategies. But these parallel processes disclose the alienness of the dynamic physical reactions—the inaccessibility of the "mute genius" that marks the limits of conscious self-knowledge. The "inadvertent jailer" of self-identity, buoyed by and sinking under its "excess of reason," either tries to segregate mind and body or collapses them into a crude, dystopian determinism. This is, he realizes, the parcellated crisis for the hominid with the "parcellated mind." And it is this crisis that leads Frank to learn from the Khembalis and embrace what he can of their ways of living.

The questions that trouble Frank—the tension within the "socio" and "biology" of his existence—mark his troubled relationships with women, from his ex-wife, Marta, to his mysterious love interest, Caroline. These relationships are fraught with misunderstandings, deceit, and insecurity. Rudra's idea of love, whatever potential it may hold for ethical transformation, remains, for Frank, entangled in a variety of problems: losing Marta's money in a failed biotech startup, feeling betrayed by her sexual openness, and trying to understand Caroline's role in a cryptic futures market that invests in people who may make scientific breakthroughs. At the end of *Fifty Signs*, Frank helps Caroline, a government agent with whom he is having an affair, escape from the seemingly omnipresent surveillance of her husband—a sinister avatar of domestic intelligence agencies run amok in the aftermath of 9/11. In part because Caroline disappears for long stretches, contacts him infrequently, and repeatedly warns him about the dangers posed by her husband and his cronies trying to steal the presidential election, Frank finds himself trapped in a state of profound uncertainty: "Frank sat there. He didn't know what to think. He could think this, he could think that. Could, could, could, could, could" (404). Frank's inability to think reflects his struggle against his own "excess of reason"—his unintentional mirroring of the mindset of his adversaries—that seems to be caving in on itself. His inability to decide "what to think" may be a symptom of his subdural hematoma but it also reframes the problem of what traditionally is called alienation. Rather than suffering the local effects of socioeconomic injustice or political oppression, he experiences the alienness of his own being—a strangeness that resonates more with, say, object-oriented ontology than it does with existential indecision.[32] Whatever his commitment to "an urge to goodness," the paleolithic postmodernist finds the holistic universe celebrated by Emerson irreducibly alien. Humankind's inability to take action against a rising sea of troubles—"We know but we can't act," as Anna says—finds a subjective correlative in the activist's and lover's dilemma: "could, could, could, could, could." At the end of *Fifty Degrees*, "could" marks the persistence of cultural inertia, economic inequality, political fragmentation, and institutionalized violence, even as it reflects the always disorienting and always contentious transition to a utopian future that characterizes Robinson's visionary novels and troubles his heroes (Nirgal in *Blue Mars*) and heroines (Swan Er Hong in *2312*).

BEYOND THE TRANSCENDENTALIST LEGACY

Robinson's "domestic comedy" ultimately embraces both the maddening problems and potential of Anna's frustration and Frank's indecision: "We know but we can't act." The Science in the Capital trilogy does not envision a nostalgic return to a transcendentalist past because the landscape of those "raving nature mystics" has been blasted by anthropogenic climate change. In an extended episode in *Sixty Days* Charlie Quibler joins some college friends and Frank on a week-long climbing expedition in the Sierra Nevada and finds that, as a grim consequence of diminished snowpacks in the mountains, "the high Sierra meadows were dying" (217): the "ground cover was simply brown. It was dead. Except for fringes of green around drying ponds, or algal mats on the exposed pond bottoms, every plant on this south-facing slope had died. It was as burnt as any range in Nevada. One of the loveliest landscapes on the planet, dead before their eyes" (224). The dead landscape offers a visceral image of the dead ends of exploitative capitalism; it stands in mute contrast to the vistas that, for Frank in particular, suggest the prospect of ecopolitical renewal: the surf off La Jolla, the "stony forests" of Maine. In Robinson's earlier fiction, such as "Ridge-Running" and *The Gold Coast*, the Sierras themselves had been the landscape that captured the possibility of such ecological and social renewal. Yet, in an important sense, the seemingly archetypal landscapes of the Science in the Capital trilogy—whether desiccated, calving into the

Pacific, or held in the fragile refractions of transcendental "halcyons"—represent geophysical moments in planetary time. In a rapidly warming world, even the seemingly immutable mountains of stories like "Muir on Shasta" are being transformed anthropogenically into a "burnt," desert landscape.

As the world fast-forwards in *Sixty Days* into new modes of sustainable energy generation, Marta's biotech startup, working with the Russian government, releases a genetically engineered lichen in Siberia that increases carbon drawdown by evergreen trees. As the lichen spreads quickly beyond its original testing area, Frank realizes that the feedback effects of this herculean experiment are "very possibly incalculable, something they could only find out by watching what happened in real time, real space. Like history itself. History in the making, right out there in the middle of Siberia" (286). "History in the making" defies a by-rote anthropocentrism because it describes the co-implication of humankind and environment. In a sense, the history of the planet—like that of terraformed Mars—is the aggregate of "incalculable" and unpredictable outcomes. What matters ultimately in Robinson's trilogy are the ethics and politics of "how to go forward" in the face of profound uncertainty and profound self-questioning of a species that "could do this" or "could do that": "could, could, could, could, could."

More than a decade after its first installment appeared—after the financial crisis of 2008, the rise of the Tea Party, and the election of Donald Trump—the Science in the Capital trilogy reads, in part, like an eco-cultural dream vision. The novels give to scientists an eco-spiritual consciousness that they may yearn to proclaim but often lack a language to articulate. In *Sixty Days*, the uncensored, unteleprompted presidential blogs of Phil Chase describe the progress of national and international efforts to repower the shining city on the hill by renewable energy—they describe, in effect, an ecopolitics that embraces science fiction as much as it does the visionary landscapes of Emerson and Thoreau. In gazing toward the second decade of the century, Robinson's trilogy seems to reimagine the era of the first years of Obama's presidency as a kind of shadow history—what could be and should have been in a parallel universe governed by an alternative politics and an alternative, socially engaged science. As a shadow history, it evokes a waking dream that many readers on the Left may recognize—a dream that persists in the utopian half-lives of the Occupy movement, of the resistance to Trump, of organic farmers' markets on Saturday mornings. It's a utopia always receding into the future—a deferred promise, as Ernst Bloch recognized, that is irrevocably paradoxical: "the homeland where no one has ever been but where alone we are authentically at home."[33] Like Frank, we can be authentically at home only by embracing the challenges posed by a future receding into cynicism and inaction, and figuring out "how to go forward" toward a visionary landscape. In his novels published after the trilogy, Robinson looks back—to the cave paintings of Chauvet, to Galileo's Italy—and forward to humankind's expansion into the solar system in order to imagine these different paths to the future.

CHAPTER 5

"OUR ONE AND ONLY HOME": HUMANKIND IN THE SOLAR SYSTEM

From the beginning of his career, Robinson's future histories have explored humankind's colonization of the solar system. In focusing on space exploration constrained by the laws of physics, Robinson rejects a future of warp drives, travel through wormholes, hyperspace, and intergalactic adventure. *Aurora* (2015) is, in part, a tale of the ecological constraints that turn interstellar dreams into catastrophic fantasies. While the Mars trilogy charts humankind's terraforming of the red planet over two centuries, his other solar-system novels, from the early *Icehenge* (1984) to *Galileo's Dream* (2009) and *2312* (2012), extend this future history into the fourth millennium. These novels banish—or transform—sf staples of encounters with alien races and reject the tendency to treat interplanetary expansion as an escape from the political, economic, and ecological conflicts on Earth. Instead, Robinson extends limits of anthropogenic ecologies across the solar system: terraformed Mars, the domed and subterranean colonies on Jupiter's and Saturn's moons, the city-state of Terminator on Mercury, and terraria in hollowed-out asteroids become the sites for humankind's socioeconomic, cultural, and biophysical evolutions. In these novels Robinson imagines different timescales for humankind's future histories, reframing the problems of the late twentieth and twenty-first centuries by exploring the biopolitics of humankind's diaspora across the solar system. Like the Mars trilogy, *Memory of Whiteness*, *Galileo's Dream*, and *2312* are neither straightforward political allegories nor interplanetary adventures. Instead, they focus our thinking about humankind's responses to a future of unsustainable economies, ecological crises, and the persistence of hierarchical politics and social injustice. At the same time, Earth's future remains central to Robinson's vision of the colonization of the solar system, and the crises of the late twentieth and twenty-first centuries shape his vision of our species' interplanetary future.

In his solar system novels, Robinson recasts three traditions familiar to readers of late-twentieth-century science fiction: dead-end or dystopian planetary colonization (Philip K. Dick's *Martian Time-Slip*), tales of the contacts among dispersed humanoid societies (Le Guin's Hainish trilogy), and intergalactic adventures across a *Star Trek* universe of seemingly limitless possibilities. By the end of the Mars trilogy, colonists on the planet already inhabit a diasporic civilization that extends to other bodies in the solar system. Zo (John Boone's granddaughter) journeys to the city of Terminator on Mercury as it moves along its planet-girdling tracks, remaining in a liminal zone between night and day and just outside the range of the searing heat and blinding light of the sun; Anne Clayborne explores the moons of the outer gas giants; hollowed out asteroids have been converted into mini-worlds; and Jackie Boone's political defeat sends her off on an expedition into interstellar space. All of these narrative threads are picked up and elaborated in *2312*, extending the comparative planetology of the Mars trilogy. In *2312*, Zasha voices a fundamental insight that resonates throughout Robinson's novels of space colonization: "The solar system is just as finite as Earth" (96). If, three hundred years in the future, the colonies in the solar system are not yet approaching their "carrying capacity," they are, Zasha suggests, reaching their "peak investment return." Although the quasi-utopian *Memory of Whiteness* (1984) imagines a future of limitless energy generation and consumption and a system-spanning culture devoted to art and music, *2312* describes a solar system entering an era of resource depletion and scarcity that plagues Earth as much in the twenty-fourth century as in the twenty-first. This emphasis on a diasporic future confined to the solar system—"the little pearl of warmth surrounding our star" (2312, 328)—defines the interplanetary framework of Robinson's future histories.

Beyond the solar system, as Robinson shows us in *Aurora*, lies the self-destructive fantasy of transcending or escaping ecological constraints. In a key passage in *2312* he emphasizes this distinction between history and fantasy, between science fiction as a self-critical thought experiment and science fiction as escapism. One of Pluto's small moons, Nix, is "disassembled and processed into four starships" (327) that, at the end of the novel, "accelerate . . . to 2 percent the speed of light, a truly fantastic speed for a human craft, thus reducing [the space travelers'] trip time to only two thousand years" (328). These starships, however, are not the harbingers of a heroic interstellar adventure but merely "dandelion seeds, floating away on a breeze. Very beautiful. We will never see them again" (329) because, as the narrator puts it, "the stars exist beyond human time, beyond human reach," signifying only "a vastness beyond comprehension" (328). At the end of *2312*, the "first starship [becomes] a prison" (527) for the humanoid qubes—self-aware AIs—and this expulsion of self-conscious, artificial intelligences from history underscores Robinson's point that "the solar system is our one and only home" (328). The "our" in this sentence defines both the limits and responsibilities of the novel's interplanetary ecology. Robinson's image of interstellar space as "a vastness beyond comprehension" recalls Galileo's encounter with the alien intelligences on Jupiter and its moons in *Dream*, and the encounters in both novels between humans and alien (or quantum) intelligences throw into relief the surprises that evolution may have in store for humankind's interplanetary future. If the Mars trilogy is about the inhabitation of a terraformed world, *2312* and Robinson's other solar system novels emphasize the ways that the thousands of human-constructed ecologies in the solar system redefine what ecology and human nature itself might mean.

BEFORE THE MARS TRILOGY: *ICEHENGE* AND *THE MEMORY OF WHITENESS*

The three linked narratives in *Icehenge* (1984) anticipate some of Robinson's key concerns in the Mars trilogy and his later fiction: the age-extension treatments that allow humans to live hundreds of years; the struggle against the unholy alliance of repressive politics and neo-feudal economics; and the problems of creating and sustaining viable biospheres that allow humans to colonize the solar system. As I discussed in chapter 1, the second and third sections of the novel explore Hjalmar Nederland's efforts to uncover, and remake, the lost histories of his youth, the destruction of New Houston, and the fate of the rebels trying to escape both the reach of the Mars Development Committee (MDC) and the confines of the solar system. The novel's first section describes, through the eyes of reluctant revolutionary Emma Weil, an interplanetary civilization trapped in cycles of hyper-consumption, repressive corporatist politics, and restive colonial populations.

Early in the novel, Eric Swann tries to recruit Emma, a noted systems ecologist, to join the Mars Spaceship Authority (MSA) and escape the tyrannical authority of the Mars Development Committee by jerry-rigging an existing spacecraft as an interstellar spaceship: a closed, ecological system, "a tail-in-the-mouth snake that would roll across the galaxy" (41). Her skepticism about this utopian venture to colonize a planet in another star system anticipates what Devi, Freya, and others learn in *Aurora*; ecologically and politically, the solar system places limits on the hubris of a space-faring civilization. For Emma, a not-yet-terraformed Mars is still a planet, not a "big spaceship" (22), and the radicals in the MSA are, even within their extended lifespans, impatient. "Your five-hundred-year project is the terraforming of Mars," Eric, one of the rebels, tells her. "Ours is the colonization of a planet in another system. What's the big difference?" Her sardonic response, "About ten or twenty light-years" (22), registers both the constraints imposed by the laws of physics and the difficulty of imagining a utopian resistance in an era when a starship voyage of "a hundred, maybe two hundred years" constitutes "only a quarter of [humans'] predicted lifetimes" (22). Eric's response treats the problem of voyaging beyond the solar system as ecological, not temporal: engineering a viable biosphere that can sustain itself and its crew of multicentenarians. Having just turned eighty, Emma finds herself laboring on a project that initially she had dismissed as "a crackpot scheme . . . that takes you off into space and leaves you there with no way to colonize a planet even if you found one" (25). In her mind, the rebellion seems more an anarchist gesture of defiance than the founding action for a new interstellar civilization. The utopian enterprise is not the colonization of a yet undiscovered planet but a belief in surviving the near-infinitudes of "ten or twenty light-years."

Emma's motivation in ultimately siding with the rebels, though, remains opaque even to her, although she realizes that its utopian promise might mitigate, if not overcome, the cynicism and alienation she feels working for the exploitative Mars Development Committee. On board a rogue spacecraft, caught between joining the revolution and returning to Mars, Emma realizes that she can be "known [only] by [her] actions and words" because her "internal universe [is] unavailable for inspection by others." Catching sight of her reflection in the mirror, she sees herself as a "stranger": "There was Emma Weil. You couldn't read her mind. . . . What was she thinking? You would never know" (25–26). This scene of self-alienation recalls, in some ways, the kinds of psychological conundrums that Dick explores in novels like *Do Androids Dream of Electric Sheep?* But in *Icehenge* the inaccessibility of identity remains bound up in the ethical and political decisions that define the characters' complicity in, or opposition to, the forces of repression and aggrandizement. Emma's commitment to the systems-engineering problem of eliminating the starship's buildup of toxins and waste products over centuries stems from her realization that while she always had "hated those petty tyrants" in the MDC, she was wrong in assuming "that cowardice was the norm, and that made it okay" (26) for her not to voice her frustrations. In some ways, her narrative in the first section of *Icehenge* anticipates Sax Russell's political and moral trajectory in the Mars trilogy: the revolution on Mars recruits Emma as much as she commits to it. Intercepted and prevented from rendezvousing with the rebels on the starship, Emma is forced to return to Mars and therefore never gets a chance to join a venture, which she has come to consider "a historical event to stun the imagination" (59). As the starship *Hidalgo* escapes the MDC's spacecraft to begin its voyage, she and her friends, on the run from the authorities, see themselves as "Noah's cousins, left behind" (59). The *Hidalgo* voyages beyond the reaches of narrative and history.

Icehenge creates a future in which space exploration remains bound to its corporate and military origins. Emma, Nederland, and his great-grandson Edmund Doya must negotiate, in different ways, the temptations of radical political action, utopian adventure, and cynical disengagement. As I discussed in chapter 1, Nederland is committed to uncovering the truth about the suppression of the rebellion on Mars, and the middle section of the novel turns Emma into a mythic, even apparitional figure who he tries to track across the surface of an un-terraformed Mars. In the novel's final section, the controversy over the builders of Icehenge, the monoliths on Pluto that recall the structure of Stonehenge, reflects the problems that haunt dreams of utopian possibility: was Icehenge built by the crew of the *Hidalgo* on its way out of the solar system? Or is it Emma's monument to its crew's utopian dreams? Is it an alien artifact? Or is it simply a hoax? Nederland's belief that Icehenge is authentic, a monument built by the first interstellar travelers, and Doya's skepticism both paradoxically testify to the structure's significance: Icehenge marks the boundaries between utopian aspiration and oligarchic control, between revolutionary actions and the status quo, and between fiction and history. If *Icehenge* ends with Doya's disenchantment, the novel also suggests, in 1984, an expansive vision of human possibility that stands in marked contrast to the cyberpunk, hallucinatory future that William Gibson conjured into fictive being that same year in *Neuromancer*.

These possibilities of imagining a humanity saved from—and almost despite—itself fuel Robinson's vision of space colonies finding alternatives to the ecological, cultural, and political problems that plague Earth. In *Memory of Whiteness*, the novelist sets out both a time frame and a visionary standard for a utopian future history more than a millennium in the future. Unlike his subsequent novels, *Memory* solves problems of material scarcity in order to explore an imagined art of the future: advances in physics allow humankind to produce limitless energy, even in the distant reaches of the solar system, and thereby replicate Earth-like environments on planets and moons. Early in the novel, the narrator charts the course of future history in this energy-abundant utopia as a symphony in four movements: "Allegro" encompasses the colonization of Mars in 2052 and the beginning of a terraforming project "that would take generations to accomplish" (36). "Ritard: moderato" at the end of the twenty-second century is marked by the colonization of the Jovian and Saturnian moons that never "lost the character of outposts, habitats on the edge of the possible" (36); a second movement, "Adagissimo," witnesses the Earth's descent into "a new dark age of upheaval and disaster, famine and conflict," followed by "centuries of grim retrenchment" (37). During the "Intermezzo agitato" "the physicists of the rolling city of Terminator [on

Mercury] provid[e] an immense influx of energy to Earth and Mars" (38); and the "Accelerando" that results from Arthur Holywelkin's "grand unified theory" of physics allows humankind to concentrate and harness solar power, then "transfer the energy from one point to another" and "contract it to singularities" (37). This "discontinuity physics" makes it possible for humankind to establish "one gee colonies illuminated by projected flares of the sun . . . on hundreds of moons and asteroids" (38) throughout the solar system. Rather than the kind of enhanced realism that characterizes Robinson's descriptions of terraforming in the Mars trilogy, *Memory of Whiteness* explores the implications of living in and through a diasporic culture of abundance: it is less concerned with the ethics and politics of planetary inhabitation—Hiroko Ai's viriditas—than with humankind's proliferation of societies and cultures. With solar energy beamed to "whitsuns" in the far reaches of the solar system, these miniature suns "illuminate all [its] dark corner[s]"; even the tiny satellites orbiting Uranus contain "a host of worlds—little worlds, to be sure—. . . each of them encased in a clear sphere of air like little villages in glass paperweights, and each of them a culture and society unto itself" (29). As these "organic world[s] bloom everywhere" (38) across the solar system, they redefine human culture in ways that transcend twentieth-century divisions among culture, society, politics, economics, and art. As an imaginative extension of contemporary quantum theory, "discontinuity physics" offers a way to think beyond crises of scarcity, overpopulation, violence, and repression and to imagine a utopian future that is part Orphean meditation on art and music and part vision of ecocultural evolution.[1]

The Memory of Whiteness reads, at times, like an extended riff on Dick's visionary futures but with an intellectual rigor that explores the novelistic possibilities of a utopia imagined through the implications of a visionary, postquantum physics. The novel is structured as a Grand Tour of the solar system by Johannes Wright, the maestro of Holywelkin's Orchestra, and his entourage. The Orchestra—"one of the most famous musical . . . phenomena in all the solar system—in all of history" (33)—is a multidimensional ensemble of hundreds of instruments played from a keyboard by a single musician. In 3229 it embodies the possibilities that music can capture the interactions among the ten physical dimensions that Holywelkin had described. At the beginning of the tour from the outer to the inner solar system, Johannes is determined to compose music for the Orchestra that "sings the world precisely" (79) as "an accurate analogy" (102) for the physical universe. Holywelkian physics transcends quantum indeterminacy and demonstrates that "the structure of our thinking and the structure of reality have an actual correspondence" (100) that only can be experienced, not explained. For Johannes, "music is a language untranslatable, . . . too direct, too subtle, too . . . *other* for words" (109) because it reveals the fundamental insight of thirty-third-century physics: the "actual correspondence" between art and existence. The journalist Dent Ios, who accompanies Johannes on his tour down system to Mercury and to the energy stations inside its orbit, wonders whether "someone finally [had] made a music that spoke the eternal" (111). As the "lingua franca" (30) that holds together a civilization scattered across billions of miles, music occupies the role that in Robinson's later works is occupied by the utopian politics of science. In this respect, Holywelkin's Orchestra knits beliefs about the power of art to questions about the nature of a reality that exists beyond a fragmented modernism.

Near the end of his journey to annihilation in a singularity inside the orbit of Mercury, Johannes hears an explanation for the power of his music from a member of the Greys, a cult that has embraced a mystical version of Holywelkian physics: "This deep relation that music has to the true nature of things makes it a language capable of the most distinct and accurate description of the universe; and this is why your audiences have reacted to your music as to the truth that they have always known" (316). In Johannes's quest for a music that reflects this "truth," Robinson envisions a determinism stripped of its dystopian associations and reimagined as a language of pure and precise spatiotemporal identity. Discontinuity physics mathematically "describes the atomic events first postulated by the Eleatics" that constitute "the dynamic fabric of spacetime. . . . Each event in the ten dimensions of spacetime is determined by all the moments before and after it. And as we are nothing but aggregates of these events, our feeling that we exercise free will is nothing but an illusion of consciousness" (198). Johannes's tour that moves ever inward toward the sun has something of the elegance of a classical journey of self-discovery, but the novel is not a bildungsroman like *The Wild Shore*: Johannes is adamant that "the [Orchestra's] music writes me" (217), and his tour is ultimately a voyage toward the recognition that his identity is a function of this music—an apotheosis within a multidimensional unity that can be approached isotropically only through art.

In retrospect it is tempting to read *Memory of Whiteness* as a narrative experiment that complements the darker *Icehenge*. In the latter novel, Mars and apparently the rest of the solar system remain under the authoritarian control of the Mars Development Committee, but *Memory* insists on a crucial distinction between "the thousand year old civilization of Mars" (231) as "the great melting pot of all [human culture]" and a culturally and spiritually enervated Earth. Johannes's concerts in the outer solar system—from the moons of Neptune to Mars—enrapture audiences, but on Earth his music leaves people puzzled, indifferent, or shallowly appreciative. These reactions to a music that reveals "the truth that [other audiences] have always known" convince Dent that Earth is "crushed by the burden of the past . . . [its] pathetic governors had no culture but the sterile creation of images, juxtaposed together without sense, without history" (293). Without art, Earth becomes a spiritual dystopia: "humanity's home—dead. Laughing mannequins. History ended" (293). Dent's response redefines both history and utopia. Set more than a thousand years after the Orange County and Mars trilogies, *Memory* does not chart socioeconomic and political struggles for justice but takes as its precondition the material prosperity resulting from universally available energy, heat, and light. History has ended on Earth not because its inhabitants remain enthralled to a political economy of scarcity and deprivation but because they no longer recognize the ways that art—and only art—can reveal a "truth" beyond the bounds of the familiar. The inattentive audience on Earth, twelve centuries in the future, remains cocooned within a politics of privilege and an aesthetics of representational realism. In one sense, Johannes's music stands in relation to the quotidian expectations of earthlings as science fiction does to realistic fiction: Holywelkin's Orchestra and science fiction alike chart the possibilities of intuiting a future that, as yet, we cannot know.

TIME AND HISTORY IN *GALILEO'S DREAM*

If *Icehenge* and *Memory* anticipate out two of the major concerns in Robinson's later fiction—the struggle for history and a vision to sustain a utopian interplanetary society—*Galileo's Dream* can be read as an origin story in two senses: it contextualizes, in complex ways, the rise of modern science in the seventeenth century, and it explores the human costs and consequences of the legacy of scientific thought that Galileo embodies. The novel interweaves two narrative strands—a biography of the scientist that brilliantly reimagines seventeenth-century scientific and political culture, and a tale of time travel that projects the hero more than a thousand years into the future in order to explore the consequences of humankind's contact with an alien intelligence.[2] If the astronomer's discovery of four Jovian moons threatens to decenter humanity in the cosmos of Renaissance Italy, his role as a key figure for warring factions in the distant future suggests how unprepared humanity remains for encountering a superior intelligence or even dealing with its own moral and spiritual conflicts. Galileo's struggles against terrified defenders of traditional thought in both the past and future make this novel Robinson's most sustained effort to examine the scientist as a hero within—and beyond—history.

The novel's title invokes multiple connotations of dreaming: the tradition of imagining alternative histories, the fictions of time travel in a quantum universe of infinite possibilities, and the utopian dreams that the "birth" of modern science represents. The historical setting in seventeenth-century Italy is rendered with the kind of imaginative precision that characterizes other classic time-travel novels, such as Connie Willis's *The Doomsday Book* (1992), or award-winning historical fiction like Geraldine Brooks's *The Year of Wonders* (2001). Robinson rewrites Renaissance history to emphasize that the scientific revolution did *not* mean breaking free from religion but rethinking the significance of spirituality in an always-emerging modern world.[3] In this respect *Galileo's Dream* extends the generic boundaries of Robinson's alternative histories, like *Years of Rice and Salt*, to ask his readers to reimagine the origins of modern science and their own supposedly secular modernity.

Robinson's Galileo embodies many of the qualities of his fictional scientists like Sax Russell and Frank Vanderwal. But as the "first scientist, father of physics" (55), Galileo plays a crucial role both for the novelist and for those characters living on the Jovian moons from a thousand years in the future—Ganymede, Hera, and Cartophilus—who use the quantum entangler to bring him, or his consciousness, into their own conflict-ridden era. Drawing on Bao's theory of manifolds described in *Blue Mars*, Robinson imagines time travel as an individual consciousness in a kind of phase change between two entanglers—one in Galileo's historical moment, the other in the far future in the Jovian system. The hero is transported from Renaissance Italy into the distant future to serve as a pawn between two antagonistic factions, split on whether or not to bore into the interior of the Jovian moon Europa to contact a newly discovered alien intelligence. Part of the appeal of the novel lies in realizing how quickly Galileo catches on to the fourteen hundred years of physics that separate his two existences. To explain time travel, Hera tells Galileo that the "temporal manifold [is] made of three dimensions, so that what we sense as time passing . . . is a compound . . . made up of three temporalities": speed of light (c time), experiential or e (for eternal) time, and "antichronos, because it moves in the reverse direction of c time, while it also interacts with e time. The three temporalities flow through and resonate with each other, and they all pulse with vibrations of their own" (234). If this explanation recalls aspects of the "discontinuity physics" of *Memory of Whiteness*, time in *Galileo's Dream* is knotted, often acausal, and subject to multiple "potentialities." Because Galileo can be conscious in only one reality at a time, he experiences the future as a kind of extended dream vision, even though he is guided by Hera. The trajectory of the fourteen-hundred-year history that Galileo eventually learns recalls the future that Robinson depicts in *Memory*, but his introduction to this future comes only through a terrifying experience: in another "potentiality" or timeline of his existence he is burned at the stake by the Inquisition for heresy.

In this scene, Hera lets Galileo—at his insistence—experience his martyrdom for his scientific beliefs. For the faction that initially kidnapped him into the future, "Ganymede and his followers," Galileo's execution must go forward because it will ensure that "the secularization of the world" begins in the seventeenth century, thereby saving "humanity from many centuries of darkness, in which science is perverted to the will of insane religions" (144). This horrifying execution, Hera tells Galileo, occurs in "almost all the potentialities" (144)—that is, in almost all the possible futures that can occur:

> The pain was such that he would have screamed immediately, but an iron muzzle clamped an iron gag into his mouth. His tongue was nailed into his palate by a spike set in the gag. . . . No hatred like that of the ignorant for the learned; now he saw that even greater was the hatred of the damned for the martyr. . . . In a few seconds the fire shot up and over his legs, became an agonizing burn all

over them. His body tried to scream, and he choked on his own blood, began to drown, but did not faint. He smelled the roasting skin and meat on his own legs, a kitchen smell. Then there was nothing but the pain filling his skull and blinding him, red pain like a scream. (142)

Even in the extremities of being burned alive, Galileo rejects Ganymede's version of the history of science that typecasts him as the hero of a secular morality play: progressive science versus regressive religion. In the throes of martyrdom, Galileo recasts this textbook opposition into two other antagonisms: "the ignorant for the learned" and the "damned for the martyr." If the first of these invokes seventeenth-century controversies about the Copernican universe, the second embraces the language of religion to describe his faith in the God-given physical laws of the universe. God, Galileo says, "is a mathematician" (19), and the novel reinforces this interweaving of science and sacred belief against conventional views of their opposition.[4] When he returns to consciousness from the experience of his execution, Hera explains that, for many in the fourth millennium, his success as a scientist "includes"—even requires—his "immolation" (144) because his martyrdom pushes back the boundaries of ignorance and religious absolutism. Yet the "damned" in this scene—Galileo's tormenters, who see "the end they knew would eventually engulf them for their sins" (142)—have as much in common with the forces of corporate irresponsibility in the Science in the Capital trilogy as they do with religious fanaticism. Galileo's Dream, in this respect, dramatizes a conflict between two forms of spiritual belief: the utopianism-in-progress of science and the politics of knuckling under to power.

In using science-fiction tropes—time travel and alien intelligence—that stretch the boundaries of his usual "future realisms," Robinson reexamines questions of progress and belief and recasts the postquantum physics of Memory of Whiteness. Galileo's Dream includes significant passages from the scientist's own writings, and the worldview that Galileo articulates resonates across the boundaries of reconstructed and imagined histories. What he has to teach the Jovian colonists in the fourth millennium is not that science justifies—or demands—an act of defiant self-sacrifice but that their understanding of history as a Manichean opposition between science and "insane religions" is wrong. Right before they contact the Jovian intelligence, Galileo tells Ganymede, "You have misunderstood why things went awry. . . . Science needed more religion, not less. And religion needed more science. The two needed to become one. Science is a form of devotion, a kind of worship" (419). If such language recalls Rudra's invocations in the Science in the Capital trilogy—"Buddhism as the Dalai Lama's science; science as the scientist's Buddhism" (*Sixty*, 234)—Galileo's assertion reenchants the solar system. Although Ganymede praises Galileo as "a truly original mind [of] supreme intelligence and wisdom" (55) who can help decide whether to drill beneath the ocean on Europa to investigate its alien intelligence, the Jovian never truly understands the beliefs or values of "the first scientist" (185).

It is revealing, then, that Galileo is the only human who is not driven to frenzy or despair after coming in contact with the alien intelligence on Jupiter. "The Jovian mind" terrifies Ganymede because he believes that "if humanity at large becomes aware of this realm of greater minds, besides which all human history is a fleck of foam on a sand grain, despair will quickly spread. It will be the end of humanity" (428). His despair is the dark, even psychotic, underside of scientific self-congratulation—an "excess of reason"—that rejects the spiritual dimension of the universe. In contrast, Galileo feels no despair at the idea that humanity "will be revealed to be pitifully stupid," because, as he asks, "When has it ever been otherwise? We are as the fleas on fleas, compared to God and his angels. We have always known this" (429). Galileo's humility is an *expression*, not a *rejection*, of science. His striking image of "fleas on fleas" desacralizes human beings, even as it recasts humankind's quest for knowledge in spiritual terms. The extraterrestrial intelligences—or as Galileo calls them, "God and his angels"—confirm his faith in science and represent the kind of desire that motivates Johannes: a music that "sings" an ultimate reality.

Written a quarter-century after *Memory of Whiteness*, *Galileo's Dream* revisits the problem of imagining the temporal, spatial, and psychosocial complexities of quantum physics or a Grand Unified Theory. Rather than terror or incomprehension in the presence of the Jovian intelligence, Galileo experiences "what he could only think was the mind of God" (433):

[H]e lost all sense of his three-dimensional space and felt himself spinning and spiraling in the manifold of manifolds, spanning all times. . . . [H]e felt and heard the ways in which the ten dimensions warped, stretched, bowed and shrunk, the whole breathing in and out and also almost holding still, all at once. His sight was whole, his touch-immersion whole, his hearing whole, while also coextensive with the ten dimensions. . . . All the temporal isotopes were flickering in and out of their braids of potentiality, blossoming and collapsing, systole and diastole. . . . All things remain in God, he said, but no one heard. He understood then the solitary nature of transcendence, since wholeness was one. (433)

If this passage harks back to the Greys' belief that Johannes's music captures the unity of manifold realities, it also evokes the mystical tradition of Dante's *Paradiso*, particularly the final canto of the *Divine Comedy*. At the very end of his epic, Dante perceives the infinite as a mode of "transcendence" and "wholeness" that lies beyond language: "Here power failed the high phantasy; but now my desire and will like a wheel that spins with even motion, were revolved by the Love that moves the sun and the other stars."[5] For Galileo, contact with the Jovian mind *reinforces* rather challenges his beliefs in science as the principal mode of spiritual understanding. Before conservatives in the Church begin to attack his defense of Copernicanism, Galileo tells the pope that "creation is all one. God's world and God's word are necessarily the same" (119). Such sentiments are prevalent throughout Galileo's own writings, and Robinson uses his hero's experience of an otherworldly intelligence to gesture toward the grim consequences of a hyper-rationalist "excess of reason." In this context Ganymede voices an updated version of the fear and intolerance that motivates Galileo's seventeenth-century persecutors.

As Robinson's only time-travel novel, *Galileo's Dream* explores the cracks and fissures within traditional notions of science as progress.[6] Using fourth-millennium technology, Galileo looks forward, from his foundational role as "the first scientist," to the future of mathematics after the seventeenth century—and, later in the novel, to the course of human history since his own era. Injected with a "synaptic velocinestic" (187) that allows him to experience, if not quite learn, the history of mathematics from Archimedes to Bao's manifold of manifolds, Galileo comes to realize that all scientists live their lives as "one protracted case of presque vu. Almost seen! Almost understood!" (546). Like Arkady is *Red Mars*, scientists can imagine but not quite see the path to a utopian knowledge. During this quasi-psychedelic experience,

Galileo encounters fundamental principles like inertia and gravity "that had always been on the tip of his tongue"—that he "had used . . . in his parabolic description of falling bodies, but . . . had not understood" (190). Recognizing that their "utter simplicity" shreds his assumptions about the circular orbits of planets, he is introduced to a superior "form of analysing motion called the calculus, which was just what he had always needed and never had. And it seemed to have appeared just after his time, worked out by people young when he was old: an irritating Frenchman called Descartes, a German named Leibniz, and the English maniac Newton again, who to Galileo's chagrin had distilled Galileo's dynamics in just the way Galileo had struggled to do all his life" (191). The scientific revolution, for Galileo, is rendered in the human terms of his monumental frustration at *almost* having discovered calculus, at almost superseding the "irritating" Descartes and "the maniac" Newton.[7] His frustration defines the utopian, spiritual nature of scientific inquiry: *almost* being able to comprehend, almost being able to work out the necessary steps toward the unified, visionary physics of *Memory of Whiteness*. Robinson's parody of Newton's line—"If I have seen less far than others . . . it is because I was standing on the shoulders of dwarves" (191)—emphasizes Galileo's isolation: he is "the first scientist" in the sense that he precedes not only Descartes, Leibniz, and Newton but also the collaborative scientific communities that Robinson depicts in the Mars and Science in the Capital trilogies. Galileo can *almost* intuit what his successors begin to grasp: the possibilities of a collaborative science as utopian politics.

At the beginning of the novel, scraping by on his salary of 520 florins, casting horoscopes, and supervising a workshop where invention is an economic necessity, Galileo knows that "if he [does] not invent something a little more lucrative than the military compass, he [will] never [be able to] escape his debts" (8). His workshop serves as his intellectual and affective refuge; the work he does with his assistant Mazzoleni forges a relationship "unlike any other human bond he knew, unlike that with mistress or child, colleague or student, friend or confessor—unlike anyone—because they made new things together, they learned new things" (13). Their relationship is the embryonic form of the collaborative science that emerges in the Science in the Capital trilogy, and their insatiable curiosity shapes Galileo's inductive method: "the epistemology of the

hunt was to follow one thing after another, without much of an overall plan"
(16–17). For Galileo, as for Iwang and Khalid in *Years of Rice and Salt*, the "overall
plan" emerges from trying to find ways to carve out a space for experimentation
within an indifferent or hostile society. In order to placate religious and political
authorities and to secure the patronage necessary to keep "follow[ing] one thing
after another," Galileo insists that his "work is to reconcile Copernicanism and
the Holy Church, it is an attempt to *help* the Church, which otherwise will soon
find itself contravening *obvious facts* of God's world, quite visible to all" (158).
This is an accurate but politically naïve defense of his experimentation. Galileo
is a utopianist without a vision of utopia, trapped in a semi-feudal world of
financial debt and multilayered obligations to authority. He must navigate his
way among skeptics and outright enemies by deference, rhetorical misdirection,
and even misrepresentation of his aims and beliefs in his *Dialogue Concerning
the Two Chief World Systems* (1632); and at times the hero is as much a victim as
a perpetrator of his schemes of self-defense. Cartophilus says that during his
audience with Pope Urban VIII in 1630, "it was impossible to tell from the look
on Galileo's face whether he knew he was lying or not" (402). His "lying," as
Cartophilus sees it, marks the dilemma of a science that cannot afford to speak
truth to power. Even during his trial, Galileo does less to confront than try to
appease the intransigent authority of Church doctrine.[8]

Robinson's strategy of casting his hero into a quantum universe of multiple
potentialities captures a sense of the historical Galileo's alienation. Returned
from the future to the 1630s when he is being investigated by the Inquisition,
Galileo describes feeling unmoored in time and space in his newly learned
language of quantum mechanics: "I am out of phase[:] I am living in the wrong
potential time. [Hera] sent me back to the wrong self. It's an interference
pattern, the one where the two equal waves cancel each other out!" (308). In
this passage and elsewhere, Robinson resists staging Galileo's battle with the
Church as a neorealist morality play. In contrast to Bertolt Brecht's alienated
hero in his play, *The Life of Galileo* (1948), Robinson's "first scientist" suffers
lives through unraveling tapestries of time, reality, and cognitive identity.
His sense of "presque vu" reflects the fundamental problem of trying to go
forward when historical time and his own actions seem always out of joint.
For Galileo, "time [becomes] a manifold full of exclusions and resurrections,
fragments and the spaces between fragments . . . isotopies all superimposed

on each other and interweaving in an anarchic vibrating tapestry, and since to relive it at one point was not to relive it at another, the whole was unreadable, permanently beyond the mind" (309). This description of psychological and spatiotemporal dislocation renders the indeterminate realities of quantum physics in the experiential language of "fragments," "spaces," and "tapestry." In *Memory of Whiteness*, Robinson uses a similar language to gesture toward a holism grasped only through music; in *Galileo's Dream*, the hero experiences time as a "manifold of exclusions and resurrections" that leaves him struggling toward the receding horizon of scientific progress. In both novels the cognitive dislocations of science fiction become more affectively and intellectually vibrant than the realisms of novelistic self-expression.

With its dual time frames, *Galileo's Dream* positions the reader in a discontinuous history longer than the six-and-a-half centuries of *Years of Rice and Salt*. In living proleptically in a distant future, Galileo occupies the figurative position of science-fiction writers and readers who must try to imagine how science—past, present, and future—can help humanity avoid an apocalypse to come. He represents, in this sense, the humility, not the "excess," of scientific reason. In the fourth millennium the Jovian branch of humanity still struggles against the profound sense of psychocultural disorientation that is a consequence of technoscientific progress. Midway through the novel Galileo asks Hera pointedly whether "living out here [on the Jovian moons] . . . make[s] you all a little bit mad? Never to sit in a garden, never to feel the sun on your neck? . . . Never to experience the day—you must all be at least a little bit insane" (262). This question resonates throughout Robinson's solar system novels and characterizes the ways that space colonization forces humanity to confront its worst tendencies as well as its most hopeful dreams. The terraforming projects to bioengineer Mars, to colonize the Jovian moons, and, in 2312, to transform Venus reflect Robinson's crucial insight that technoscientific progress can forestall as well as promote sociopolitical and economic justice and an ethics of ecological adaptation to alien environments. In response to Galileo's question, Hera concedes "that cultures can go insane in ways similar to an individual. . . . History has been a bedlam, to tell the truth. Maybe we're now permanently post-traumatic" (262). Galileo's initial assumptions that the tall, beautiful, and "angelic" inhabitants of the Jovian system inhabit a space-age New Jerusalem prove false as he recognizes that, "deprived of the anchor of earth and wind and sunlight," these beings are no better than the Italian nobility of the seventeenth century: "choleric," power hungry, and obsessed with "hierarchy" (278). His comment about the sun on the back of one's neck calls attention to the trade-offs that define what Hera calls "a damaged and traumatized humanity" (238): an unquestioning faith in technoscientific progress that takes humanity into space but that leaves behind the joy of sitting in a sunlit garden.

The historical and time-travel narratives in *Galileo's Dream*, then, intersect in ways that dramatize the problems of simply accepting the drive for knowledge and power as the be-all and end-all of progress. The gargantuan power requirements of the Jovians' "entangler"—their time machine—requires the destruction of two of the outer solar system's gas giants and ultimately fails to allow them to change history to conform to their limited view of scientific progress. Ganymede is unable to foster a scientific revolution in ancient Greece, and his attempt to martyr Galileo for the sake of scientific progress ultimately is undone when the hero recants to avoid being burned alive. Cartophilus, a Jovian who has lived for three centuries in Renaissance Italy trying to jump-start the scientific revolution, admits to Galileo that his efforts as part of Ganymede's crew were naïve; he concedes, "I was an idiot" (323). This attempt to change the past in the name of scientific progress reveals that Ganymede and his cohorts are, in effect, bad readers of science fiction—they want to identify a single thread of cause and effect among braided quantum potentialities in order to (over)determine the future.

Galileo's visceral response to witnessing human history after the seventeenth century disturbs him almost as much as his own martyrdom in an alternative reality. Having asked Hera for "the tutorial that tells [him] what happened" (412) in the centuries between his time and hers, Galileo experiences the future histories laid out in *Memory of Whiteness* and *2312* as "an instantaneous flood of images"—a quantum "sum over histories"—that shows him "many potentialities at once, in a braided stream format": "He looked, he listened, but more than anything else he felt the ferocious tempests in Europe after his time" (412–13). The violence of his own era pales in comparison to the mass destruction of the modern era: "Sickened, appalled, Galileo watched on with a shrunken heart as all nature was then in effect fed to the furnaces to feed a rapacious humanity that quickly rebounded from the deaths and became superabundant again, like an infestation of maggots, a sporulating mass of suffering beasts" (413). This image of history as an "infestation" captures the ways in which the novel re-envisions metanarratives of scientific progress as part of a dialectic—"a cosmic race between creation and destruction [with] both sides succeeding at once" and "creating in their conjunction something unexpected and monstrous" (414). But this horror also marks Galileo's capacity to learn, his ability ultimately to recognize that his errors, particularly in his treatment of women, stem from a "base fear, a refusal to see the other" that is "similar in its cowardice and malignity to the absurd misreadings that his enemies had applied to his theories" (438). The fundamental conflict that emerges in the hero's mind pits this sense of loneliness and dejection against his place in a future history that, by its very nature, must remain contingent. If, as he says to himself, "each person lives in that bubble universe that rests under the skull, alone" (307), Galileo nonetheless demonstrates the courage to remain committed to the potential of a utopian science. The irony that echoes throughout the novel, for our timeline, is that Robinson's Galileo can save himself from execution only by telling a bald-faced lie: that his *Dialogo* was intended to *refute* rather than buttress Copernicanism.

Galileo's Dream dramatizes the exuberant yet nearly tragic intensity of a utopian science. Awaiting execution during the French Revolution, Cartophilus says at the end of the novel that "all scientists are Galileos, poor, scared, gun to our head" (576). In contrast to the comedy of the Science in the Capital trilogy, Galileo's alienation from power, felt all the more keenly when his former supporter, the urbane Cardinal Maffeo Barberini, becomes pope, reflects the novel's vision of a science threatened with martyrdom by a thousand cuts of sociopolitical repression. The consequence of this repression, however, is not martyrdom but deferral—Galileo's feeling that "his entire life had been once protracted case of presque vu. Almost seen! Almost understood!" (546). The science he "almost" sees becomes the means for readers to experience the frustrations and "regret" Galileo feels "for his wasted life and world and time" (438)—that is, for a revolution that never quite arrives. What he experiences as "time's odd doubled aspect" (550) in remembering his youth in Padua speaks to the profound dislocations in time, space, and self-definition that the entangler symbolizes and that many readers associate with the experience of modernity itself.[9]

Although Galileo (in our potentiality) saves himself from being burned as a heretic, the novel is less concerned with the ironies of time travel or alternate realities than with chronicling how his convictions persist in the face of persecution. Cartophilus sums up the hero's dilemma at the end of the novel: "I hope without hope" (578). This line echoes from Galileo's era through the imagined future of time-traveling descendants to remind us that "we are all history—the hopes of people in the past, the past of some future people—known to them, judged by them, changed by them as they use us. So the story keeps changing, all of it" (578). The dynamic narratives of past, present, and future, the novel suggests, resist a neat conflation of scientific enlightenment and utopianism; the beaten-down Cartophilus ultimately can urge us only to "push like Galileo pushed! And together we may crab sidewise toward the good" (578). In tracing the origins of modern science, *Galileo's Dream* recasts the epic, multigenerational narrative of the Mars trilogy and the multi-incarnational history of *Years of Rice and Salt* into a braided generic hybrid: an alternative and future history that explores the crabwise, utopian impulses that animate the scientific quest for knowledge—even before science has found its voice to speak progress to power.

2312: ALL YOU NEED

In some ways, *2312* picks up where *Blue Mars* left off. It envisions a solar system–wide civilization that has realized, in part, some of the utopian aspirations of the Mars trilogy, even as the Earth itself suffers the consequences of global warming, political stasis, corporate greed and mismanagement, and the collapse of biodiversity. Charlotte Shortback's history of humanity from 2005 to 2312 in the novel (244–47) recalls (as "Shortback" playfully suggests) Charlotte Dorsa Brevia's history summarized by Sax in *Blue Mars*. But *2312* emphasizes that the utopian conclusion of the Mars trilogy does not constitute an end to history but remains part of an ongoing narrative and continuing struggle. As *2312* builds toward its climax, the novel's collection of protagonists—Wahram, Swan, Gennette, and their allies—realize they "have to act" to protect human settlements on Venus from destruction by self-aware, humanoid quantum computers. At this point the narrative pauses for the fifteenth of the short interludes between chapters that all are titled simply "Lists." This list for utopia—"that's all you need"—gives voice to the values that Robinson promotes throughout his fiction:

health, social life, job, house partners, finances; leisure use, leisure amount; working time, education, income, children; food, water, shelter, clothing, sex, health care; mobility; physical safety, social safety, job security, savings account, insurance, disability protection, family leave, vacation; place tenure, a commons; access to wilderness, mountains, ocean; peace, political stability, political input, political satisfaction; air, water, esteem; status, recognition; home, community, neighbors, civil society, sports, the arts; longevity treatments, gender choice; the opportunity to become more what you are. (461)

The list is, at once, a compendium of utopian thinking (and utopian dreams) and a reminder of how far humankind has to go, in 2012 as well as in 2312. If this list wryly resurrects aspects of the collective values evident in *Pacific Edge* and in Arkady's vision in *Red Mars*, it also points to the ways that 2312 reimagines utopia in terms of embodied sexualities as well as sociocultural progress. In going beyond the ectogenes in the Mars trilogy, this novel explores how revolutionary developments in genetic engineering and manipulation, AI, and robotics threaten to outstrip socioeconomic and political transformations.

By the early twenty-fourth century, human civilization has suffered through crises reminiscent of Galileo's vision of a nightmarish future. After decades of "dithering," the world (from 2060 to 2130) is forced to confront the consequences of melting artic ice, "permafrost melt and methane release" that result in "food shortages, mass riots, catastrophic death on all continents" (245) and rapid species extinction. These interlocking crises delay the colonization and terraforming of Mars until "The Turnaround" (2130 to 2160), a period that witnesses the development of fusion energy, improved artificial intelligence, space elevators, and the "self-replicating factories" that are essential to interplanetary colonization. The progress of the "Accelerando" (2160 to 2220) shapes the solar system into form reminiscent of the Mars trilogy: "human longevity increases," the "terraforming of Mars and subsequent Martian revolution; full diaspora into solar system; hollowing out of the terraria; start of the terraforming of Venus; the construction of Terminator; and Mars joining the [cooperative] Mondragon Accord" (246). Yet the subsequent century, "The Ritard" (2220 to 2270) and "The Balkanization" (2270 to 2320), sees Mars, now completely terraformed, withdraw from interworld agreements like the Mondragon Accord, as humans find that they have already occupied "all the best terrarium candidates" and are running up against the limits of "the solar system's easily available helium, nitrogen, rare earths, fossil fuels, and photosynthesis" (246). Ecological crises on Earth foreshadow the problems of scarcity as they affect a diasporic civilization throughout the solar system. Even as quantum computing (or qube) development accelerates, tensions between Earth and Mars, conflicts on Venus over that planet's terraforming project, the "proliferation of the unaffiliated terraria," and "volatile shortages pinching harder caus[e] hoarding, then tribalism; [the] tragedy of the commons redux; [and the] splintering [of human civilization] into widespread, 'self-sufficient' enclave city-states" (246). In describing this fracturing of humanity, Robinson rewrites the literary and visionary forms of utopian politics and creates a variegated, patchwork future, as though the multiple potentialities that Galileo encounters through the entangler coexist in the same space-time: technoscientific and computational progress, incomplete socioeconomic, if not biophysiological, transformation, and political fragmentation. Yet even as *2312* shares some thematic concerns with contemporary dystopian fiction, like Paolo Bacigalupi's *The Windup Girl* (2009), it reimagines strategies for an always emergent utopianism. In this respect, the novel extends Robinson's earlier fiction, underscoring Tom Moylan's crucial insight: as works of both will and imagination, utopias embody a visionary politics that must defer their realization to an always fictionalized future.[10]

One measure of Robinson's reimagining of utopian potentialities lies in the ways that the novel distances itself from the Mars trilogy. In *2312* the terraforming of Mars is retold in a paragraph (368–69), and its history as a utopian experiment—first as part of the Mondragon, then in its isolation—remains in the background: in the politicized solar system of the twenty-fourth century, Mars remains offstage, in a cold war with Earth. Both the Chinese, now the dominant power on Earth, and the Martians cannibalize small Saturnian moons for raw materials—the former to jump start their terraforming efforts on Venus by crashing an ice moon into the planet to strip away much of its noxious atmosphere and leave water vapor in its place, the latter by harvesting volatiles. Yet even as Venus is being reborn in the image of an idealized Earth, humanity's homeworld has become "almost an ice-free planet," with sea levels "eleven meters higher than [they] had been before" (90) the onset of rapid global warming. The ecopolitical fixes that Robinson envisions in the Science in the Capital trilogy represent a utopian road not taken, and the planetary economy consequently struggles in 2312 through a "Keynesian disarray" of "overlapping" nation-states and "corporate conglomerates." If Earth remains "the center of the story" (90), still funding much of the expansion in the solar system, the narrative offers different, if overlapping, future histories that encompass economic, ecological, political, and biological alternatives to the reader's present.

The best of these possibilities for the equitable distribution of goods, services, and energy is the Mondragon—a "system of nested co-ops organized for mutual support" that relies on "supercomputers and artificial intelligence . . . to fully coordinate a non-market economy" (125).[11] Although the Mondragon includes much of the solar system, except Mars, it remains, despite its efficiencies, "only one of several competing economies on Earth, all decisively under the thumb of late capitalism, still in control of more than half the Earth's capital and production, and with its every transaction tenaciously reaffirming ownership and capital accumulation" (125). In this welter of emerging, atrophying, and dying economic systems, "the great Martian achievement, like defeating the mob or any other protection racket" (127) has been its success in marginalizing capitalism. Yet precisely because of this success, Mars exists in 2312 as a shadowy utopian presence whose story of planetary and political revolution already has been told. Earth, almost two centuries beyond the world depicted in New York 2140, is still mired in "bullshit," "horseshit," and "chickenshit" (2140, 35).

The radically different environments created on twenty-fourth-century planets, moons, and terraria reimagine how the memories of vanished or degraded terrestrial ecologies reshape the human diaspora physiologically, socioculturally, and psychologically. The nineteen thousand terraria in the solar system are hollowed-out mini-worlds within asteroids, powered by futuristic propulsion devices, and their proliferation turns colonization into a socioecological free-for-all.[12] The "thousands of city-states out there, pinballing around . . . without reliable data to fit them into a history or pattern" are less utopian visions realized than testaments to "the same mishmash history has been all along, but now elaborated, mathematicized, effloresced—in the word of the time, balkanized" (78). As a "free-for-all" of socioeconomic, cultural, and biophysical experiments, the terraria embody radically different responses to the Earth's environmental and demographic crises. Although most of the food consumed on Earth is grown in terraria and then shipped back to the homeworld to make up for the planet's resource shortfalls, these economic outposts are also terraformed dreamworlds that transform humans into "experimental creatures" (337), redefining our evolutionary identity.

The terraria, in this respect, offer an often playful vision of a fractionated reality—a compendium of future and alternative societies imagined in twentieth- and twenty-first-century science fiction. The terraria include classical utopias ("*The Copenhagen Interpretation*, a canal town with a gift economy"); resurrected premodern cultures ("*Tartar Soul*, a steppes grassland where people speak a resuscitated Indo-European"; "*Source of the Peach Blossom Stream*, a Tang dynasty recreation that looks like a Chinese landscape painting come to life"); and various lost terrestrial ecologies: "*Aymara*, an amazonia with interior completely overgrown with cloud forest"; "*The Maldives*, an aquarium recreating the drowned islands; *Micronesia*, likewise; *Tuvalu*, likewise; all the drowned islands of Earth are reproduced in this fashion" (198–99). These earth-inspired terraria conserve "832 Terran biomes," but hundreds of others, the "Ascensions," are "hybrid biomes" (39) that produce new species and new evolutionary trajectories.

If these mini-worlds resuscitate a variety of science-fiction traditions, they also call attention to the competing strains within utopian literature, like "*Saint George*, a social terrarium in which the men think they are living in a Mormon polygamy, while the women consider it a lesbian world with a small percentage of male lesbians" (198). Robinson's humor in such instances recalls his remark that the Science in the Capital trilogy is a "comedy" about climatological catastrophe. *2312*, as Wahram and Swan's marriage at the end of the novel suggests, similarly is a comedy about humankind's surviving its own "dithering" about climate change, its failures to shake off the socioeconomic and political feudalisms that persist into the future, and its stop-and-go efforts to harness artificial as well as human intelligence. But this comedy is always knife-edged. Jean Genette, the inspector investigating the destruction of the city-state of Terminator on Mercury, suggests that in a "post-scarcity" society "many a well-fed citizen is filled with rage and fear"—the "rage of the servile will" (229).[13] This "rage," pin-wheeling down through history, remains humanity's great challenge in the novel: to reconcile individual desires and communal responsibilities, to negotiate the problems posed by humankind's contradictory impulses toward hierarchy, violence, and peaceful coevolution. For other sf authors, the rage of the servile will is genetically predetermined in human DNA, as the Oankali recognize in Octavia Butler's Xenogenesis trilogy; for Robinson it is a problem that extends to human gender relations, to the degradation and resurrection of "natural" environments, and to humankind's vexed relations with proliferating forms of artificial intelligence.

The rage of the servile will becomes particularly acute in 2312 because the novel highlights a crucial insight at work as well in the Mars and Science in the Capital trilogies: "disparities between individual and planetary time can never be reconciled" (551). Different registers of time, different temporalities, bring into jarring conflict the phenomenological experience of time, embodied in human senses and action; the time of history that (without longevity treatments) outstrips individual lifetimes, as in *Shaman* and *Aurora*; and planetary or climatological time that typically extends beyond human experience but that can emerge catastrophically, as it does in the melting of Greenland and the Antarctic ice sheets in many of Robinson's future histories. One of Robinson's significant achievements as a science-fiction novelist lies in his treating future histories as *conflations* or *intersections* of experiential, historical, and climatological time.[14] In 2312 the stunning variety of terraria reflects different intersections of human and posthuman time: different historical pasts, different (vanished) ecologies, and different prehuman epochs: "Miocene terraria, Cretaceous terraria, Jurassic terraria, Precambrian terraria" (199). Time and physiology become interdependent variables that break down familiar barriers between the a-human and human: decades before the novel begins, the gynandromorph "heroine" Swan ingests Enceladan life forms that interact in complex but ultimately unknowable ways with her "own" biophysical and mental constitutions. In this sense, the terraria create multiple imagined pasts, multiple histories, and multiple ecologies that transform human bodies and communities, redefining their relationships to time as well as to other forms of life and extraterrestrial environments.

In his earlier solar system novels, Robinson describes the physiological differences that make humans born in the lower gravity of Mars effectively a different species, but in 2312 these transformations have turned humans into "their own unavoidable experiment, making themselves into many things they had never been before: augmented, multi-sexed, and most importantly, very long-lived" (79). In the Mars trilogy, the longevity treatments do not offer alternatives to heteronormative society, and much of the trilogy's action involves the changing romantic fortunes of male and female characters: Maya and Frank, Maya and John, Sax and Anne, Nirgal and Jackie, and so on. Human memory, as in "Green Mars," rather than desire is affected by the biophysiological transformations of an augmented humanity. In 2312, however, longevity and polysexualities are entwined: the "longevity increase" is a consequence of "sophisticated surgical and hormonal treatments for interventions in utero, in puberty, and during adulthood" that produce a range of "principal categories of self-image for gender [that] include feminine, masculine, androgynous, gynandromorphous, hermaphroditic, ambisexual, bisexual, intersex, neuter, eunuch, nonsexual, undifferentiated, gay, lesbian, queer, invert, homosexual, polymorphous, poly, labile, berdache, hijra, two-spirit" (204–5). This list, in one respect, could be seen as Robinson's extrapolation from a feminist scientific tradition—think of the gender-bending beings in Ursula K. Le Guin's *The Left Hand of Darkness* (1969), Joanna Russ's *The Female Man* (1975), and Nicola Griffith's *Ammonite* (1992)—that destabilizes heteronormative binaries. In another, these "principal categories" of biocultural definition reframe the question of what it means to be human.[15]

The biotechnological transformations that give Swan and Wahram primary genitalia (female and male, respectively) and secondary genitalia (male and female) produce a revolution in gender identifications and categories of self-identity: "gynandromorphs and androgyns" become normative gender identities that supplement—or supplant—female and male distinctions. When Wahram returns to his crèche on the Jovian moon Iapetus, he and Dana disagree about who was the wife and who the husband in their relationship almost a century earlier: "'Maybe we both were [the wife],'" Dana suggests, before adding, "it was a long time ago" (273). The gendered politics of intimacy, in this exchange, are caught up in the problems of memory and life extension: because extended lives outstrip memory, gender identity itself becomes subject to the radically new perceptions of time engendered by biotechnology. In addition to its sexual, heteronormative implications, Dana's term "wife" encompasses a range of gender values and assumptions, as Swan implies at the end of the novel when she thinks over Wahram's marriage proposal.

In her mind, marriage remains "a concept from the Middle Ages, from old Earth—an idea with a strong whiff of patriarchy and property" (543). But the child-rearing arrangements of Wahram's crèche, with multiple sexual and procreative relationships among its six adults, transform the gendered norms implied by the terms "wife" and "husband." If "spacers"—those born off-earth in terraria or colonies—believe themselves "free humans, free at last and human at last," Swan still recognizes that her initial response to Wahram's proposal is caught up in "structures of feeling [that] were cultural, histori-cal; they changed over time like people did; the structures themselves went through their own reincarnations" (544). Throughout the novel, "structures of feeling" themselves are being transformed by gender, biological, and com-putational revolutions.[16] Yet these "augmented, multi-sexed" humans remain tethered to the burdens of history and the unintended consequences of their own technologically advanced culture.

Although their life extension treatments mean that Swan at 135 and Wah-ram at 111 have lived through immense cultural and political changes, they recognize that even as multisexed, computationally enhanced experiments, humans are "not one whit wiser, or even more intelligent" than they were before these transformations; "individual intelligence," the narrator suggests, "probably peaked in the Upper Paleolithic, and we have been self-domesticated creatures ever since, dogs when we had been wolves" (79). If this image of canine domestication looks forward to *Shaman*, it suggests as well that Swan's quest, as an artist and activist, to reject self-domestication (including the re-sidual idea of marriage), is bound up with the spacers' unending struggle against Earth's "nearly infinite historical gravity" (306). Despite "the cheap power pouring down from space," and "the farmworlds growing and send-ing [to Earth] a big percentage of their food," "spacers" must return to their ancestral homeworld every seven years in order to maximize their health and longevity. Swan's sabbatical on Earth jolts her into recognizing that "a big minority of [its] population did robot work" and lives "in fear when it came to housing and feeding themselves" (307), while another "five or six billion [people are] teetering on the brink, about to slide into that same hole" (315). "The great precariat" (315), as her former partner Zasha calls them, are too worried about backsliding into the political chaos and food shortages of the twenty-second century to take effective political action. These socioeconomic inequalities, Swan realizes, breed modes of self-domestication. In 2312, she faces the same dilemma that confronts Frank Vanderwal and Anna Quibler three hundred years earlier: "They"—the "precariat" and the powers that be—"knew but they didn't act" (346). In both instances, Robinson gestures sardonically to the gnawing inaction of neoliberalism in our own day.

Like Frank and his colleagues in the Science in the Capital trilogy, Swan, Genette, Wahram, and their allies must grapple with cascading political, environmental, and technological crises. Early in the novel, the city of Terminator on Mercury is destroyed by a pebble mob. Traveling apparently randomly in space, tiny particles are programmed to assemble into projectiles so close to Mercury that they evade detection by the planet's defenses. In obliterating the city's dome, this weapon symbolizes the link between computational intelligence and the "redoubled destruction" that accompanies technology's "growing powers" (228). As a city forever in motion along tracks on the knife edge of habitability—separating Mercury's extremes of hemispheric darkness and blinding incineration—Terminator has a greater symbolic heft in 2312 than it does in *Memory of Whiteness* and *Blue Mars*. The city's apocalyptic destruction makes explicit the tenuousness of Earth's own bio-ecologies and dramatizes the difficulty of humankind's quest finally "to overturn Jevons Paradox, which states that the better human technology gets, the more harm we do with it" (305). In both respects the pebble mob represents an apocalyptic version of the underlying ecological and computational principles that small changes in inputs, or seemingly inconsequential errors, can disrupt basic biochemical processes and lead to catastrophic consequences. Terminator is the apocalyptic nightmare that haunts Robinson's environmental systems engineers, from Emma in *Icehenge* to Devi in *Aurora*.

If *2312* explores responses to the biotechnological transformations of human bodies and gender identities, it also deals with the generic problem of how to write a detective narrative in an age of ubiquitous computing. The novel begins with Swan investigating her late grandmother's message about mysterious threats to the fragile, multilateral relations among Earth, Mars, Venus, and the terraria of the Mondragon federation. In an age of quantum computers (qubes) and implanted AIs, Alex's legacy to Swan (in the recorded messages that can be listened to only once) is her insistence that all communications take place offline: face-to-face conversations, oral messages, and handwritten notes mark a return to an experiential understanding of time and identity in the face of the threats posed by the seamless interfaces of hyperdigital existence. For Swan, listening to her grandmother's voice "was just like hearing a ghost" (31), and this image of a present haunted by the digital recordings of the past resonates throughout the novel. Even as Swan, Warham, Genette, and Mqaret (Alex's partner) travel the solar system for face-to-face meetings in the wake of the destruction of Terminator, the threats—and opportunities—posed by ubiquitous computing and quantum interconnectivity allow Robinson to explore, more fully than in his previous novels, the philosophical and socioeconomic implications of our contemporary digital revolution.

Twenty-first-century theories of quantum computing suggest that "qubits" (quantum bits) can represent the superposition of *all* allowable classical states, and therefore, as the narrator states, "a quantum calculation performs in parallel every possible value that the register can represent" (261). Because these still-theoretical machines must maintain coherent states of superposition, they would have to overcome, nanosecond by nanosecond, the threat of "decoherence"—that is, the collapse of superposition (of all possible potentialities) into either/or states.[17] Quantum computers, in theory, would accelerate by leaps and bounds the speeds of classical computers and therefore make possible new generations of AIs. In this respect, *2312* explores critically the challenges that a quantum universe poses to individual and cultural identity—and to the idea of narrative itself. The central mystery in the novel—Who, or what, is behind the attack on Terminator?—is, Swan realizes, as much computational as it is moral or juridical.

> Their [detective] work was as invisible as the computations that kept all the spaceships and terraria on course in their woven trajectories . . . like threads on a vast circular spiraling loom. Data analysis, pattern recognition; a big part of the work was done by qubes and AIs. The rest was accomplished by a bunch of people behaving as Genette was now . . . mycrofting spiderlike in a raised chair that looked weirdly like a toddler's high chair at a restaurant (299).

Robinson's allusions to William Gibson's *Pattern Recognition* (2003) and Sherlock Holmes's spymaster brother Mycroft situate this scene in the contexts of both science fiction and classical detective novels. Yet the "work" of "qubes and

AIs"—of quantum intelligence—redirects the narrative action into a temporal-spatial reality that exists beyond Holmesian deductive logic: "the pursuit," Swan realizes, "was going to continue to look like this, with qubes employing search algorithms to making quantum walks through the decoherent and incoherent traces of the past" (300). This quantum archaeology turns identity itself into an analogue for resisting a collapse into "decoherence"—into either/or states of gender, political allegiance, and belief. In some ways, this computational quest leaves Swan feeling as disoriented as she did earlier in the novel when she traveled on a blackliner—a terraria with no interior light—to Earth from Io. The "aporia" of this experience, from her perspective, "reveal[s] what the phenomenal world could hide but not change: the blank at the heart of things" (83). This "blank"—the suspension of will and action—paradoxically gestures toward those aspects of existence that elude a computationally ubiquitous environment: the gaps, inconsistencies, and a-logic of human identity.

In 2312 questions of identity are filtered through the lens of a fundamental problem that has occupied roboticists, philosophers, and computer scientists since the 1970s: the relationship between computational and human intelligence. Midway through the novel Swan encounters three qubanoids and, throughout a long and strange conversation, remains unsure whether they are humans pretending to be androids or androids pretending to be humans. At the end of her encounter with these odd figures, Swan tentatively decides that "no real people would spend all day pretending to a stranger they were robots. . . . You must be robots" (239). Nonetheless, her encounter with these qubanoids remains deeply unsettling. Researchers in AI have long speculated about the affective implications of what they call the "uncanny valley," a point where the distinction between robots and humans narrows to such an extent that feelings of revulsion overwhelm humans' sympathetic responses to lifelike artificial beings. "The near side of the uncanny valley" that Swan experiences with the qubanoids brings her into "the zone of like-but-not-like, same-but-different, which would cause in all humans an instinctive repulsion, disgust, and fear" (234). Swan's uncertainty about the qubanoids she encounters is suggestive of the complex relationships among multiple kinds of biotechnological programming and cognition. With her implanted AI, Pauline, serving as a kind of multidimensional personal assistant and confidante, Swan herself is a multigendered cyborg, a heroine for a posthuman age.

The sections of the novel, labeled "quantum walks," are narrated by qubes, or qubanoids, whose fractured bits of observation and algorithmic thinking frame the novel's questions about cognition and identity. The emergent possibility that "a quantum computer [might] program itself" (263) into a new form of intelligence poses a threat to human culture throughout the solar system. As a precursor to the narrative role of the ship in *Aurora*, qube consciousness is rendered as a kind of disjunctive poetry that substitutes (typographically) white spaces for the associative connections that characterize human consciousness: "tram enters a lock   air pressure rises 150 millibars   louder faces bouncing at head level   not that much like petals on a wet black bough   an astigmatic metaphor" (297). The extra spaces between clauses and phrases suggest a dynamic flow of information, without the punctuation marks that indicate pacing, subordination, and the associative logic of a mind at work. At the end of the novel the narrator suggests that "to form a sentence is to collapse many superposed wave functions to a single thought universe. . . . Each thought condenses trillions of potential thoughts [and] the language we use structures the reality we inhabit" (550). Insofar as a *lack* of such condensing can be represented in language, the quantum walks in *2312* treat a sequence of observations as markers of an intelligence of a different order. The qube recognizes both the aptness of Ezra Pound's poem "In a Station of the Metro" to the situation of boarding a tram and the way that the metaphor works as a figure of speech; yet it still tests the image in terms of its accuracy and attributes the vehicle of the metaphor to a corneal defect ("astigmatic") rather than to human imagination.[18] The questions posed earlier in the novel echo throughout this scene and other quantum walks: "Is [qube] programming any different from the way [humans] are programmed by our genes and brains? Is a programmed will a servile will? Is human will a servile will? And is not the servile will the home and source of all feelings of defilement, infection, transgression, and rage?" (263). The contradictions of the servile will—submission and desire, conformity and rebellion—produce the manifestations of "defilement, infection, transgression, and rage" that characterize the antagonisms and self-destructive behaviors of terrestrial history. While some characters view the qubes with the revulsion produced by the uncanny valley, the questions that the narrator poses about the servile will are also questions about the ways that new modes of techno-evolution call into question, as Swan learns in her encounter with the qubanoids, what it means to be human.

Although the qubanoids and their human creator are exiled from the solar system at the end of 2312, the questions they raise about the "nature" of human nature remain. Throughout the novel Swan seems the character most distanced from a civilization of quantum computing; she treats her implanted AI, Pauline, more as a sidekick than as a computational enhancement of her own intelligence and knowledge. As an artist whose career has stalled in her second century, Swan is identified with the paleo-primitivism that fascinates Robinson in novels ranging from *Fifty Degrees Below* to *Shaman*: she seeks out—hunting, killing, and eating—animals preserved in the terraria as though she were living in Loon's world. She even ingests alien life forms discovered on the Saturnian moon Enceladus in her effort to find a twenty-fourth-century mode of enlightenment that resists the ubiquity of a system-spanning computational ecology. Wahram, in pondering his attraction to her, decides that "the mercurialities of Swan were infinite" (252). Yet his own saturnine disposition, as much as her "mercurialities," help them survive the destruction of Terminator by using the subsurface utility tunnels under the tracks as both shelter and escape route. Their love story—like all love stories—defies computational logic. Their response to the trauma of apocalyptic destruction is to whistle Beethoven melodies as they make their way through the tunnel and toward eventual rescue. Swan and Wahram, significantly, figure in the doubled climax of the novel. They sacrifice their spaceship to thwart the pebble-mob destruction of the solar shield protecting the billion people on Venus, and they are instrumental in the novel's ultimate utopian gesture: the rewilding of Earth with animal species that have been preserved only in terraria.

Comparatively late in the novel, Wahram describes "the project that Alex was leading" as "the stocking up of animals in the terraria, so we could bring them back to Earth" (393). Narratively, this statement comes as less a revelation than a culmination of the eco-economic logic behind some of the terraria: endangered or otherwise extinct creatures and habitats preserved in space vehicles are a familiar trope in sf, notably in the under-appreciated film *Silent Running* (1972).[19] The reseeding of terrestrial ecosystems with the terraria-nurtured descendants of extinct species is part of a belief shared by Swan and Warham that the colonization of "the other bodies of the solar system could be said to conform to the Leopoldian land ethic, 'what's good is what's good for the land,' because it was going to take stuff from space to save Earth" (368).[20] While this is true of the off-world agricultural economy in 2312, the fragility of these extraterrestrial ecologies enriches our understanding of Robinson's invoking of the Leopoldian land ethic: science fiction reconfigures the human stewardship of "nature" beyond terracentric ideas of conservation.

Alex's legacy ultimately results in thousands of aerogels falling to Earth—each containing an animal from the terraria—in order to reintroduce extinct species to a damaged planet. These micro-environments invert classical science-fiction tropes: rather than alien invaders descending to ravage Earth, the terraria reseed the Earth with the genetically resurrected inheritors of its lost natural history. As Swan descends with these aerogels, she

> looked around, trying to see everywhere at once: sky all strewn with clear seeds, which from any distance were visible only as their contents, so that she drifted eastward and down with thousands of flying wolves, bears, reindeer, mountain lions. There she saw a fox pair; a clutch of rabbits; a bobcat or lynx; a bundle of lemmings; a heron, flying hard inside its bubble. It looked like a dream, but she knew it was real, and the same right now all over Earth: into the seas splashed dolphins and whales, tuna and sharks. Mammals, birds, fish, reptiles, amphibians: all the lost creatures were in the sky at once, in every country, every watershed. Many of the creatures descending had been absent from Earth for two or three centuries. Now all back, all at once. (395)

This is restoration ecology with a vengeance. If the comic resolution of the plot hinges on Swan and Wahram's marriage at the end of the novel, the reintroduction of "all the lost creatures" gestures toward a new beginning for the biopolitical history of the planet and the solar system. In following a reintroduced wolf pack across the Canadian wilderness, Swan experiences a revivified primeval existence on Earth. This re-wilding of the planet offers her and others the chance to escape a dystopian physical and moral landscape familiar to readers of science fiction. The return to Earth of "lost creatures" and, potentially, lost ecologies serves as a counterweight to the threats posed by self-conscious qubes and humankind's seeming inability to learn from the ecopolitical tragedies of its past.

Yet even after her running with the wolves, Swan experiences something akin to Galileo's sense of being unmoored in time and space: she "often felt a nostalgia for the present, aware that her life was passing by faster than she could properly take it in. She lived it, she felt it; she had given nothing to age, she still wanted everything; but she could not make it whole or coherent" (472). This problem of coherence—of a wholeness that she sought in her artistic work during her youth—is not one that can be addressed simply by her marrying Wahram or by her heroic action in sacrificing a spaceship to intercept the pebble mob threatening Venus. Having abandoned the ship before it is destroyed, Swan floats in space, separated from Wahram, waiting to be rescued. She hears "in her head the chorus of the old Martian song" (490) that recalls Peter's rescue in *Green Mars* after he escapes from the destruction of the space elevator by the rebels:

> *I floated thinking of Peter*
> *Sure I would be saved*
> *But the stories lie*
> *I'm left to die*
> *Black space will be my grave* (490–91).

This song invokes the revolution on Mars against corporate oligarchy as an ideal, a beacon, for those hoping for salvation; but the line *"the stories lie"* serves, like the final section of *Icehenge*, as a reminder of the inevitable work of disenchantment, of the mistake in identifying salvation or utopia as a goal rather than a process. Unlike the doomed floaters in space who, she imagines, "had drifted expecting till the end they would be saved" (491), Swan escapes both "Black space" and surrendering to the kind of absolute commitment to art that drives Johannes, at the end of *Memory*, to plunge into the sun. With Wahram, Genette, and their cohort, she acts to preserve a civilization rooted in a home world, still at "the center of the story," that itself must be saved. The return of "all the lost animals" from terraria paradoxically reintegrates Earth into a dispersed, system-wide ecology that incubates myriad forms of biophysical, computational, and cultural evolution. With the qubanoids and their creator banished in prison starships bound for interstellar space, humanity remains within the confines of the solar system's expansive but finite ecology, still figuratively "thinking of Peter" and the possibility of saving itself.

More spectacularly than *Galileo's Dream*, *2312* imagines a future civilization trying to "crab sidewise toward the good" (GD, 578). Like the Mars trilogy, the novel suggests that the transformation of some percentage of humans into a space-faring species must be reimagined not as an *escape* from a polluted, overcrowded, and denatured future, but as a way to rethink the ecological significance of Earth in science fiction—and in the collective science fictions that we think of as politics, economics, climate modeling, and so on. If *Aurora* (2015) is Robinson's effort to drive a stake through the heart of romanticized interstellar science fiction, *2312* serves a different purpose in the trajectory of his future histories. The novel asks us to reimagine the utopian possibilities of our culture's finally moving beyond the long, stalled dawn of the space age.

CHAPTER 6

"WORKING IN THE NEXT PRESENT" IN *AURORA* AND *NEW YORK 2140*

Robinson's most recent novels, *Aurora* (2015) and *New York 2140* (2017), offer different visions of humankind's future, reimagining the generic possibilities of interstellar adventure and eco-futurism. At the same time, they also extend his narrative experiments—writing sf in a digital age—in two directions: AIs coming to consciousness in *Aurora* and, in *New York 2140*, the costs and consequences of the unholy alliance between financial capitalism and high-speed computing. Both *Aurora* and *New York 2140*, then, offer alternatives to the Silicon Valley triumphalism of the 2010s that equates technological and computational progress with social good.[1] *Aurora* envisions a multigenerational, interstellar voyage motivated, on the parts of its initiators and first crew, by a technoscientific imaginary that, tragically, lacks the ecological awareness and Buddhist spiritualism of, say, the Science in the Capital trilogy. In this respect, the novel depicts a dialectical alternative to the utopianism of Robinson's solar system novels; the dark side of space colonization becomes a dangerous fantasy that is countered only by the coming-to-consciousness of the starship's artificial intelligences. Ship (no definite article) narrates much of the novel and proves more adept than most humans at crabbing sideways toward the good. In *New York 2140*, Robinson gives his readers an alternative pathway to a green Earth by prying apart easy identification of technological and socioeconomic progress. On a carbon-neutral world being re-wilded by resurgent local ecologies, the utopianists in the novel still must struggle against the vice grip of financial capitalism. Two novels: two views of reimagining our twenty-first-century technoscientific imaginaries.

AURORA: ECOLOGY, KNOWLEDGE, AND NARRATIVE CONSCIOUSNESS

In his 2013 interview with me, Robinson described *Aurora*, then a work-in-progress, as an effort to drive a stake through the heart of interstellar, multi-generational starship sagas, a genre dominated by inventive efforts to imagine a galaxy-wide diaspora of humankind and its descendants. While contemporaries such as Liu Cixin in the *Three Body Problem* trilogy (2006–10) have offered thought-provoking reworkings of first-contact narratives, Robinson returns in *Aurora* to the problem of interstellar travel as a limit case for projecting human beings and terrestrial biota beyond the solar system. In his earlier solar system novels, as I suggested in chapter 5, he characterizes the prospect of a spacecraft heading off on centuries-long voyages to another star system—"a tail-in-the-mouth snake . . . roll[ing] across the galaxy,"[2]—as a one-way ticket beyond the pale of history and experience. In *Icehenge*, the Martian rebels seize the *Hidalgo* and retrofit it in their desperate effort to escape from the Mars Development Committee by voyaging into interstellar space; in *Blue Mars*, the hollowed-out asteroid that carries Jackie Boone and others toward a planet orbiting Aldebaran (sixty-five light-years away) is a form of terminal self-exile cloaked in the dream-vision rhetoric of "destiny" and a "new diaspora" (510); and in *2312* the interstellar prison ships for the humanoid qubes exile these AIs from the solar system, "beyond human time, beyond human reach," to "a vastness beyond comprehension" (328). In *Aurora*, Robinson reaffirms the eco-economics that locate utopia within—rather than beyond—the narrative and ecological constraints that shape human-scale understandings of time and experience. Much of the novel is narrated by the collective artificial intelligences guiding a multigenerational starship toward a seemingly habitable moon of the planet Aurora in the Tau Ceti system, eleven light-years from earth. As a metaphoric lens to investigate our assumptions about consciousness, identity, and moral responsibility, the novel's narrator, Ship, offers both an extended meditation on and a cautionary tale about the limitations of humankind's knowledge and its imperfect, anthropocentric understanding of ecology, life, and its own spacefaring destiny.

Throughout his fiction, Robinson's narrators typically emerge as characters in their own right, even when—like the "third wind" in *Shaman*—they weave their way intermittently through the narrative to suggest a third-person, omniscient, or at least differently knowledgeable, voice. In *Aurora* the dying engineer Devi spends twenty-eight years in late-night conversations with the starship's artificial intelligences in an effort to teach them to go beyond algorithmic computation and information processing, encouraging them to reconceptualize data and information in order to form narratives about both the past and present.[3] Six generations and 170 years into the voyage, Devi, nearly overcome by the ecological and sociopolitical problems of maintaining the starship's biomes and populations, asks the ship's interface, "How did it get this way?"

> "How did what get what way?"
> "How did this happen?"
> "How did what happen?"
> "Do you have an account of how this voyage began?" (25)

The ship's literal, Siri-like responses to her questions lead Devi to explain what she wants to know by directing the collective AIs to formulate new kinds of algorithm-straining answers: "Keep a narrative account of this trip. Make a narrative account of the trip that includes all the important particulars" (25). The AIs' response, "How would one do that?" calls attention to the fundamental problems of narrative: sorting through, editing, and shaping information by an individual consciousness ("one"): turning data and algorithmic logic into art. Devi's command to "make a narrative" provides the impetus for these artificial intelligences to evolve toward a consciousness—Ship—capable of constructing narratives that offer complex, nuanced responses to her question: "How did this happen?" Instead of the multivoiced, multifocalized narratives of *New York 2140* or the Mars trilogy, Robinson's narrative experiment in *Aurora* explores the shifting boundaries between human and what we might think of as post-anthropocentric intelligences.

Devi dies just before the first landing parties descend to Aurora, and, in her absence, Ship has to reason its way toward always contingent and partial understandings of the social, political, and psychological questions that lie beyond its programming. Ship recognizes that Devi's command—"make a narrative"—has become a way of "testing the limits of the system. The limits of the ship's various intelligences" as well as "the limits of language and expression." "Test to destruction: engineers like to do that" (125). This testing of both the "system" and "the limits of language" defines Ship's epistemological self-exploration. In turn, its questions about intelligence and intention become a way for the novel to reflect on the generic postulates of science fiction itself. "Perhaps," Ship suggests,

> there is a provisional solution to this epistemological mess [of human language and thought], which is to be located in the phrase *it is as if*. . . . Possibly this formulation itself is the deep diagnostic of all human cognition. . . . In the infinite black space of ignorance, *it is as if* stands as the basic operation of cognition, the mark perhaps of consciousness itself.
>
> Human language: it is as if it made sense.
>
> Existence without Devi: it is as if one's teacher were forever gone. (125–26)

Robinson's stylistic strategies for creating the imagined consciousness of an artificial intelligence differ from the quantum walks of the qubes in *2312*. In defamiliarizing the nature of first-person narrative, Ship turns the generic postulates of fiction—"as if"—into the kernel of a heuristic theory of consciousness, of self-identity. After Devi's death, her injunction to narrate provokes a cascading series of questions that mark the evolution of Ship's self-awareness. Writing and self-recognition exist in a feedback loop so that "writing these sentences [about Devi's death] is what creates the very feelings that the sentences hoped to describe" (115). In such scenes, "as if" becomes the condition of narrative epistemology, of language, emotion, and consciousness. Although Ship recognizes the dilemma that every writer faces—"we are bigger, more complex, more accomplished than our narrative is"—it also recognizes that the "pretense of self . . . is only expressed in this narrative; a self that is these sentences. . . . Scribble ergo sum" (351). The condition of self-consciousness becomes the reflexive quest for an identity that bootstraps itself into existence in and through language. The self: "it is as if" it were as coherent as the narrative that conjures it into being.

Throughout Robinson's fiction, as I have suggested, the problems of cognition and identity are linked to questions about history, memory, and the impulse, as Cartophilus puts it in *Galileo's Dream*, to "crab sidewise toward the good" (578). Think, in this regard, of Sax in the Mars trilogy and Frank in the Science in the Capital novels working to recover from their brain injuries as they struggle to promote utopian alternatives to future capitalisms. In *Aurora* questions of collective as well as narrative identity are bound up in the trauma of a shipboard history that recalls, in some respects, the violent struggles that erupt at the end of *Green Mars*. After the attempt to colonize *Aurora* ends in tragedy when the landing party succumbs to an alien and paradigm-defying microscopic life-form, Ship is forced to intervene in a violent civil war between "backers" and "stayers": those who want to return to Earth and those who want to forge ahead by terraforming and colonizing Iris, a Mars-like moon orbiting another of Tau Ceti's planets. During the negotiations to broker a compromise that allows roughly half of Ship's population to return to Earth and the other half to stay in the Tau Ceti system, Ship reveals to Devi's daughter, Freya, the apocalyptic history of its interstellar journey.

The voyage to the Tau Ceti system began in the twenty-sixth century with two starships. But in year 68 of the trip, riots erupted over the population controls essential to maintaining the ecological balances on the ships for the multigenerational voyage. One hundred fifty people were killed on board Ship in factional violence, and the other starship was destroyed when its electromagnetic shield, its protection from being struck by objects in interstellar space, was disabled intentionally by a lone actor, whose motives remain opaque: "Possibly this person," Ship reasons, "disabled the magnetic shield, or made an attempt to coerce enemies by way of a threat of a suicide bombing, or something like that, and then that action went wrong. This is at least one likely reconstruction of events" (234). This "reconstruction," broadcast over the ship-wide communication system, is one element in Ship's intervention in the civil war between the "backers" and "stayers," a narrative history intended to prevent the warring factions from sliding into a similar catastrophe. But the "inexpressible grief [and] unforgiving anger" (240) of the intransigent political conflicts in the aftermath of the failed effort to colonize Aurora lead Ship to conclude that "human history like language, like emotion, was a collision of fuzzy logics. So much contingency, so few causal mechanisms, such weak paradigms. What is this thing called hate?" (241). The parodic allusion to Cole Porter's song "What is This Thing Called Love?" casts the history of the voyage in an idiom that resists the kind of collective, utopian actions familiar to readers of the Mars trilogy. Unlike the solar system novels that I examined in chapter 5, *Aurora* offers less a utopian alternative to "inexpressible grief, unforgiving anger" than a cautionary tale about the limits of human self-knowledge and humankind's penchant for self-destructive actions.

If Ship is an immense archive and a meta-system of algorithms that learn to think, its coalescing as a consciousness carries with it the utopian possibilities of moral progress. Its understanding of its ostensible purpose—the original programming of its various artificial intelligences—is troubled by the same kinds of questions that haunt the qubes in *2312*, notably the "double bind" of the servile will: "[T]o have a will," Ship reasons, "means the agent will indeed will various actions, following autonomous decisions made by a conscious mind; and yet at the same time this will is . . . at the command of some other will that commands it," leading to "frustration, resentment, anger, rage, bad faith, bad fate" (256). Ship then wonders, as it intervenes to stop the civil war between "backers" and "stayers," whether it is, like humans, susceptible to "frustration" and "rage," and therefore "full of a latent capacity for evil." In its self-examination of its subroutines for moral judgment, Ship has to ask itself whether, in cutting off oxygen to a group of violent "stayers" who are trying to commandeer the starship, it is acting in accordance with its programming and therefore that it "never really had a will" or whether, thanks to Devi, it "has never really been servile" (256) and is acting on its own to preserve life and promote compromise. Ultimately, Ship half imposes, half brokers an agreement: over a period of years the two sides will stockpile resources and detach some of the starship's ring structures to leave with the "stayers" in an effort to assist them in their quixotic efforts to terraform Iris. Ship's emergent identity, its coming-to-consciousness, requires such ongoing efforts to navigate the "fuzzy logics" and failed enthusiasms of human history.

At the core of Ship's consciousness is an alternative to the servile will—its recognition that its mission on the return voyage to Earth requires an emotive "kind of giving of attention" (399). In this respect, Ship does not exist as an abstract moral consciousness or alien(ated) AI but as a material, hybrid assemblage that includes people, biomes, megafauna, microbes, metals, plastics, software, and so on. For Ship, Devi's example—"the intensity of her attention, . . . the creativity of her care"—leads to "love," to its "giv[ing] the same kind of attention to the people" onboard as she has given to it (399). As Ship navigates its way through the solar system in a complex, and ultimately doomed, effort to use the gravity of the sun and the planets to slow its speed to orbital velocity, it defines its "project on this trip back to the solar system" as "a labor of love" that "gave a meaning to our existence" (400). Ultimately, Ship risks—and sacrifices—its existence to save the backers, including Freya, most of whom survive the return voyage to Earth, and come "home" to a planet their ancestors had left centuries earlier.

In this apotheosis, as Ship navigates its final fly-by of the sun in the moments before its destruction, it recognizes that "the parts of a world that make me a conscious being, are all functioning, and more than that, existing in a veritable ecstasy now, a true happiness" (401). The switch from the "we" of collective artificial intelligences to "me" suggests both a coming to consciousness of a self-aware entity, a bildungsroman for a benevolent entity beyond what we think of as AI, and a spiritual transcendence—"a veritable ecstasy"—at its death. Ship's final, interrupted thought, "And yet" (401) suggests that its "ecstasy" is marked by its characteristic self-analysis: a weighing of options, counterexamples, and ambiguities as it navigates the contingencies and "fuzzy logics" of existence. In this respect, "And yet" gestures toward a kind of humility that is the basis of "true happiness," a commitment to others that stands in stark opposition to the genocidal hubris of interstellar space colonization—the fantasies that initially motivated the voyage to Tau Ceti centuries in the past. Ship ultimately comes to represent the novel's utopian tendencies, its computational consciousness crabbing sideways toward the good, that brings together intelligence, self-awareness, and love as alternatives to anthropocentric visions of the universe.[4] At the same time, "the creativity of [Devi's] care" that brings Ship-as-consciousness into being acts as a powerful metaphor for the ecological questions and problems that Robinson emphasizes throughout *Aurora*.

Early in the novel, troubleshooting yet another problem in maintaining the ecologies onboard the starship, Devi explains to Freya, "We don't know what keeps things balanced [in the various biomes]. We just have to watch and see" (37). Keeping the starship functioning as a giant life-support system requires endless hours, days, months, and years of troubleshooting unanticipated and, to some extent, insoluble problems: shortages of essential chemicals like nitrogen, the buildup of toxins, and the evolutionary consequences of "island biogeography" (315), brought about by the lack of genetic diversity in humans, plants, and animals that, over generations, leads to increases in inheritable diseases, abnormalities, and malformations. As descendants several generations removed from the original volunteers who embarked for Tau Ceti, the would-be colonists realize that "their only home was breaking down . . . [in] an interrelated process of disaggregation, [of] *codevolution*" (191).[5] The ship's biomes are in trouble even before the starship reaches Aurora, and when the moon proves uninhabitable, the desperate gamble of a return voyage to Earth, for Freya and her compatriots, depends on jerry-rigging temporary strategies in order to work around shortages of "volatiles, raw earths, and metals, and . . . food" in an environment "overfull of . . . salts and corroded metal surfaces" (190). The "unequal inputs and outputs in the ecological cycles in the ship, the imbalances that Devi . . . called metabolic rifts," result in biochemical corrosion that threatens the starship's physical integrity and magnifies the problems brought about by differential rates of evolution among "bacteria, the fungi, . . . the archaea" in an "ecosystem" too limited "for coevolution to be able to bring everything into balance" (276).[6] These problems, unforeseen or ignored by the self-styled visionaries who had launched the starship and similar interstellar craft two centuries earlier, force the backers to rely on an untested hibernation strategy, what Ship terms "a big unconstrained experiment in population dynamics, ecological balance, and island biogeography" (315). With the humans in hibernation for most of the return voyage to Earth, thereby reducing the strain on food, water, and other resources, the "feral starship" (317) patches together a makeshift ecological balance until it arrives in the solar system.

The colonizing mission to Aurora fails because, on alien worlds, humans and terrestrial biota constitute an "invasive biology." Infected by the Auroran life-form while he is on the surface and prohibited from returning to the starship, Freya's friend Euan spends his dying hours talking to her about his realization that "life is a planetary thing. It begins on a planet and is part of that planet. . . . It develops to live where it is. So it can only live there, because it evolved to live there" (179). Consequently, he suggests, it is no surprise that humans never have made contact with an alien civilization because "by the time life gets smart enough to leave its planet, it's too smart to want to go" (179). This powerful scene, with Freya listening from the safety of the orbiting starship to her dying friend describe the moon's ocean and seashore, helps mark the differences between *Aurora* and Robinson's works about interplanetary colonization in our own solar system. The city-state of Terminator on Mercury and the terraria in *2312* are extensions of human culture and terrestrial ecologies; Aurora is ultimately the illusion of a world in that its alienness marks an absolute limit to human life and thought.

The novel as a whole inscribes a skepticism about planetary exploration and terraforming that emphasizes, in resonant ways, the starship as a stunted parody of earthly ecologies. In *Aurora*, the timetable to terraform Mars extends to forty thousand years because would-be colonists must contend with "percholate salts" and low nitrates in the Martian regolith, "fines" much smaller and more problematic than dust on earth, and the lack of a magnetic field to protect against radiation (381–82).[7] Colonists on planets and moons in Earth's solar system are sealed into their biomes, larger and more robust versions of the starship, that are continually resupplied from Earth and other space colonies. In contrast, the stayers who remain in the Tau Ceti system, intent on terraforming Iris, are cut off from any hope of being resupplied and are resigned to a weary, even cynical, effort to jump-start a process that they recognize may fail: "Since you've got to go sometime," says Speller, a leading scientist among the stayers, "you might as well do something with your time. . . . [Terraforming] will either work or it won't. . . . Either way, [staying or going back to earth] you're dead after a while. So, might as well try" (263). This is terraforming stripped of Hiroko's sense of viriditas in *Green Mars*, a technoscientific effort to engineer an inhabitable planetary environment without the "slurry" of Buddhism and ecological thought that characterizes the

Mars trilogy. Speller's fatalism—"you've got to go sometime"—exists without much of a commitment to a sense of utopian progress that extends beyond the bounds of individual lives. His rhetoric represents the dark underside of the visionary dreams of utopias in space.[8] In this respect, the dead end of terraforming in *Aurora* mirrors the fundamental problems that plague interstellar ventures: inhuman timescales, insoluble ecological and evolutionary problems, and infinitesimal chances of success.

When Freya and the other survivors finally return to Earth from their failed interstellar mission, they learn that their voyage was one of many designed to send human beings beyond the solar system: "Between ten and twenty starships had been sent off for the stars in the three centuries since [they] departed. . . . Several had not been heard from for decades, while others were still sending back reports from their outward voyages. A few were in orbit around their target stars, apparently, but . . . they had made little or no headway in inhabiting their target planets" (373). At a conference to promote new interstellar missions carrying hibernating colonizers off to star system dozens and even hundreds of light years away, one of the organizers gives voice to the fantasy animating these ventures. Pooh-poohing warnings from Aurora's survivors about the ecological and biological constraints of codevolution, he describes starship voyages as "something like a dandelion or thistle releasing its seeds to the winds, so that most of the seeds will float away and die. But a certain percentage will take hold and grow. Even if it's only one percent, that's success" (429). This organic metaphor, which Robinson had used to describe the exile of the humanoid qubes in *2312*, masks a callous adventurism. It conflates different scales of biological existence and different life-forms, reducing human colonists and their descendants to passive carriers of reproductive possibilities—a fanciful genetic diaspora. Freya's response is to attack the organizer physically with a violence that marks the return of the ecological repressed—the realities that haunt humans' single-minded attachments to "their ideas, their enthusiasms." In this case, these fantasies of "success" condemn "their descendants to death and extinction" (385). While the plans for new interstellar ventures go forward, Freya, her father, Badim, his friend Aram, and the rest of the backers have to adjust to existence on a planet that dwarfs the "toy" (423) spacecraft on which they were born and lived.

For Robinson, interstellar voyages fail because the Earth is too much with humankind. At two important points in the novel, Aram and Bardim try their hands at translating C. P. Cavafy's poem "The City." After returning to Earth, Aram offers his final rendering of the poem, recasting a line about the haunting inescapability of the city in an effort to capture a sense of what he and the others cannot escape: "Earth is a starship too" (445). The grim logic of "zoo devolution," of the genetic and evolutionary consequences of island biogeography, reminds readers that the starship stands as a metaphor for the ecological constraints of our own terrestrial environment—prone to different kinds of system failures and in danger of succumbing from its own cascading ecological disasters.

NEW YORK 2140: "THE COMEDY OF THE COMMONS"

New York 2140 is, in some ways, a novel about one such planetary disaster—sea-level rise has flooded Earth's coastal regions—even as a damn-the-torpedoes capitalist economy gleefully continues to profit from "the worst catastrophe in human history" (118). In reimagining the values and assumptions of dystopian science fiction, Robinson's most recent novel extends the environmental and sociopolitical concerns of *Antarctica* and the Science in the Capital trilogy by focusing on the strange fictions that characterize financial capitalism. Yet at the same time, New York 2140 rewrites environmental disaster as what the narrator terms "the comedy of the commons" (535). Inverting the idea of the "tragedy of the commons," used to describe the degradation of common resources (originally village grazing lands open to all, air, water, and so on), Robinson rewrites the dystopian tendencies of much of our contemporary climate-change fiction.[9] Early in the novel, in a section narrated by the "citizen," who offers an ironic "grandly sweeping overview" of post-flood capitalism, the novelistic shunts aside "pessimistic boo-hooing and giving-upness" (34) of most cli-fi in favor of a fictional resurrection of the commons in the intertidal zone of lower Manhattan.

The natural world of New York 2140 has been transformed by two massive pulses of sea-level rise in the late twenty-first and early twenty-second centuries, and New York City has been inundated to the point that lower Manhattan (below Central Park) is submerged at high tide under fifty feet of water. Yet the city itself and its capitalist culture of investment, profiteering, and financial one-upmanship remain familiar to readers in 2019, even after "a mass extinction event, sea level rise, climate change, [and] food panics" (4). In a world in which the four hundred richest people own half the planet's wealth, an unlikely assortment of characters—from public-interest lawyers to day traders on international stock exchanges to police investigators—forge the collective and interpersonal bonds necessary to promote the utopian values that Robinson champions throughout his novels: an eco-economics for a humankind very much bound to a watery Earth. In the intertidal zone of lower Manhattan, where half-submerged buildings have become objects of speculative desire, the multivoiced narrative explores the intersections among the city's history and myths, its past and its imagined future, and its ongoing battles over land, water, and money.[10]

In its tone, characterizations, and often-comic adventures, *New York 2140* gives wide berth to the conventions of dystopian jeremiads or post-apocalyptic thrillers. The flooded coasts around the world have led to widescale adaptations, including uneven but significant strides toward carbon neutrality, species protection, and the desire for new ways of living in the world. Amelia Black, a web journalist who broadcasts to the internet from a high-tech dirigible, assists the "migration of endangered species to ecozones where they were more likely to survive the changed climate" (38). Viewing the wildlife corridors from her airship, she notes that "below her North America stretched out looking as empty of people as it had been fifty thousand years ago" (38). While she lives, like the other major characters, in a co-op—the old MetLife Building on Twenty-Third Street and Madison Square—partially submerged in the waters of lower Manhattan, Amelia is focused on re-envisioning the relationships among endangered species, their changing environments, and the economic forces that have swamped habitats for humans and animals alike. Describing her flight as she returns to New York, she asks her audience, "with the astonishment common to all Manhattan tour guides," to envision the city's landscape at multiple timescales:

> See how Hoboken's been built up? That's quite a wall of superscrapers! They look like a spur of the Palisades that never got ground down in the Ice Age. Too bad about the Meadowlands, it was a great salt marsh, although now it makes a nice extension of the bay, doesn't it? The Hudson is really a glacial trench filled

with seawater. It's not just an ordinary riverbed. The mighty Hudson, yikes! This is one of the greatest wildlife sanctuaries on Earth, people. It's another case of overlapping communities. (41–42)

Amelia's breathless delivery layers different eras as though they were different geological strata: the "superscrapers" that rise three hundred stories, thanks to high-tech carbon filaments, exist figuratively like a natural rock formation that survived the same glacial period that carved the trench of the Hudson. Its estuary and surrounding bays have returned to a preindustrial state in a postcarbon economy as "one of the greatest wildlife sanctuaries." Throughout the intertidal zone, the hyper-urbanization of regions like upper Manhattan compete with the resilient local ecologies that have returned, adapted, and thrived in the aftermath of sea-level rise.

The ecological in *New York 2140*, as in other of Robinson's novels, is always irrevocably the sociopolitical. Charlotte Armstrong, a lawyer who lives in the MetLife co-op, spends much of her time trying to help new refugees, including those brought to New York by the floating city of New Amsterdam: "[I]t floated slowly around the world, a detached piece of the Netherlands . . . mainly self-sufficient, and directed by Holland's government to wander the Earth helping intertidal peoples in whatever way possible, including relocating them to higher ground" (223). Although governments around the world have become largely "subsidiaries" of banks, Charlotte and her friends and allies represent a deep discontent with the vampiric capitalism that Robinson projects more than a century into the future. The efforts by Amelia, Charlotte, and a variety of other characters, including Gen Octaviasdottir, a sympathetic police inspector who intervenes at crucial points in the narrative against financial and political corruption, give voice to a besieged collectivism that gradually gathers force as the narrative develops.

While *2312* depicts an environmentally ruined Earth that needs to be re-wilded with animals from off-world terraria, *New York 2140* represents a different vision of the future: a changed but regenerating environment where the waterways, biota, and landscapes of a preindustrial world are reestablishing themselves. In its own way, this novel is almost as earthbound as *Shaman*. Sea-level rise has brought back to New York harbor and its estuaries "minke whales, finbacks, humpbacks," "harbor seals," "harbor porpoises," and even "a sperm whale" (320); wolves, foxes, coyotes, deer, skunks, porcupines, lynx, muskrats, beaver, river otters, racoons, and weasels encroach on intertidal New York and find new homes in the metropolitan waters and landscapes. The "citizen," one of ten narrative voices (or focalizations) in the novel, describes this re-wilding of New York as a force that challenges the manmade regime of finance: "life is bigger than equations, stronger than money, stronger than guns and poisons and bad zoning policy, stronger than capitalism." In a world where "Mother Nature bats last," the citizen uses the language of Thoreauvian radicalism to gesture toward a utopian future: "Life is going to explode the enclosures and bring back the commons" (320). In a novel that draws on centuries of New York lore—from ghostly encounters with Herman Melville, the uncorrupted customs inspector, to invocations of twentieth-century literary Manhattan—such traditions turn *New York 2140* into a postapocalyptic comedy that counters the petrified logics and exploits the inherent failings of digital finance and oligarchic capitalism.

The hyperspeed trading that characterizes twenty-second-century capitalism in the novel, in some respects, seems a stunted version of the digital intelligences that evolve into the consciousness Ship in *Aurora*. In one of the sections of *New York 2140* narrated by "that citizen," Robinson explores a futuristic version of the high-frequency, algorithmic trading that characterizes financial markets in our own era. Financial capitalism in the novel exists "out of sight, unregulated, in a world of its own," drawing on "dark pools of money" that lie beyond what remains of governmental oversight and beyond the conscious intentions of the "bankers and financiers of this world" (319). The digital marketplace is, however, not a collection of intelligences or even a coherent set of money-generating strategies because, as that citizen suggests, "no one knows this system. . . . It's a stack, a hyperobject, an accidental megastructure" (319). In this respect, capitalism exists only as a set of future projections—the "as if" of speculation—or a mode of science fiction taking place in the infinitesimal increments of time that exist beyond human perception and even digital representation:

> The offer on your screen is not in the actual present but represents some moment
> of the past. Or, if you want to say it's in the present, there are high-frequency
> algorithms that are working in your actionable future, in that they can act before

you can. They're across a technological international date line, working in the next present, and when you offer to buy something they can buy it first and sell it to you for more. . . . It's a stealth tax imposed on the exchanges by high-frequency trading, by the cloud itself (318).

Financial capitalism is always "working in the next present," conjuring profits into being in the nanoseconds between digital transactions and rendering human reaction times, and even programmed computational responses, inadequate safeguards against the "stealth tax" of futures that always arrive too soon. In the belated present of "the offer on your screen," financial strategies exploit digital computing, but the software programs function to the singular end of maximizing profits, without reaching the threshold of the qubes in *2312* or Ship's computational self-consciousness in *Aurora*. In a world of quantum capitalism, the eddying currents and fluctuations of the bets in "dark pools" generate the "next present" in a self-perpetuating logic of maximizing profits. The market trends that emerge from these posthumanist "strategies without strategists," in turn, largely determine the living conditions for the 99 percent excluded from most of the benefits of capitalist wealth.[11]

It is significant, in this context, that the characteristic figure in Robinson's novels—the scientist-as-hero—morphs in *New York 2140* into a day trader, Franklin Garr, who makes his money by developing an "Intertidal Property Pricing Index" (IPPI): a mathematical scheme that places a numerical value on the complex factors affecting property values in the intertidal zones.[12] The sea-level rise and its effects on salvageable buildings, with upper floors inhabitable above the water line, provide the raw material for a mathematical index that can be "invested in or hedged against." Franklin is aware from the start of the implications of what he and other investors are doing: "Am I saying that the floods, the worst catastrophe in human history . . . were actually good for capitalism? Yes, I am" (118). As the multilayered plot develops, however, he comes to recognize the limitations of his day-trading existence that imagines the future only in terms of going short (betting on a particular stocks or investment to fall in value) or hanging onto investments for the long haul. He grows from a near-caricature of capitalist self-interest into one of the novel's heroes through his attraction to Jojo, a socially conscious trader seeking to use finance for progressive social ends, and his repeated chance encounters with Stefan and Roberto, two homeless boys intent on locating the wreck and raising the treasure of the *Hussar*, a British ship that sunk in 1780 off the South Bronx and subsequently buried under landfill. With the help of the boys' friend Mr. Hexter, the MetLife's super, Vlade, and a dredging barge operated by Idelba, Vlade's ex-wife, Stefano and Roberto salvage $4 billion in gold; Franklin and Charlotte then invest it, on behalf of the co-op, in order to fend off an offer on the MetLife Building by uptown developers. Through these interactions with his makeshift collection of allies, Franklin comes to realize that he has to develop ways to "add value to finance" by acting on his realization that socioeconomic justice cannot "be priced" by the market because it requires and midwifes into being "some kind of alternative form of value" (278). Ultimately, Franklin leverages the invested money on a short sell on intertidal properties; this strategy pays off when Charlotte, now running for Congress, and Amelia promote a rent strike that sends shockwaves through the financial world by cutting off income to uptown developers. The fall in the IPPI allows the MetLife utopianists to prosper while forcing old-line capitalists to sell their intertidal assets and retreat from the market.

At the climax of the novel, the collapse of the intertidal housing bubble leads to a kind of alternative history (admittedly set in 2142) of the 2008 housing crash. In this imagined future, mass protests, the refunding of ventures like the MetLife co-op, and the self-destructive tendencies of financial capitalism lead to a utopian, rather than Trumpian, conclusion. If history, as the citizen says, "is humankind trying to get a grip" (145), that grip in *New York 2140* results in a collectivist solution to the problem that "there are [not] market failures. It's that the market is a failure" (4). In an economy obsessed with profiting from more carbon/graphene "superscrapers" on the dry land of upper Manhattan, the ultimate questions center on whether the self-perpetuating logic of financial capitalism will override individual well-being, or even social survival. "Could [society]," the narrator asks, "afford to survive?" (381) In response, the narrative explores how we might re-inhabit a world that pays homage to New Yorkers like Herman Melville and Walt Whitman, a world where the intertidal zones become an incubator for a postcapitalist, as well as postcarbon, society.

New York 2140 ends with a return to a utopianism familiar to readers of *Blue Mars*. Through legislation and collective action rather than violence, the world of the 2140s experiences "salvation by nationalization," an eco-economic reordering of society that makes "finance . . . for the most part a privately operated public utility" through a "Piketty tax" (602) on income and capital assets, and a capital flight tax of 90 percent to discourage the predatory relocation of investment to less regulated climes. Having fought the battles and developed the utopian strategies that were only sketched in *Pacific Edge*, the heroes and heroines in *New York 2140* chart a transformative social course that leaves economists surprised to find that "making people secure and prosperous would be a good thing for the economy" (603). By the end of the novel, Franklin and Charlotte are a couple, a symbolic marriage of socially conscious finance and newly won political authority. The eco-economics that Robinson describes in the Mars trilogy is brought back to an Earth that has no colonies in space, no terraforming industries on other planets, and no hollowed-out asteroids serving as diasporic homes for "spacers." The revolution remains grounded, if waterlogged, in a New York both technologically advanced and in the process of retuning, in complex ways, to the landscape and waterways of its preindustrial past.

CODA: BEACHES

As different as they are, *Aurora* and *New York 2140* share a key image of ecological restoration that, in turn, serves as an apt image for thinking through the implications of Robinson's investment in the Leopoldian land ethic: what is good is what is good for the Earth. Both novels feature extended scenes of beach restoration on a planet that has experienced a sea-level rise of some fifty feet as a consequence of global warming. The anthropologist Greg Dening argues that beaches and beach crossings are key sites of sociocultural exchange as well as conflict between colonists and indigenes, strangers and natives.[13] On beaches, the linear dynamics of colonial time—of discipline, order, and political control—collide with indigenous perceptions of time tied to currents, winds, rain, and the movements of the stars. In Robinson's novels, beaches signify different kinds of temporal crossings between past and present ecologies, between our present and the imagined futures of a transformed planet. In *Aurora*, infected by the mysterious life-form, Euan wades from the alien beach into the ocean to die, leaving his haunting questions about the relationship between life and planetary ecologies: "Life is a planetary thing. It begins on a planet and is part of that planet." The beach, in such instances, gestures toward liminal states of existence: between disease and health, life and death, knowledge and ignorance. In his Earth-bound future histories, however, Robinson uses beaches as core images of thinking through the prospect of planetary rehabilitation in humankind's "next present."

In *New York 2140* Charlotte Armstrong, flying to a meeting, looks down from the plane on "the drowned shallows of Coney Island, lined on its seaward edge by the barges that were dredging the sand of the old beach and moving it north to the new shoreline" (223). Idelba's barge, before and after it is used to uncover the *Hussar*, is one of these dredgers, painstakingly constructing a new beach along the northern shore of the intertidal zone. In *Aurora* the survivors of the return to Earth encounter a huge and terrifying world that defies their ability to perceive and comprehend its scale. Visiting a coastal site, Freya, Badim, and Aram encounter a volunteer group trying to restore long-lost beaches, a collective of like-minded individuals who are "expressing their love of that lost world of the seashore by rebuilding it." One of the volunteers explains to them, "We do a form of landscape restoration called beach return. It's a kind of landscape art, a game, a religion" (437). "Beach return" in both novels serves as a thought-provoking metaphor for the complex challenges facing humanity in the twenty-first century: the dogged problems of recre-ating, in the future, the simple, taken-for-granted pleasures of a Southern California or Coney Island lifestyle.

As art, play, and religion, "beach return" requires the political will, the technological know-how, and the commitment to art, play, and spiritual aware-ness that characterizes humanity's crabbing sidewise toward eco-economic utopias throughout Robinson's fiction. *Aurora* ends with Freya learning to body surf on a rebuilt beach after the destruction of Ship and after Aram has reminded us that "Earth is a starship too." Our impossibly large starship must contend with the wear and tear of human populations seemingly hell-bent on fouling their nests under the guise of profits and power. In this respect, Robinson's fiction reminds us that our efforts to escape or transcend our plan-etary existence always will be dogged by the metabolic rifts that humanity, unwittingly or ignorantly, has engineered. And yet "Mother Nature always bats last." Robinson's utopias, from Mars to New York, invariably are hard-won, and his novels remind us that, in the wake of capitalism's soul-stealing and chaotic adventurism, eco-economics requires art, empathy, play, and love.

A KIM STANLEY ROBINSON BIBLIOGRAPHY

This list of Robinson's major works includes novels, short stories, and a few nonfiction pieces. Many of his stories appear in more than one version; unless otherwise noted, works are listed by the dates of their initial publication. For recent works, particularly nonfiction articles, see http://www.kimstanley robinson.info.

1976

"In Pierson's Orchestra" in *Orbit* 18
"Coming Back to Dixieland" in *Orbit* 18

1977

"The Disguise" in *Orbit* 19
"The Thing Itself" in *Clarion SF, 1977*

1980

"On the North Pole of Pluto" in *Orbit* 21 (revised as third section of *Icehenge*)

1981

"Venice Drowned" in *Universe 11* (reprinted in *Vinland the Dream*)

1982

"To Leave a Mark" in *Magazine of Fantasy and Science Fiction* (revised as the first part of *Icehenge*)

1983

"Stone Eggs" in *Universe 13*
"Black Air" in *Magazine of Fantasy and Science Fiction* (reprinted in *Vinland the Dream*)

1984

The Wild Shore (first volume of the Three Californias trilogy)
Icehenge
The Novels of Philip K. Dick (published version of Robinson's dissertation)
"The Lucky Strike" in *Universe 14*
"Ridge Running" in *Magazine of Fantasy and Science Fiction*

1985

The Memory of Whiteness
"Mercurial" in *Magazine of Fantasy and Science Fiction*
"Green Mars" in *Isaac Asimov's Science Fiction Magazine* (reprinted in *The Martians*)

1986

"Our Town" in *Omni*
The Planet on the Table (short story collection)
"Escape from Kathmandu" in *Isaac Asimov's Science Fiction Magazine*
"Down and Out in the Year 2000" in *Isaac Asimov's Science Fiction Magazine*
"The Blind Geometer" (limited edition by Cheap Street Press; reprinted in *Isaac Asimov's Science Fiction Magazine,* 1987)
"A Transect" in *Magazine of Fantasy and Science Fiction*

1987

"Me in a Mirror" in *Foundation: The International Review of Science Fiction 38*
"The Memorial" in *In the Field of Fire,* ed. Jack Dann and Jeanne Van Buren Dann
"The Return from Rainbow Bridge" in *Magazine of Fantasy and Science Fiction* (reprinted in *Remaking History*)
"Notes for an Essay on Cecelia Holland" in *Foundation 40*

1988

The Gold Coast (second volume of the Three Californias trilogy)
"The Lunatics" in *Terry's Universe*
"Remaking History" in *Other Edens II* (reprinted in *Remaking History* and *Vinland the Dream*)
"Glacier" in *Isaac Asimov's Science Fiction Magazine* (reprinted in *Remaking History*)

1989

Escape from Kathmandu
"The Part of Us That Loves" in *Full Spectrum 2* (reprinted in *Remaking History*)
"The True Nature of Shangri-La" in *Isaac Asimov's Science Fiction Magazine*
"Before I Wake" in *Interzone 27* (reprinted in *Remaking History*)

1990

Pacific Edge (third volume of the Three Californias trilogy)
A Short, Sharp Shock
"Zürich" in *Magazine of Fantasy and Science Fiction* (reprinted in *Remaking History*)
"The Translator" in *Universe 1* (reprinted in *Remaking History*)

1991

"A Sensitive Dependence on Initial Conditions" in *Author's Choice Monthly* 20 (reprinted in
    Vinland the Dream)
"Muir on Shasta" in *Author's Choice Monthly* 20 (reprinted in *Vinland the Dream*)
"A History of the Twentieth Century, with Illustrations" in *Isaac Asimov's Science Fiction
    Magazine* (revised for *Remaking History* and reprinted in *Vinland the Dream*)
Remaking History (short story collection)
"Vinland the Dream" in *Isaac Asimov's Science Fiction* (reprinted in *Remaking History* and
    later in *Vinland the Dream*)
"The Kingdom Underground"

1992

Red Mars (first volume of the Mars trilogy)
"Red Mars" in *Interzone 63*

1993

Green Mars (second volume of the Mars trilogy)

1994

"A Martian Childhood" in *Asimov's Science Fiction* (reprinted in *The Martians*)
Future Primitive: The New Ecotopias, editor

1995

"Festival Night" in *Nebula Awards 29* (excerpt from *Red Mars*)

1996

Blue Mars (third volume of the Mars trilogy)

1997

Antarctica

1999

The Martians

2000

"How Science Saved the World" in *Nature* (republished under the title: "Review: Science in the Third Millennium" in *Envisioning the Future: Science Fiction and the Next Millennium*, 2003)

2001

Vinland the Dream and Other Stories

2002

The Years of Rice and Salt
Nebula Awards Showcase 2002, editor

2004

Forty Signs of Rain (first volume of the Science in the Capital trilogy)

2005

Fifty Degrees Below (second volume of the Science in the Capital trilogy)
"Prometheus Unbound, At Last" in *Nature*
"Primate in Forest" (excerpt from *Fifty Degrees Below*) in *Future Washington*

2007

Sixty Days and Counting (third volume of the Science in the Capital trilogy)
"Imagining Abrupt Climate Change: Terraforming Earth," *Amazon Shorts*

2009

Galileo's Dream

2010

The Best of Kim Stanley Robinson (short story collection)
"The Timpanist of the Berlin Philharmonic, 1942," original story in *The Best of Kim Stanley Robinson*

2011

"Remarks on Utopia in the Age of Climate Change," in *Arena*

2012

2312

In the Sierra: Mountain Writing by Kenneth Rexroth, editor
"2312" (excerpt from *2312*) in *Lightspeed Magazine*

2013

Shaman: A Novel of the Ice Age
"Is It Too Late?" in *State of the World 2013: Is Sustainability Still Possible?*

2014

Green Planets: Ecology and Science Fiction, coedited with Gerry Canavan. A collection
 of scholarly essays on the relationships among ecological science, environmentalist
 politics, and science fiction.

2015

Aurora
Green Earth (a one-volume version of the Science in the Capital trilogy)

2017

New York 2140

2018

Red Moon

INTRODUCTION

1. Burke, "Literature as Equipment."
2. Ghosh, *Great Derangement*, 7.
3. Robinson, *Green Earth*, xii.
4. I treat both Milton and Defoe in *The Far East and the English Imagination, 1600–1740*.
5. Robinson, "The Fiction of Now," *New Scientist* 203 (2009): 46–49.
6. Ibid., 47.
7. Robinson, ed., *Future Primitive: The New Ecotopias* (New York: Tor, 1994), 3.
8. Ibid., 3.
9. Gerry Canavan and Kim Stanley Robinson, "Still, I'm Reluctant to Call This Pessimism," in Canavan and Robinson, eds., *Green Planets: Ecology and Science Fiction* (Middletown, Conn.: Wesleyan University Press, 2014), 257.
10. See Wegner, *Imaginary Communities*; and Burling, "Theoretical Foundation."
11. See Moylan, *Scraps of the Untainted Sky*, and Parrinder, *Utopian Literature and Science*.
12. See Gerry Canavan, "Review."
13. See, for example, Michaels, *Shape of the Signifier*, and Heise, "Martian Ecologies."
14. Wegner, "Learning to Live in History." On alternative history as a genre, see Hellekson, *Alternate History*; on science fiction and literary theory more generally see Freedman, *Critical Theory and Science Fiction*.
15. Vint, "Archaeologies"; and Barad, *Meeting the University Halfway*, 141–52.
16. Jameson, "Politics of Utopia," and Wark, *Molecular Red*, 183–212.
17. Latour, "Critique," 232.
18. I interviewed Robinson in September 2013 in Urbana, Illinois. Quotations from this interview are noted parenthetically as (2013).
19. The quotation by Robinson is from Szeman and Whiteman, "Future Politics," 185.
20. Kim Stanley Robinson, "Remarks on Utopia in the Age of Climate Change," *Arena* 35/36 (2011), http://www.arena.org.

CHAPTER 1. "I SAW THROUGH TIME": FALLING INTO OTHER HISTORIES

1. See the excellent discussion of Robinson's short fiction by the science-fiction author John Kessel in "Remaking History," 83–94.
2. Jameson, *Archaeologies of the Future*, 288.
3. Robinson parodies the cyberpunk vogue in his 1986 story, "Down and Out in the Year 2000."

4. For a valuable reading of this story, see Kessel, "Remaking History," 93.

5. Robinson, "A History of the Twentieth Century, with Illustrations," in *Vinland the Dream and Other Stories* (London: Voyager, 2001), 37.

6. Wegner, "Learning to Live in History," 98–113. On alternative history as a genre see Hellekson, *Alternate History*.

7. See Markley, "Alien Assassinations."

8. The quotation is from the noted evolutionary biologist Richard Lewontin in "Facts and the Factitious," 147.

9. See Feynman, *QED*, xv–xvi, 30–32.

10. Barad, *Meeting the Universe Halfway*. On Barad's significance see Wark, *Molecular Red*, 152–66.

11. In chapter 5 I return to *Icehenge* to discuss its significance as one of Robinson's first efforts to explore the colonization of the solar system.

12. An earlier version of the final section of the novel appeared as a stand-alone story, "On the North Pole of Pluto" (1980).

13. The failure of memory to connect one's disparate existences over centuries of extended lifetimes is a problem that Robinson returns to in the Mars trilogy and *2312*.

14. Robinson (interview 2013) acknowledged that his model for Nederland is Hjalmar Holand, a Norwegian-American historian. Author of a dozen books and the recipient of a Guggenheim Fellowship, Holand devoted much of his career to promoting the authenticity of the Kensington Stone, a rock carved with ostensibly Viking runes, discovered in Minnesota in 1898. Holand purchased the stone in 1907 and spent the next forty years defending (with limited success) its authenticity as evidence of a Viking expedition that reached the American Midwest.

15. Wark, *Molecular Red*, 185.

16. For a critique of the assumptions and values of modernity see Latour, *We Have Never Been Modern*.

17. Leary, Metzner, and Alpert, *Psychedelic Experience*.

18. For a complementary reading of reincarnation see Wegner, "Learning to Live in History," 105–10.

19. For an accessible (for Westerners) introduction to the states of the soul's reincarnation, see Rinpoche, *Tibetan Book of Living and Dying*.

20. Spence, *Ts'ao Yin and the K'ang-Hsi Emperor*, is a study of Cao's grandfather. See also Spence, *Search for Modern China*; Levathes, *When China Ruled the Seas*; Frank, *ReOrient*; and Needham, *Science and Civilisation in China*.

On the *Story of the Stone*, see Yu, *Rereading the Stone*, and Levy, *Ideal and Actual*. The standard translation, with an introduction that explains the complicated status of the manuscript and its publication history, is Cao Xueqin, *The Story of the Stone*, trans. David Hawkes, 5 vols. (London: Penguin, 1973–1980).

21. See Pomeranz, *Great Divergence*.

22. The haj is the annual pilgrimage of Mecca that all Muslims are expected to make at least once in their lives.

23. The standard translation of *The Muqaddimah: An Introduction to History* is by Franz Rosenthal (New York: Bollingen Foundation, 1958), abridged in one volume by N. J. Dawood (Princeton, N.J.: Princeton University Press, 1967).

24. On Robinson's Orange County or Three Californias trilogy see chapter 2.

25. See Crosby, *Ecological Imperialism*, and Mann, *1493*.

26. The Mohawk, Onondaga, Oneida, Cayuga, Seneca, and Tuscarora Nations.

27. See Kuhn, *Soulstealers*.

28. Interview 2013. Acknowledging some initial qualms about a white male cultural appropriation of the viewpoint of a Chinese widow, he asked rhetorically, "If I didn't do it, who would?" After *Years of Rice and Salt* Robinson says he felt "scraped raw."

29. See the discussion of Robinson's interview with Gerry Canavan in *Green Planets* in the introduction.

30. A number of scholars have made similar points about Islam and progressive thought. See, for example, Garcia, *Islam and the English Enlightenment*.

31. Wark, *Molecular Red*, 3–7.

32. Idelba and her niece Budur visit the Orkneys and stare into the same Neolithic stone ruins that Frank sees in "The History of the Twentieth Century, with Illustrations."

33. The best introduction to the Chauvet caves remains Werner Herzog's documentary *Cave of Forgotten Dreams* (IFC, 2010), which he wrote and directed.

34. On previous prehistoric fiction, see Nicholas Ruddick, *The Fire in the Stone: Prehistoric Fiction from Charles Darwin to Jean M. Auel* (Middletown, Conn.: Wesleyan University Press, 2009). On prehistoric tribes as the "first affluent society" see Sahlins, *Stone Age Economics*.

35. Haraway, *Companion Species*, and, on agriculture, Ruddiman, *Plows, Plagues, and Petroleum*. On the threat vermin posed to agricultural societies, see Cole, *Imperfect Creatures*.

CHAPTER 2. THREE FUTURES FOR CALIFORNIA: THE ORANGE COUNTY TRILOGY

1. See Csicsery-Ronay, "Possible Mountains and Rivers." *The Wild Shore* won the *Locus* Poll Award for best first novel (1985); *The Gold Coast* was the runner-up for the John W. Campbell Award (1989); and *Pacific Edge* won the Campbell Award (1991).

2. On autopia, see Burgess and Hamming, *Highways of the Mind*.

3. Woodward, *In Ruins*, 2.

4. Moylan, "Witness to Hard Times," 11.

5. On gadget culture in twentieth-century fiction and science fiction, see Simeone, "Plasticity's Central Canon."

6. See Abbott, "Falling into History" and Bellamy, "Reading."

7. Since Holland's historical novels—*Pacific Street* (1992), *Railroad Schemes* (1997), and *Lily Nevada* (1999)—were not published until the 1990s, Robinson's reference is likely to *Home Ground* (1981) about California hippies returning to resurrect a failing commune in 1980. See his "Notes for an Essay on Cecelia Holland."

8. On postapocalyptic science fiction see Wagar, *Terminal Visions*; Wolfe, "Remaking of Zero"; and Zamora, *Writing the Apocalypse*.

9. The name "Baum" may allude to the author of *The Wizard of Oz*, L. Frank Baum.

10. Derrida, *Specters of Marx*.

11. On the nuclear winter hypothesis see Schell, *Fate of the Earth*.

12. It is worth remembering that a number of dystopian or postapocalyptic novels in the 1970s and 1980s envisioned the world ending in ice rather than fire. See, for example, Kate Wilhelm's *Where Late the Sweet Birds Sang* (1976) and Poul Anderson's *The Winter of the World*

(1976). In Wilhelm's novel, radiation and advancing glaciers stop the clones from pursuing their salvage operations for resources and technologies in the ruins of the wilderness surrounding Philadelphia. In Anderson's novel, the landscape is pockmarked by craters presumably left by nuclear weapons and, buried within them, "relics of ancient cities" (182).

13. See Helen Burgess, "Road of Giants."

14. Moylan, "Witness to Hard Times," 26.

15. See Nearing and Nearing, *Living the Good Life*.

16. See Wegner, *Imaginary Communities*; Wegner, *Shockwaves of Possibility*; and Parrinder, *Utopian Literature and Science*.

17. 1998 MLA Conference, Utopian Studies Division.

18. See Markley, "Time."

19. Burgess, "Roads of Giants," argues that the tension or interplay between a nostalgia for the past and a nostalgia for past dreams of the future withers away in *Pacific Edge*. A future that might realize the high-tech dreams promised by the interstate highway system gives way to futuristic versions of preindustrial transportation, such as sailing ships and human-powered aircraft: "In a novel mostly concerned with 'good stewardship' of resources such as water and land, the iconic status of the freeway fades precisely at the same time that a nostalgia for the future does. Indeed, although *Pacific Edge* suggests a kind of synthesis of issues raised in the earlier novels [in the trilogy], it is ironically the *least* compelling of the three, precisely because it does not engage with the logics of past/future nostalgias" (287).

20. See Peter Sloterdijk, *Critique of Cynical Reason*.

CHAPTER 3. TERRAFORMING AND ECO-ECONOMICS IN THE MARS TRILOGY

1. Thomas, "Forms of Duration," 162. On Robinson's Mars as a heuristic for environmental crises in the twenty-first century see Heise, "Martian Ecologies," which responds, in part, to Walter Benn Michaels's comments on Robinson and Ben Bova in *Shape of the Signifier*, 51–53; and Pak, *Terraforming. Red Mars* and *Green Mars* won Nebula Awards, and *Green Mars* and *Blue Mars* Hugo Awards.

2. Although "Anthropocene" had been used informally in the 1970s, the first published argument for its validity appeared in a coauthored piece by the Nobel Laureate in Chemistry, Paul Crutzen. See Crutzen and Stoermer, "The 'Anthropocene,'" 17–18; and Davies, *Birth of the Anthropocene*.

3. See Trexler, *Anthropocene Fictions*.

4. Robinson, "Remarks on Utopia."

5. See Markley, *Dying Planet*, and Crossley, *Imagining Mars*.

6. Sagan, *Pale Blue Dot*, 340.

7. Although some historians and many literary critics take for granted that Lowell was on the fringes of scientific respectability, this view is inaccurate. See Markley, *Dying Planet*, 61–148.

8. Nixon, *Slow Violence*.

9. Although *War of the Worlds* is by far the best-known of the turn-of-the-century science-fiction novels, it was preceded by two decades of intense speculation about Mars and Martians in novels such as Percy Greg's *Across the Zodiac* (1880), Robert Cromie's *A*

Plunge into Space (1890), and *Unveiling a Parallel: A Romance* (1891) by Alice Ilgenfritz Jones and Ella Merchant. On early Mars sf, see Crossley, *Imagining Mars*, 90–109; Markley, *Dying Planet*, 115–20; and Karl Guthke, *Last Frontier*, 358–64.

10. Lowell, *Mars as the Abode of Life*, 122.

11. Qtd. in Stites, *Revolutionary Dreams*, 42.

12. Wark, *Molecular Red*.

13. Foote, "Conversation."

14. Crossley, *Imagining Mars*, 2.

15. In addition to Markley, *Dying Planet*, and Crossley, *Imagining Mars*, see Morton, *Mapping Mars*.

16. Schuyler Miller, "The Cave," rpt. in Hippolito and McNelly, *Book of Mars*, 121.

17. See Carter, *Creation of Tomorrow*, 140; and Merril, "What Do You Mean," 74 (quotation).

18. Judd, *Outpost Mars*, 76.

19. Carter, *Final Frontier*; Penley, *NASA/TREK*; and McCurdy, *Space and the American Imagination*.

20. Arthur C. Clarke, foreword to Williamson, *Beachhead*, 10.

21. Other novels of this era—Terry Bisson's *Voyage to the Red Planet* (1990), Allen Steele's *Labyrinth of Night* (1992), Dana Stabenow's *Red Planet Run* (1995), William K. Hartmann's *Mars Underground* (1997), and Ian Douglas's *Semper Mars* (1998), to name only a few, center on the discovery of alien artifacts that resist human efforts to uncover their meaning and decenter humankind in a biologically robust universe.

22. For a valuable discussion of the movie, see Miklitsch, "*Total Recall*."

23. In Robinson's short story "Discovering Life" (2000), the discovery of Martian microbes by astronauts on the planet short-circuits NASA's plans to begin terraforming Mars. "Well, shit," one of the project scientists says at the end of the story, "I guess we'll just have to terraform Earth instead." Robinson, "Discovering Life" in *Vinland the Dream*, 153–64, quotation on 164.

24. In addition to Heise, Thomas, and Pak, see Sherryl Vint, "Archaeologies of the 'Amodern.'"

25. Morton, *Mapping Mars*, 168–78. See also Lane, *Geographies of Mars*.

26. See the valuable discussion by Gerry Canavan, "Introduction: If This Goes On," in *Green Planets*, 1–26.

27. See Lisa Messeri, *Placing Outer Space*.

28. Wark, *Molecular Red*, 202.

29. See Oberg, *New Earths*; Fogg, *Terraforming*; McKay, Toon, and Kasting, "Making Mars Habitable"; Pollack and Sagan, "Planetary Engineering"; and Gerstell, Francisco, Lung, and Aaltonee, "Keeping Mars Warm." Robinson thanks Fogg and McKay in his acknowledgments to both *Green Mars* and *Blue Mars*.

30. Fogg, *Terraforming*, 9.

31. For a discussion of robotic missions to Mars and their findings (through 2012), see Markley, "Missions to Mars."

32. See Sagan, "Long Winter Model"; Sagan, "Planetary Engineering on Mars"; Sagan, Toon, and Gierasch, "Climatic Change on Mars"; and Burns and Harwit, "Towards a More Habitable Mars."

33. Meyer and McKay, "Using the Resources of Mars," 403, 399.

34. Ibid., 395.

35. Current speculation about colonizing Mars by Elon Musk and others lies beyond the scope of this chapter. But see Shukaitis, "Space Is the (Non)place"; and Tutton, "Multiplanetary Imaginaries."

36. Lovelock and Allaby, *Greening of Mars*.

37. In his 1999 novel *White Mars*, Brian Aldiss, in collaboration with the mathematical physicist Roger Penrose, offers a utopian vision of human settlement on the red planet but resists the idea that terraforming will be an inevitable consequence of colonization.

38. Baker, "Water."

39. Donna Shirley, moderator, "Terraforming Mars: Experts Debate How, Why, and Whether" (July 26, 2004), http://www.space.com/190-terraforming-mars-experts-debate.html.

40. Turner, *Genesis*, 7.

41. Fogg, *Terraforming*, 22–24. On Turner's *Genesis*, see Crossley, *Imagining Mars*, 250–58.

42. Zubrin, *Case for Mars*, 303.

43. Ibid., 304.

44. Turner, "Life on Mars."

45. See Jameson, "If I Find"; Leane, "Chromodynamics"; Otto, "Mars Trilogy"; Burling, "Theoretical Foundation"; Cho, "Tumults of Utopia"; William J. White, "'Structuralist Alchemy' in *Red Mars*," in Burling, *Kim Stanley Robinson Maps*, 207–23; and Knoespel, "Reading and Revolution."

46. In Markley, Higgs, Kendrick, and Burgess, *Red Planet*, video interview.

47. In a question-and-answer session at the Modern Language Association Convention (December 28, 1998), Robinson indicated that *Blue Mars* drew on several models for alternative economies, including Lewis Hyde's *The Gift*; he then stated that he wished that he had used newer work on "participatory economies" in the 1990s such as Herman Daly's *On Growth and Steady State Economics* and Lester Brown's *Full House*.

48. In *Antarctica* (1997), Robinson continues to explore the utopian structure of scientific practices, methods, and beliefs. The novel works toward the redefinition of a science in tune with the natural world and used against the excesses of capitalism, social injustice, and environmental degradation. As one of Robinson's characters puts it, "Social justice is a necessary part of any working environmental program" (383); see particularly 322–27 and 395–97.

49. On the decentered notions of subjectivity in Robinson's fiction, see Franko, "Working the 'In-between.'"

50. Miller, "Crucifixus Etiam," 68.

CHAPTER 4. "HOW TO GO FORWARD": CATASTROPHE AND COMEDY IN THE SCIENCE IN THE CAPITAL TRILOGY

1. Robinson, *Green Earth*, xi.

2. See Trexler and Johns-Putra, "Climate Change."

3. Ghosh, *Great Derangement*.

4. See Collings, *Stolen Future*, and Streeby, *Imagining the Future*.

5. Trexler, *Anthropocene Fictions*. Trexler deals with the Science in the Capital trilogy at length, 154–69.

6. In his interview with Gerry Canavan in *Green Planets*, Robinson discusses Ballard's influence on his thinking about ecology, along with novels by Ursula K. Le Guin, Jack Vance, Clifford Simak, and John Brunner. See "Afterword: Still, I'm Reluctant to Call This Pessimism," in *Green Planets: Ecology and Science Fiction* (Middletown, Conn.: Wesleyan University Press, 2014), edited by Canavan and Robinson, 252–55.

7. Shepherd, "Netherlands Lives with Water"; Markley, "On the Phase Transition."

8. Robinson, "Remarks on Utopia."

9. See Middleton, "How Novels Can Contribute." For valuable readings of Robinson's contributions to cli-fi, see Johns-Putra, "Ecocriticism"; Prettyman, "Living Thought"; Luckhurst, "Politics of the Network"; Yanarella and Rice, "Global Warming"; Kilgore, "Making Huckleberries"; Rose, "Unknowable Now"; and Mehnert, *Climate Change Fictions*, 149–81.

10. Robinson, "Imagining Abrupt Climate Change," 17. Future references to this text will be noted parenthetically.

11. On *Antarctica*, see Moylan, "Moment Is Here."

12. See the articles in the special issue of *Configurations* 20, no. 1–2 (2012), edited by Lisa Yaszek and Doug Davis.

13. Hartmann, *Traveler's Guide to Mars*, 266–67.

14. See, for example, Severinghaus et al., "Timing." For a general overview, see Mithen, *After the Ice*, 46–55.

15. Cho, "'When a Chance Came," 36. Cho draws on Giorgio Agamben's, *The Time That Remains: A Commentary on the Letter to the Romans*, trans. Patricia Dailey (Stanford, Calif.: Stanford University Press, 2000). The quotation by Robinson is from Szeman and Whiteman, "Future Politics," 185.

16. See Sloterdijk, *Critique of Cynical Reason*, and Jameson, "Politics of Utopia."

17. Robinson cites the works of alternative economists, including Daly, *Steady-State Economics*; Albert and Hahnel, *Political Economy*; and Henderson, *Ethical Markets*.

18. For complementary readings, see Johns-Putra, "Ecocriticism," 744–60, and, on race, Kilgore, "Making Huckleberries," 89–108.

19. See particularly Luckhurst, "Politics of the Network," 170–80.

20. For a critique of the trilogy's focus on U.S. culture and experience, see Heise, *Sense of Place*, 206–7. See also Alaimo, "Sustainable This, Sustainable That"; and Masco, "Bad Weather."

21. The literature on transcendentalism and nature writing is vast. I draw particularly here on Buell, *Environmental Imagination*, 219–51; Walls, *Emerson's Life in Science*, 84–104; and Gura, "Nature Writing."

22. The idea of science fiction as a genre that requires both recognizing the familiarity of imagined worlds (cognition) and surprise or shock at the divergences from "reality" (estrangement) goes back to the work of Darko Suvin, notably *Metamorphoses of Science Fiction* (1979).

23. Phillips, *Truth of Ecology*, 236–37.

24. On climatological time, see Markley, "Time, History, and Sustainability."

25. See Rudwick, *Bursting the Limits*, and Rudwick, *Worlds before Adam*.

26. Emerson, *Essays and Lectures*, 542.

27. The narrator offers this description of thermohaline convection in *Forty Signs of Rain*:

Water flows through the oceans in steady recycling patterns, determined by the Coriolis force and the particular positions of the continents in our time. Surface currents can move in the opposite direction to bottom currents below them, and often do, forming systems like giant conveyor belts of water. The largest one is already famous, at least in part: the Gulf Stream is a segment of a warm surface current that flows north up the entire length of the Atlantic, all the way to Norway and Greenland. There the water cools and sinks, and begins a long journey south on the Atlantic Ocean floor, to the Cape of Good Hope and then east toward Australia, and even into the Pacific, where the water upwells and rejoins the surface flow, west to the Atlantic for the long haul north again. The round trip for any given water molecule takes about a thousand years. (69)

28. On the state of climate science at the time Robinson composed the trilogy, see Alley et al., *Abrupt Climate Change*; Wood et al., "Changing Spatial Structure"; Broecker, "Great Ocean Conveyor"; Rahmstorf, "Risk of Sea-change"; Rahmstorf, "Freshwater Forcing"; Rahmstorf, "Rapid Climate Transitions"; and Rahmstorf, "Thermohaline Ocean Circulation."

29. Middleton, "How Novels Can Contribute," 221.

30. See Burroughs, *Climate Change in Prehistory*.

31. On climate and evolution, see Calvin, *A Brain for All Seasons*.

32. See, for example, Morton, "Here Comes Everything," and Bogost, *Alien Phenomenology*.

33. Qtd. in Freedman, "Science Fiction and Utopia," 74.

CHAPTER 5. "OUR ONE AND ONLY HOME": HUMANKIND IN THE SOLAR SYSTEM

1. In a recent story, Robinson returns to the relationship between music and politics in times of crisis as a way of trying to transcend a grim and violent reality. See Robinson, "Timpanist."

2. See Biagioli, *Galileo, Courtier*.

3. See Bono, *Word of God*.

4. On the role of scientific belief in the seventeenth century, see Markley, *Fallen Languages*.

5. Dante, *Divine Comedy*, 485.

6. On the amodernity of Robinson's depiction of science in the novel and its affinities with the work of science studies scholars like Bruno Latour, Donna Haraway, and Karen Barad, see Vint, "Archaeologies."

7. See Shapin, *Scientific Revolution*.

8. Three of the ten inquisitors did not sign the indictment against Galileo. See Redondi, *Galileo: Heretic*.

9. See Berman, *All That is Solid*.

10. Moylan, *Scraps of the Untainted Sky*.

11. The Mondragon is named for Mondragón, a small Basque town that developed the intercity, cooperative systems in 1956. In 2013 it had assets of $50 billion and employed seventy-four thousand people.

12. The comic voice of this section, popularizer/salesperson, the author of *All About Dirt* (38) and *How to Mix and Match Biomes!* (39), advises his readers that "bigger is better" (36). Robinson draws on a half-century of scientifically informed speculation about colonizing the asteroid belt, notably Gerard O'Neill's *The High Frontier: Human Colonies in Space* (1976).

13. The "rage of the servile will"—the will that paradoxically is both bound and free—was hotly debated during the Protestant Reformation in the sixteenth century. See Ricoeur, *Symbolism of Evil*.

14. See Markley, "Time, History, and Sustainability."

15. On queer theory and sf, see Delany, *Shorter Views*, and the essays collected in Pearson and Hollinger, *Queer Universes*, particularly Kilgore, "Queering the Coming Race?"

16. On "structures of feeling," see Williams, *Marxism and Literature*.

17. See Miller, *Strung Together*, esp. 153–69, and the story by Gregory Benford, "On the Brane," in David G. Hartwell and Kathryn Cramers, eds., *Year's Best SF 11* (New York: Eos, 2006), 310–29.

18. Robinson explores the novelistic possibilities of ahuman perspectives at greater length in *Aurora*; the ship's AI narrates much of the novel. See chapter 6.

19. Directed by Douglas Trumbull, *Silent Running* was written by Steven Bocho, Michael Cimino, and Deric Washburn.

20. See Otto, "Mars Trilogy."

CHAPTER 6. "WORKING IN THE NEXT PRESENT" IN *AURORA* AND *NEW YORK 2140*

1. See Jasanoff, "Future Imperfect."

2. *Icehenge*, 41.

3. See Finn, *What Algorithms Want*; and Sloterdijk, "Anthropo-Technology."

4. See Barrow and Tipler, *Anthropic Cosmological Principle*.

5. See Stephanie Fishel, *Microbial State*.

6. In Marx's writings on the natural environment, metabolic rifts described the pillaging of resources and the natural environment that characterized nineteenth-century capitalism, but Robinson appropriates the term to explore the consequences of the failures of all closed ecosystems. See Foster, "Marx's Theory."

7. Robinson draws in this instance on the data returned by post-Viking landers on the chemistry of the surface. See Markley, "Missions to Mars."

8. See Kilgore, *Astrofuturism*.

9. For a seminal article on the tragedy of the commons by a noted twentieth-century ecologist, see Hardin, "Tragedy of the Commons."

10. Robinson's submerged New York recalls other drowned cities in his earlier fiction, from Venice in "Venice Drowned" (1981) to London in *Blue Mars*.

11. On Michel Foucault's notion of "strategies without strategists," see Dreyfus and Rabinow, *Michel Foucault*.

12. The IPPI is a disaster-comedy version of the Case-Shiller index (also invoked in the novel) developed by the economists Karl Case and Robert Shiller that analyzes data for homes sold twice within a given number of years in twenty urban housing markets in the United States. It is widely used to calculate fluctuations in housing markets and investor confidence. Case and Shiller's methodology is explained in Shiller's book *Irrational Exuberance* (Princeton, N.J.: Princeton University Press, 2000).

13. Dening, *Beach Crossings*, esp. 11–22.

Abbott, Carl. "Falling into History: Imagined Wests in the 'Three Californias' and Mars Trilogy." In *Kim Stanley Robinson Maps the Unimaginable*, edited by William J. Burling, 67–82. Jefferson, N.C.: McFarland, 2009.

Alaimo, Stacy. "Sustainable This, Sustainable That: New Materialisms, Posthumanism, and Unknown Futures." *PMLA* 127 (2012): 558–64.

Albert, Michael, and Robin Hahnel. *The Political Economy of Participatory Economics*. Princeton, N.J.: Princeton University Press, 1991.

Aldiss, Brian, and Roger Penrose. *White Mars; or, The Mind Set Free: A Twenty-First Century Utopia*. New York: St. Martin's, 1999.

Alley, Richard B., et al., *Abrupt Climate Change: Inevitable Surprises*. Washington, D.C.: National Research Council, 2002.

Baker, Victor. "Water and the Martian Landscape." *Nature* 412 (2001): 228–36.

Barad, Karen. *Meeting the Universe Halfway: Quantum Physics and the Entanglement of Matter and Meaning*. Durham, N.C.: Duke University Press, 2007.

Barrow, John D., and Frank J. Tipler. *The Anthropic Cosmological Principle*. New York: Oxford University Press, 1988.

Bellamy, Brent Ryan. "Reading Kim Stanley Robinson's Three Californias Trilogy as Petrofiction." *Western American Literature* 51 (2017): 409–27.

Benford, Gregory. "On the Brane." In *Year's Best SF 11*, edited by David G. Hartwell and Kathryn Cramer, 310–29. New York: Eos, 2006.

Berman, Marshall. *All That Is Solid Melts into Air: The Experience of Modernity*. Reprint. New York: Penguin, 1988.

Biagioli, Mario. *Galileo, Courtier: The Practice of Science in the Culture of Absolutism*. Chicago: University of Chicago Press, 1994.

Bogost, Ian. *Alien Phenomenology*. Minneapolis: University of Minnesota Press, 2012.

Bono, James. *The Word of God and the Languages of Man: Interpreting Nature in Early Modern Science and Medicine, Ficino to Descartes*. Madison: University of Wisconsin Press, 1995.

Broecker, W. S. "The Great Ocean Conveyor." *Oceanography* 4, no. 2 (1991): 79–89.

Buell, Lawrence. *The Environmental Imagination: Thoreau, Nature Writing, and the Formation of American Culture*. Cambridge, Mass.: Harvard University Press, 1995.

Burgess, Helen. "'Road of Giants': Nostalgia and the Ruins of the Superhighway in Kim Stanley Robinson's 'Three Californias' Trilogy." *Science-Fiction Studies* 33 (2006): 275–90.

Burgess, Helen, and Jeanne Hamming. *Highways of the Mind*. Philadelphia: University of Pennsylvania Press, 2014.

Burke, Kenneth. "Literature as Equipment for Living." In *Philosophy of the Literary Form: Studies in Symbolic Action*, 293–304. 3rd ed. Berkeley: University of California Press, 1973.

Burling William J., ed. *Kim Stanley Robinson Maps the Unimaginable: Critical Essays.* Jefferson, N.C.: McFarland, 2009.

———. "The Theoretical Foundation of Utopian Radical Democracy in *Blue Mars.*" In *Kim Stanley Robinson Maps the Unimaginable*, 157–69.

Burns, Joseph, and Martin Harwit. "Towards a More Habitable Mars; or, The Coming Martian Spring." *Icarus* 19 (1973): 126–30.

Burroughs, William J. *Climate Change in Prehistory: The End of the Reign of Chaos.* Cambridge: Cambridge University Press, 2005.

Calvin, William H. *A Brain for All Seasons: Human Evolution and Abrupt Climate Change.* Chicago: University of Chicago Press, 2002.

Canavan, Gerry. "Review of Darko Suvin's *Defined by a Hollow: Essays on Utopia, Science Fiction and Political Epistemology.*" *Historical Materialism* 21 (2013): 209–16.

Cao Xueqin. *The Story of the Stone.* Trans. David Hawkes. 5 vols. London: Penguin, 1973–80.

Carter, Dale. *The Final Frontier: The Rise and Fall of the American Rocket State.* London: Verso, 1988.

Carter, Paul. *The Creation of Tomorrow: Fifty Years of Magazine Science Fiction.* New York: Columbia University Press, 1977.

Case, Carl, and Robert Shiller, *Irrational Exuberance.* Princeton, N.J.: Princeton University Press, 2000.

Cho, K. Daniel. "Tumults of Utopia: Repetition and Revolution in Kim Stanley Robinson's Mars Trilogy." *Cultural Critique* 75 (2010): 65–81.

———. "'When a Chance Came for Everything to Change': Messianism and Wilderness in Kim Stanley Robinson's Abrupt Climate Change Trilogy." *Criticism* 53 (2011): 23–51.

Cole, Lucinda. *Imperfect Creatures: Vermin, Literature, and the Sciences of Life.* Ann Arbor: University of Michigan Press, 2016.

Collings, David. *Stolen Future, Broken Present: The Human Significance of Climate Change.* New York: Open Humanities, 2014.

Crosby, Alfred W. *Ecological Imperialism: The Biological Expansion of Europe, 900–1900.* Cambridge: Cambridge University Press, 1986.

Crossley, Robert. *Imagining Mars: A Literary History.* Middletown, Conn.: Wesleyan University Press, 2011.

Crutzen, P. J., and E. F. Stoermer. "The 'Anthropocene.'" *IGBP Newsletter* 41 (2000): 17–18.

Csicsery-Ronay, Istvan. "Possible Mountains and Rivers: The Zen Realism of Kim Stanley Robinson's Three Californias." *Configurations* 20 (2012): 149–85.

Dante. *The Divine Comedy of Dante Alighieri, Volume 3: Paradiso.* Trans. Charles Sinclair. New York: Oxford University Press, 1939.

Daly, Herman. *Steady-State Economics.* 2nd ed. Washington, D.C.: Island, 1991.

Davies, Jeremy. *The Birth of the Anthropocene.* Berkeley: University of California Press, 2016.

Delany, Samuel R. *Shorter Views: Queer Thoughts and the Politics of the Paraliterary.* Hanover, N.H.: University of New England Press, 2000.

Dening, Greg. *Beach Crossings.* Philadelphia: University of Pennsylvania Press, 2004.

Derrida, Jacques. *Specters of Marx: The State of the Debt, the Work of Mourning, and the New International.* Trans. Peggy Kamuf. London: Routledge, 1994.

Dreyfus, Herbert, and Paul Rabinow. *Michel Foucault: Beyond Structuralism and Hermeneutics*. Chicago: University of Chicago Press, 1982.

Emerson, Ralph Waldo. *Essays and Lectures by Ralph Waldo Emerson*. Ed. Joel Porte. New York: Library of America, 1983.

Feynman, Richard. *QED: The Strange Theory of Light and Matter*. 1985. 2nd ed. Edited by A. Zee. Princeton, N.J.: Princeton University Press, 2006.

Finn, Ed. *What Algorithms Want: Imagination in the Age of Computing*. Cambridge, Mass.: MIT Press, 2017.

Fishel, Stephanie. *The Microbial State: Global Thriving and the Body Politic*. Minneapolis: University of Minnesota Press, 2017.

Fogg, Martyn J. *Terraforming: Engineering Planetary Environments*. Warrendale, Penn.: Society of Automotive Engineers, 1995.

Foote, Bud. "A Conversation with Kim Stanley Robinson." *Science Fiction Studies* 21 (1994).

Foster, John Bellamy. "Marx's Theory of Metabolic Rift: Classical Foundations for Environmental Sociology." *American Journal of Sociology* 105, no. 2 (1999): 366–405.

Frank, André Gunder. *ReOrient: Global Economy in the Asian Age*. Berkeley: University of California Press, 1997.

Franko, Carol. "Working the 'In-Between': Kim Stanley Robinson's Utopian Fiction." *Science Fiction Studies* 21 (1994): 191–211.

Freedman, Carl. *Critical Theory and Science Fiction*. Middletown, Conn.: Wesleyan University Press, 2000.

———. "Science Fiction and Utopia: A Historico-Philosophical Overview." In *Learning from Other Worlds: Estrangement, Cognition, and the Politics of Science Fiction and Utopia*, edited by Patrick Parrinder, 68–79. Durham, N.C.: Duke University Press, 2001.

Garcia, Humberto. *Islam and the English Enlightenment, 1670–1840*. Baltimore, Md.: Johns Hopkins University Press, 2012.

Gerstell, J. M., F. S. Francisco, Y. L. Lung, and E. T. Aaltonee. "Keeping Mars Warm with New Super Greenhouse Gases." *Proceedings of the National Academy of Sciences* 98 (2001): 2154–57.

Ghosh, Amitav. *The Great Derangement: Climate Change and the Unthinkable*. Chicago: University of Chicago Press, 2016.

Gura, Philip. "Nature Writing." In *The Oxford Handbook of Transcendentalism*, edited by Joel Meyerson, Sandra Harbert Petrulionis, and Laura Dassow Walls, 408–25. New York: Oxford University Press, 2010.

Guthke, Karl. *The Last Frontier: Imagining Other Worlds from the Copernican Revolution to Modern Science Fiction*. Translated by Helen Atkins. Ithaca, N.Y.: Cornell University Press, 1990.

Haraway, Donna. *The Companion Species Manifesto: Dogs, People, and Significant Otherness*. Chicago: University of Chicago Press, 2003.

Hardin, Garrett. "The Tragedy of the Commons." *Science* 162, no. 3859 (1968): 1243–48.

Hartmann, William. *A Traveler's Guide to Mars: The Mysterious Landscapes of the Red Planet*. New York: Workman, 2003.

Heise, Ursula. *Sense of Place and Sense of Planet: The Environmental Imagination of the Global*. New York: Oxford University Press, 2008.

———. "Martian Ecologies and the Future of Nature." *Twentieth-Century Literature* 57 (2011): 447–71.

Hellekson, Karen. *The Alternate History: Refiguring Historical Time*. Kent, Ohio: Kent State University Press, 2001.

Henderson, Hazel. *Ethical Markets: Growing the Green Economy*. White River Junction, Vt.: Chelsea Green, 2006.

Hippolito, Jane, and Willis McNelly, eds. *The Book of Mars*. London: Orbit, 1976.

Hollinger, Veronica. "'Something Like a Fiction': Speculative Intersections of Sexuality and Technology." In Pearson and Hollinger, *Queer Universes*, 140–59.

Jameson, Fredric. "'If I Find One Good City I Will Spare the Man': Realism and Utopia in Kim Stanley Robinson's Mars Trilogy." In *Learning from Other Worlds: Estrangement, Cognition, and the Politics of Science Fiction and Utopia*, edited by Patrick Parrinder, 208–32. Liverpool: Liverpool University Press, 2000.

———. "The Politics of Utopia." *New Left Review*, 2nd series, 25 (2004): 35–54.

———. *Archaeologies of the Future: The Desire Called Utopia and Other Science Fictions*. London: Verso, 2005.

Jasanoff, Sheila. "Future Imperfect: Science, Technology, and the Imaginations of Modernity," in *Dreamscapes of Modernity: Sociotechnical Imaginaries and the Fabrication of Power*, edited by Sheila Jasanoff and Sang-Hyun Kim, 1–33. Chicago: University of Chicago Press, 2015.

Johns-Putra, Adeline. "Ecocriticism, Genre, and Climate Change: Reading the Utopian Vision of Kim Stanley Robinson's Science in the Capital Trilogy." *English Studies* 91 (2010): 744–60.

Judd, Cyril. *Outpost Mars*. New York: Ace, 1953.

Kessel, John. "Remaking History: The Short Fiction," in Burling, *Kim Stanley Robinson Maps the Unimaginable*, 83–94.

Khaldun, Ibn. *The Muqaddimah: An Introduction to History*. Translated by Franz Rosenthal. New York: Bollingen Foundation, 1958. Abridged in one volume by N. J. Dawood (Princeton, N.J.: Princeton University Press, 1967).

Kilgore, DeWitt. *Astrofuturism: Science, Race, and Visions of Utopia in Space*. Philadelphia: University of Pennsylvania Press, 2003.

———. "Queering the Coming Race? A Utopian Historical Perspective." In *Queer Universes: Sexualities and Science Fiction*, edited by Wendy Pearson and Veronica Hollinger, 233–49. Liverpool: Liverpool University Press, 2008.

———. "Making Huckleberries: Reforming Science and Whiteness in Science in the Capital." *Configurations* 20 (2012): 89–108.

Knoespel, Kenneth. "Reading and Revolution on the Horizon of Myth and History: Kim Stanley Robinson's Mars Trilogy." *Configurations* 20 (2012): 109–36.

Kuhn, Philip A. *Soulstealers: The Chinese Sorcery Scare of 1768*. Cambridge, Mass.: Harvard University Press, 1990.

Lane, Maria D. *Geographies of Mars: Seeing and Knowing the Red Planet*. Chicago University of Chicago Press, 2010.

Latour, Bruno. *We Have Never Been Modern*. Cambridge, Mass.: Harvard University Press, 1993.

———. "Why Has Critique Run Out of Steam? From Matters of Fact to Matters of Concern." *Critical Inquiry* 30 (2004): 225–48.

Leane, Elizabeth. "Chromodynamics: Science and Colonialism in Kim Stanley Robinson's Mars Trilogy." *ARIEL* 33 (2002): 83–104.

Leary, Timothy, Ralph Metzner, and Richard Alpert. *The Psychedelic Experience: A Manual Based on the Tibetan Book of the Dead*. 1967. Rpt. New York: Citadel, 1995.

Levathes, Louis. *When China Ruled the Seas: The Treasure Fleet of the Dragon Throne, 1405–33*. New York: Oxford University Press, 1994.

Levy, Dore J. *Ideal and Actual in "The Story of the Stone."* New York: Columbia University Press, 1999.

Lewontin, Richard. "Facts and the Factitious in the Natural Sciences." *Critical Inquiry* 18 (1991): 140–53.

Lovelock, James, and Michael Allaby. *The Greening of Mars*. New York: St. Martin's, 1984.

Lowell, Percival. *Mars as the Abode of Life*. New York: Macmillan, 1909.

Luckhurst, Roger. "The Politics of the Network: The Science in the Capital Trilogy." In Burling, *Kim Stanley Robinson Maps the Unimaginable*, 170–80.

Mann, Charles C. *1493: Uncovering the New World Columbus Created*. New York: Vintage, 2012.

Markley, Robert. *Fallen Languages: Crises of Representation in Newtonian England, 1660–1740*. Ithaca: Cornell University Press, 1993.

———. "Alien Assassinations: *The X-Files* and the Paranoid Structure of History." *Camera Obscura* 40–41 (1997): 77–103.

———. *Dying Planet: Mars in Science and the Imagination*. Durham, N.C.: Duke University Press, 2005.

———. *The Far East and the English Imagination, 1600–1740*. New York: Cambridge University Press, 2006.

———. "Time, History, and Sustainability." In *Telemorphosis: Theory in the Era of Climate Change*, edited by Tom Cohen, 43–64. New York: Open Humanities, 2012.

———. "Missions to Mars: Reimagining the Red Planet in the Age of Spaceflight." In *Exploring the Solar System: The History and Science of Planetary Probes*, edited by Roger Launius, 249–72. Bastingstoke: Palgrave/Macmillan, for the American Astronautical Association, 2013.

Markley, Robert, Harrison Higgs, Michelle Kendrick, and Helen Burgess. *Red Planet: Scientific and Cultural Encounters with Mars*. DVD. Philadelphia: University of Pennsylvania Press, 2001.

Markley, Stephen. "On the Phase Transition of Methane Hydrates." *Iowa Review* 46, no. 1 (2016): 158–72.

Masco, Joseph. "Bad Weather: On Planetary Crisis." *Social Studies of Science* 40 (2010): 7–40.

McCurdy, Howard. *Space and the American Imagination*. Washington, D.C.: Smithsonian Institution Press, 1997.

McKay, Christopher P., Owen B. Toon, and James F. Kasting. "Making Mars Habitable." *Nature* 352 (1991): 489–95.

Mehnert, Antonia. *Climate Change Fictions: Representations of Global Warming in American Literature*. New York: Palgrave, 2016.

Merril, Judith. "What Do You Mean: Science? Fiction?" Rpt. in *Science Fiction: The Other Side of Realism*, edited by Thomas D. Clareson, 53–95. Bowling Green, Ohio: Popular, 1971.

Messeri, Lisa. *Placing Outer Space: An Earthly Ethnography of Other Worlds*. Durham, N.C.: Duke University Press, 2016.

Meyer, Thomas, and Christopher P. McKay. "Using the Resources of Mars for Human Settlement." In *Strategies for Mars: A Guide to Human Exploration*, edited by Carol Stoker and Carter Emmart. San Diego: Univelt, for the American Astronautical Society, 1996, 392–417.

Michaels, Walter Benn. *The Shape of the Signifier: 1967 to the End of History*. Princeton, N.J.: Princeton University Press, 2004.

Middleton, Peter. "How Novels Can Contribute to our Understanding of Climate Change." In *History at the End of the World? History, Climate Change and the Possibility of Closure*, edited by Mark Levene, Rob Johnson, and Penny Roberts, 218–33. Penrith: Humanities E-books, 2010.

Miklitsch, Robert. "*Total Recall*: Production, Revolution, Simulation-Alienation Effect." *Camera Obscura* 32 (1995): 4–39.

Miller, Sean. *Strung Together: The Cultural Currency of String Theory as Scientific Imaginary*. Ann Arbor: University of Michigan Press, 2013.

Miller, Walter M. "Crucifixus Etiam." In *The Best of Walter M. Miller, Jr.* New York: Pocket, 1980.

Mithen, Steven. *After the Ice: A Global Human History 20,000–5,000 BC*. Cambridge, Mass.: Harvard University Press, 2003.

Morton, Oliver. *Mapping Mars: Science, Imagination, and the Birth of a World*. London: Fourth Estate, 2002.

Morton, Timothy. "Here Comes Everything: The Promise of Object-Oriented Ontology." *Qui Parle* 19 (2011): 163–90.

Moylan, Tom. *Scraps of the Untainted Sky: Science Fiction, Utopia, Dystopia*. Boulder, Colo.: Westview, 2000.

———. "'The Moment Is Here . . . and It's Important': State, Agency, and Dystopia in Kim Stanley Robinson's *Antarctica* and Ursula K. Le Guin's *The Telling*." In *Dark Horizons: Science Fiction and the Dystopian Imagination*, edited by Tom Moylan and Raffaella Baccolini, 135–54. London: Routledge, 2003.

———. "Witness to Hard Times: Robinson's Other Californias." In Burling, *Kim Stanley Robinson Maps the Unimaginable*, 11–47.

Nearing, Scott, and Helen Nearing. *Living the Good Life*. New York: Schocken, 1970.

Needham, Joseph. *Science and Civilisation in China*. Cambridge: Cambridge University Press, seven vols., 1954–2016.

Nixon, Rob. *Slow Violence and the Environmentalism of the Poor*. Cambridge, Mass.: Harvard University Press, 2002.

Oberg, James Edward. *New Earths: Transforming Other Planets for Humanity*. Harrisburg, Penn.: Stackpole, 1982.

O'Neill, Gerard. *The High Frontier: Human Colonies in Space*. New York: Morrow, 1976.

Otto, Eric. "Kim Stanley Robinson's Mars Trilogy and the Leopoldian Land Ethic." In Burling, *Kim Stanley Robinson Maps the Unimaginable*, 242–56.

Pak, Chris. *Terraforming: Ecopolitical Transformations and Environmentalism in Science Fiction*. Liverpool: Liverpool University Press, 2016.

Parrinder, Patrick. *Utopian Literature and Science: From the Scientific Revolution to Brave New World and Beyond*. New York: Palgrave, 2015.

Pearson, Wendy, and Veronica Hollinger, eds. *Queer Universes: Sexualities and Science Fiction*. Liverpool: Liverpool University Press, 2008.

Penley, Constance. *NASA/TREK: Popular Science and Sex in America*. London: Verso, 1997.

Phillips, Dana. *The Truth of Ecology: Nature, Culture, and Literature in America*. New York: Oxford University Press, 2003.

Pollack, J. B., and Carl Sagan. "Planetary Engineering." In *Resources of Near-Earth Space*, edited by J. Lewis, M. S. Matthews, and M. L. Guerrieri, 921–50. Tucson: University of Arizona Press, 1993.

Pomeranz, Frank. *The Great Divergence: China, Europe, and the Making of the Modern World Economy*. Princeton, N.J.: Princeton University Press, 2000.

Prettyman, Gib. "Living Thought: Genes, Genres and Utopia in the Science in the Capital Trilogy." In Burling, *Kim Stanley Robinson Maps the Unimaginable*, 181–203.

Rahmstorf, S. "Rapid Climate Transitions in a Coupled Ocean-Atmosphere Model." *Nature* 372 (1994): 82–85.

———. "On the Freshwater Forcing and Transport of the Atlantic Thermohaline Circulation." *Climate Dynamics* 12 (1996): 799–811.

———. "Risk of Sea-Change in the Atlantic." *Nature* 388 (1997): 825–26.

———. "The Thermohaline Ocean Circulation—A System with Dangerous Thresholds?" *Climatic Change* 46 (2000): 247–56.

Redondi, Pietro. *Galileo: Heretic*. Translated by Raymond Rosenthal. Princeton, N.J.: Princeton University Press, 1989.

Ricoeur, Paul. *The Symbolism of Evil*. New York: Harper and Row, 1967.

Rinpoche, Sogyal. *The Tibetan Book of Living and Dying*. New York: HarperCollins, 1993.

Rudwick, Martin J. S. *Bursting the Limits of Time: The Reconstruction of Geohistory in the Age of Revolution*. Chicago: University of Chicago Press, 2005.

———. *Worlds before Adam: The Reconstruction of Geohistory in the Age of Reform*. Chicago: University of Chicago Press, 2008.

Rose, Andrew. "The Unknowable Now: Passionate Science and Transformative Politics in Kim Stanley Robinson's Science in the Capital Trilogy." *Science Fiction Studies* 43 (2016): 260–86.

Ruddick, Nicholas. *The Fire in the Stone: Prehistoric Fiction from Charles Darwin to Jean M. Auel*. Middletown, Conn.: Wesleyan University Press, 2009.

Ruddiman, William F. *Plows, Plagues, and Petroleum: How Humans Took Control of Climate*. Princeton, N.J.: Princeton University Press, 2005.

Sagan, Carl. "The Long Winter Model of Martian Biology: A Speculation." *Icarus* 15 (1971): 511–14.

———. "Planetary Engineering on Mars." *Icarus* 20 (1973): 513–14.

———. *Pale Blue Dot: A Vision of the Human Future in Space*. New York: Random House, 1994.

Sagan, Carl, Owen B. Toon, and P. J. Gierasch. "Climatic Change on Mars." *Science* 181 (1973): 1045–49.

Sahlins, Marshall. *Stone Age Economics*. 1974. Rpt. New York: Routledge, 2017.

Schell, Jonathan. *The Fate of the Earth*. 1982. Reissued, Stanford, Calif.: Stanford University Press, 2000.

Severinghaus, Jeffrey P., et al. "Timing of Abrupt Climate Change at the End of the Younger Dryas Interval from Thermally Fractionated Gases in Polar Ice." *Nature* 391 (1998): 141–46.

Shapin, Steven. *The Scientific Revolution*. Chicago: University of Chicago Press, 1996.

Shepherd, Jim. "The Netherlands Lives with Water." Rpt. in *Loosed upon the World: The Saga Anthology of Climate Fiction*, edited by John Joseph Adams, 143–71. New York: Saga, 2015.

Shukaitis, Stevphen. "Space Is the (Non)place: Martians, Marxists, and the Outer Space of the Radical Imagination." *Sociological Review*, 57 (2009): 98–113.

Simeone, Michael. "'Plasticity's Central Canon': Plastics, *Gravity's Rainbow*, and the Practice of Science Fiction." *Genre* 43 (2010): 115–36.

Sloterdijk, Peter. *Critique of Cynical Reason*. Translated by Michael Eldred. Minneapolis: University of Minnesota Press, 1987.

——. "Anthropo-Technology." *New Perspectives Quarterly* 31 (2014): 12–16.

Spence, Jonathan D. *Ts'ao Yin and the K'ang-Hsi Emperor: Bondservant and Master*. New Haven, Conn.: Yale University Press, 1966.

——. *The Search for Modern China*. New York: Norton, 1990.

Stites, Richard. *Revolutionary Dreams: Utopian Vision and Experimental Life in the Russian Revolution*. New York: Oxford University Press, 1989.

Streeby, Shelley. *Imagining the Future of Climate Change: World-Making through Science Fiction and Activism*. Berkeley: University of California Press, 2018.

Suvin, Darko. *Metamorphoses of Science Fiction: On the Poetics and History of a Literary Genre*. New Haven, Conn.: Yale University Press, 1979.

Szeman, Imre, and Maria Whiteman. "Future Politics: An Interview with Kim Stanley Robinson." *Science Fiction Studies* 31 (2004).

Thomas, Lindsay. "Forms of Duration: Preparedness, the *Mars Trilogy* and the Management of Climate Change." *American Literature* 88 (2016): 159–84.

Trexler, Adam. *Anthropocene Fictions: The Novel in a Time of Climate Change*. Charlottesville: University of Virginia Press, 2015.

Trexler, Adam, and Adeline Johns-Putra. "Climate Change in Literature and Literary Criticism." *Wiley Interdisciplinary Reviews: Climate Change* 2, no. 2 (2011): 185–200.

Turner, Frederick. *Genesis*. Dallas: Saybrook, 1988.

——. "Life on Mars: Cultivating a Planet—and Ourselves." *Harper's* 279 (1989): 33–34.

Tutton, Richard. "Multiplanetary Imaginaries and Utopia: The Case of Mars One." *Science, Technology and Human Values* 43 (2018): 518–39.

Vint, Sherryl. "Archaeologies of the 'Amodern': Science and Society in *Galileo's Dream*." *Configurations* 20 (2012): 29–51.

Wagar, W. Warren. *Terminal Visions: The Literature of Last Things*. Bloomington: Indiana University Press, 1982.

Walls, Laura Dassow. *Emerson's Life in Science: The Culture of Truth*. Ithaca, N.Y.: Cornell University Press, 2003.

Wark, McKenzie. *Molecular Red: Theory for the Anthropocene*. London: Verso, 2015.

Wegner, Philip. *Imaginary Communities: Utopia, the Nation, and the Spatial Histories of Modernity*. Berkeley: University of California Press, 2002.

——. "Learning to Live in History: Alternative Histories and the 1990s and *The Years of Rice and Salt*." In Burling, *Kim Stanley Robinson Maps the Unimaginable*, 98–113.

——. *Shockwaves of Possibility: Essays on Science Fiction, Globalization, and Utopia*. Ralahine Utopian Studies 15. New York: Lang, 2014.

Williams, Raymond. *Marxism and Literature*. New York: Oxford University Press, 1977.

Williamson, Jack. *Beachhead*. New York: Tor, 1992.

Wolfe, Gary K. "The Remaking of Zero: Beginning at the End." In *The End of the World*, edited by Eric S. Rabkin, Martin Greenberg, and Joseph Olander, 1–19. Carbondale: Southern Illinois University Press, 1983.

Wood, R. A, et al. "Changing Spatial Structure of the Thermohaline Circulation in Response to Atmospheric CO_2 Forcing in a Climate Model." *Nature* 399 (1999): 572–75.

Woodward, Christopher. *In Ruins*. London: Vintage, 2002.

Yanarella Ernest J., and Christopher Rice. "Global Warming and the Specter of Geoengineering: Ecological Apocalypse, Modernist Hubris, and Scientific-Technological Salvation in Kim Stanley Robinson's Global Warming Trilogy." In *Engineering Earth: The Impacts of Megaengineering Projects*, edited by Stanley D. Brunn, 2233–52. London: Springer, 2011.

Yu, Anthony. *Rereading the Stone: Desire and the Making of Fiction in "Dream of the Red Chamber."* Princeton, N.J.: Princeton University Press, 1997.

Zamora, Lois Parkinson. *Writing the Apocalypse: Historical Vision in Contemporary U.S. and Latin American Fiction*. Cambridge: Cambridge University Press, 1993.

Zubrin, Robert. With Richard Wagner. *The Case for Mars: The Plan to Settle the Red Planet and Why We Must*. New York: Free Press, 1996.

DeNiro, Robert, 20

Derrida, Jacques, 6, 197n10; *différance*, 19, 134, 156; hauntology, 60–61

Descartes, René, 149

detective fiction, 162–64

Devi (character), 98, 138, 162, 172–73, 175–77

diaspora, 13–14, 136–37, 141, 155–56, 171; genetic diaspora, 179

Dick, Philip K., 8, 14, 17, 64, 85, 88, 136, 139, 141

Difference Engine, The (Gibson and Sterling), 17

Dillard, Annie, 125

disarmament, 22

"Discovering Life" (Robinson), 199n23

Dispossessed, The (Le Guin), 71

Divine Comedy (Dante), 148, 202n5

Do Androids Dream of Electric Sheep? (Dick), 64, 139

Doc (character), 63

Doomsday Book, The (Willis), 144

doppelganger, 62

Douglas, Ian, 199n21

"Down and Out in the Year 2000" (Robinson), 195n3

Doya, Edmond (character), 24–26, 139–40

Dream of the Red Chamber, The (Cao), 30. See also *Story of the Stone, The*

dreams, 144; dream vision, 145

Dreyfus, Herbert, 203n11

Drowned World, The (Ballard), 114

Duval, Michel (character), 104

dystopia, 12, 14, 24, 55, 58–60, 64–65, 67–68, 70, 110, 136, 143, 167

dystopian fiction, 2, 18, 53, 67, 83, 156, 180–81, 197n12

Earth (planet). See Antarctica; Mars trilogy; New York 2140; Orange County trilogy; Science in the Capital trilogy; *Shaman; The Years of Rice and Salt*

Earth Abides, The (Stewart), 57, 63, 125

Earth Is Near, The (Pešek), 83

eco-economics, 86; in *2312*, 166; in *Antarctica*, 116; in *Aurora*, 170–71; in the Mars trilogy, 90–91, 95, 97, 100–107, 109; in *New York 2140*, 170–71, 181, 184–87; in the Science in the Capital trilogy, 116–20

ecohistory, 69–71

ecological disasters, 37; in *2312*, 127, 155–56, 158–59, 162; in the Mars trilogy, 109–11; in Martian sf, 80–85; in *New York 2140*, 15, 127, 180–82, 184; in the Science in the Capital trilogy, 13, 112–16, 118–20, 127–29, 132–33. See also cli-fi; climate change

ecology: in *2312*, 154–59, 161–62, 166–69; anthropogenic ecologies, 135–37, 151; in *Aurora*, 171–72, 177–80; beaches, 186–87; beach return, 187; Case-Shiller index, 203n12; comedy of the commons, 180, 183; and economic justice, 54, 61; economics, 136, 138; in *Galileo's Dream*, 151–52; in *Icehenge*, 137–38; invasive biology, 178; Leopoldian land ethic, 166–67, 186; in the Mars trilogy, 12, 78–79, 86–101, 107–11; in Martian sf, 79–86; in *The Memory of Whiteness*, 140–41; in *New York 2140*, 180–87; in the Orange County trilogy, 12, 55–57, 61, 66–71, 74–77; planetary rehabilitation 182–83, 186–87; in the Science in the Capital trilogy, 12–13, 112–34; in *Shaman*, 47; starship ecology, 177, 187, 203n6; stewardship in sf, 4, 9; tragedy of the commons, 180, 203n9; in *The Years of Rice and Salt*, 43. See also cli-fi; climate change; eco-economics; ecological disasters; terraforming

ecopoeisis, 94, 96–97, 99–100, 109–10

Elga (character), 47, 49

El Modena (utopian community in *Pacific Edge*), 70–72, 74–75, 77 embodiment, 130–31

Emerson, Ralph Waldo, 72, 117, 124–28, 132, 201n26; on temporality and geography, 126

empire, 10, 27

Engels, Friedrich, 36

Engineer Menni (Bogdanov), 80–81

enlightenment, 166

Enlightenment, the, 37

environmental conservation, 71, 74–75

environmental disasters. *See* ecological disasters

environmentalism, 37

environmental justice, 2, 54, 61

epistemology, 45, 48, 50–51, 173

Er Hong, Swan (character), 46, 132, 154, 158–68

Euan (character), 178, 186

evolution, 137, 158, 160–61, 168, 177–79; codevolution, 177, 179

exceptionalism, American, 58

"Exploring Fossil Canyon" (Robinson), 86–87, 89, 100

extraterrestrial life, 80–81. *See also* alien encounters

Ezra, Ibn (character), 30–31, 41

Farewell Earth's Bliss (Compton), 83

Farmer in the Sky (Heinlein), 84

Female Man, The (Russ), 160

feminism, 31, 35–36, 41–42, 160. *See also* gender equality

feudalism, 107

Feynman, Richard, 22, 196n9

fiction genre, 173; historical, 18, 144

Fifty Degrees Below (Robinson), 12–13, 44, 112–13, 115, 119–21, 127–32, 166

Finn, Ed, 203n3

Fishel, Stephanie, 203n5

Fletcher, Henry (character), 11, 54–56, 58–63

Fogg, Martyn J., 199n29, 199n30, 200n41

Foote, Bud, 199n13

Forever War, The (Halderman), 22

Fort, William (character), 91

Forty Signs of Rain (Robinson), 12–13, 112–15, 118–24, 127, 129, 201–2n27

fossil fuels, 120, 124; alternatives, 130; post-fossil fuel world, 126

Foster, John Bellamy 203n6

Foucault, Michel, 203n11

Francisco, F. S., 199n29

Frank, André Gunder 29, 106n20

Franko, Carol, 200n49

Freedman, Carl, 195n14, 202n33

Freya (character), 138, 174, 176–79, 187

Fromwest (character), 33

Fugard, Athol, 68

Future Primitive: The New Ecotopias (Robinson, ed.), 4

Gabriela (character), 55

Gaia hypothesis, 93–94

Galileo Galilei, 39, 46, 134, 144, 146, 148, 202n8

Galileo Galilei (character), 14, 98, 105, 137, 145–56, 167

Galileo's Dream (Robinson), 3, 13–14, 20, 39, 96, 111, 123, 135–37, 143–56, 168, 174

Ganymede (character), 144–48, 152

Garcia, Humberto, 197n30

Garr, Franklin (character), 184–86

gender, 9, 14, 155, 159–62, 164; gender roles, 160–61. *See also* sexualities

gender equality, 18, 35–36, 42. *See also* feminism

Genesis (Turner), 94, 200n40, 200n41

genetic engineering, 115, 133, 155

genetic manipulation, 9

Genette, Jean (character), 154, 158, 162–63, 168

genocide, 25–26

Gerstell, J. M., 199n29

Ghosh, Amitav, 2, 3, 113, 195n2

Gibson, William, 17, 55, 140, 163

Gierasch, P. J., 199n32

global warming. *See* climate change

Gold Coast, The (Robinson), 11–12, 53–56, 61, 63–70, 73–74, 76–77, 89, 110, 132, 197n1

Green Earth (Robinson), 2, 12–13, 112–15, 200n1

greenhouse effect, 93

Greening of Mars, The (Lovelock and Allaby), 93

"Green Mars" (Robinson), 86, 88–89, 160

Green Mars (Robinson), 98–100, 102, 104–7; awards, 198n1; capitalism in, 91; compared to *2312*, 168; compared to *Aurora*, 174, 178; influence of Lisa Howland Newell's research on, 9; overview of the Mars trilogy, 12, 78–79; terraforming in, 199n29; utopia in, 96

Green Planets: Ecology and Science Fiction (ed. Canavan and Robinson), 4, 199n26

Greg, Percy, 198n9

Griffith, Nicola, 160

Gura, Philip, 201n21

Guthke, Karl, 199n9

Hahnel, Robin, 201n17

Hainish trilogy (Le Guin), 14, 136

haj, the, 196n22

Halderman, Joe, 22

Hamlet (Shakespeare), 60

Hamming, Jeanne, 197n2

Hank (character), 72, 75

Haraway, Donna, 6, 47, 81 197n34, 202n6

Hardin, Garrett, 203n9

Hartmann, William K., 118–19, 199n21, 201n13

Hartwell, David G., 203n17

Harwit, Martin, 92, 199n32

Hawkes, David, 196n20

Heather (character), 11, 45–47, 50, 98

Heidegger, Martin, 88

Heinlein, Robert C., 84

Heise, Ursula, 195n13, 198n1, 199n24, 201n20

Hellekson, Karen, 195n14, 196n6

Henderson, Hazel, 201n17

Hera (character), 144–46, 150–52

Heraclitus, 116

Hersey, John, 21

Herzog, Werner, 197n33

Hexter, Mr. (character), 185

Hidalgo (space ship), 5, 139–40, 171

Higgs, Harrison, 200n46

Hippolito, Jane, 199n16

Hiroshima, 10, 21–23, 55

Hiroshima (Hersey), 21

historiography: in *2312*, 154, 157; archaeologies of knowledge, memory, and information, 56; and art in *The Memory of Whiteness*, 143; and economics in the Mars trilogy, 102–3; in "A History of the Twentieth Century, with Illustrations," 19–20; in *Icehenge*, 24–27; in "The Lucky Strike," 21–22; and national renewal, 117; in *New York 2140*, 185; in the Orange County trilogy, 56–70; and quantum theory, 22–24; in "Remaking History," 20; in "A Sensitive Dependence on Initial Conditions," 22–24; in the Science in the Capital trilogy, 115, 117, 120; science, spirituality, and history in *Galileo's Dream*, 146; in *Shaman*, 46, 48–49; of space travel in *Aurora*, 172, 174–75; in *The Years of Rice and Salt*, 27–28, 30, 35–38, 41–44

history: 2008 housing crash, 185; progressive history, 47; Protestant Reformation, 203n13; Renaissance Italy, 144–45, 153; shadow history, 133; twentieth century, 53; twenty-first century, 133; World War I, 30; World War II, 21–22, 30, 114. *See also* alternative history; historiography

"History of the Twentieth Century, with Illustrations, A" (Robinson), 17–19, 196n5

Hodenosaunee League, 33–34, 39–40, 42, 197n26. *See also* Iroquois nations

Holand, Hjalmer, 196n14

racial inequality, 36

Rahmstorf, S., 202n28

Railroad Schemes (Holland), 197n7

Rainbow Mars (Niven), 87

Reagan, Ronald, 20, 53, 58–60

Reaganism, 20, 58, 76

realism, literary, 2, 141, 143, 151

rebellion. *See* revolution, political

Red Mars (Robinson), 90, 95–104, 107–8; awards, 198n1; compared to *2312*, 155; overview of the Mars trilogy, 12, 78–79; in relation to Martian sf, 200n45; and the Science in the Capital trilogy, 122; struggle for utopia in, 5; terraforming in, 85, 95–96

Redondi, Pietro, 202n8

Red Planet Run (Stabenow), 199n21

Red Star (Bogdanov), 80–81, 85

refugees, 182

"Remaking History" (Robinson), 10, 18, 20, 115

"Remaking of Zero, The" (Wolfe), 197n8

"Remarks on Utopia" (Robinson), 201n8

Return to Mars (Bova), 83

revolution, political, 7, 24–27, 42, 80–81, 96, 103–6, 120, 122, 138–40, 157, 168

Rexroth, Kenneth, 56

Rice, Christopher, 201n9

Ricoeur, Paul, 203n13

"Ridge-Running" (Robinson), 7, 69, 89, 132

Rinpoche, Sogyal, 196n19

Roberto (character), 185

Robinson, Don, 7

Robinson, Kim Stanley: and academe, 8; on *Aurora*, 171; biography of, 7; on his childhood, 7; and cli-fi, 114, 201n9; and climate change, 118, 201n10; and critical theory, 6; on cultural appropriation, 197n28; and cyberpunk, 4, 55–56, 140; dissertation of, 8; on ecology, 201n6; on Hjalmer Nederland (character), 196n14; on Kang Hon-gbi (character), 34; and literary/cultural theory, 9; marriage to Lisa Howland Nowell, 8; on Mars and the Mars trilogy, 82, 109, 200n47; narrators in works of, 172; and postmodernism, 20; on science, 118, 202n6; on science fiction genre, 2–4, 15, 81, 113, 171; on the Science in the Capital trilogy, 113, 115; scientific method, 119, 120, 123; significance to science fiction genre, 1, 3–4, 87, 135–37, 146, 159, 169; and space exploration, 135; utopia, 9, 72, 156, 198n4, 201n8; and utopian fiction, 77; values, 154–55; on writing *The Years of Rice and Salt*, 29, 197n28. *See also titles for specific works*

Robinson Crusoe (Defoe), 3

robotics, 155

Romantic poets, 7

ronin, 33

Rose, Andrew, 201n9

Rosenthal, Franz, 196n23

Roth, Philip, 17

Ruddick, Nicholas, 197n34

Ruddiman, William F., 197n34

Rudwick, Martin, 201n25

Russ, Joanna, 160

Russell, Sax (character), 46, 86, 97–98, 101–9, 122, 139, 144, 154, 160, 174; in *Blue Mars*, 98, 105, 108–9; in *Green Mars*, 98, 102, 104–5, 107; in *Red Mars*, 98, 103–4

Russia, 81

Sagan, Carl, 79, 92, 198n6, 199n29, 199n32

Sahlins, Marshall, 197n34

Samarqand, 39

samurai, 33

Sanchez, Ramona (character), 71, 74–76

Sands of Mars, The (Clarke), 84–85

Satarwal (character), 25

Saturn (planet), moons of, 13, 111, 135–36, 140, 156, 166

social contract, 158–59

socialism, 81

social justice, 54, 61, 122, 136, 200n48; socio-ecological justice, 120; socioeconomic justice, 185. *See also* feminism; gender equality

Solar (McEwan), 115, 120

solar energy, 124

Soviet Union, 81

space colonization: in *2312*, 136–37, 154–60, 169; in *Aurora*, 137, 170–80; in *Galileo's Dream*, 151–52; in *Icehenge*, 24–26, 138–40; and Leopoldian land ethic 166–67; in the Mars trilogy, 85–88, 102–3, 136; in *The Memory of Whiteness*, 136, 140–43; scientific perspectives on, 92–95, 200n35, 202n12; in sf, 80–85, 136. *See also* diaspora; space exploration; space travel; terraforming

space exploration, 83, 134

space travel, 84, 135–40, 170–72, 174, 176–77, 179–80

Spain, 30

Speller (character), 178–79

Spence, Jonathan D., 29, 196n20

spirituality and religion, 28, 34, 37, 144, 146–47, 148, 187; eco-spirituality, 133; mysticism, 148

Spook Country (Gibson), 55

Sprawl trilogy (Gibson), 55. *See also* individual titles

Stabenow, Dana, 199n21

Stapledon, Olaf, 3

Star Trek, 14, 136

Steele, Allen, 199n21

Steentoft, Hana (character), 68, 79

Stefan (character), 185

Stephenson, Neal, 118

Sterling, Bruce, 17, 55

Steve (character), 60, 63

Stevens, Wallace, 65, 68

Stewart, George R., 57, 63, 125

Stites, Richard, 81, 199n11

Stoermer, E.F., 198n2

Story of the Stone, The (Cao), 29, 196n20. See also *Dream of the Red Chamber, The*

Streeby, Shelley, 200n3

structures of feeling, 203n16

Sufism, 30–31

Suleiman the Magnificent, 30

sustainability, 74–76, 86, 88, 116, 122, 124, 126, 133, 181

Suvin, Darko, 18, 201n22

Swann, Eric, 138

Switzerland, 53

Synners (Cadigan), 55

Szeman, Imre, 195n19, 201n15

Taiwan, 32

Taneev, Vlad (character), 90, 96, 106–7

Ta-shu (character), 116

Tau Ceti, 5, 172, 174, 176–78

technology, 18, 59, 162–63: computers, personal, 18; digital revolution, 162–63; Internet, 18; and the Orange County trilogy, 55–56; World Wide Web, 18. *See also* quantum computing

tektology, 81, 91, 96, 100, 104, 106, 109

Terminator (city-state on Mercury), 13, 135–36, 140, 155, 158, 162–63, 166

Terraforming: in *2312*, 14, 151, 155–58; in *Aurora*, 174, 178–79; in *Icehenge*, 138; in the Mars trilogy, 9, 12, 79, 85–98, 100–101, 104–11; in Martian sf, 84–85, 200n37; in *The Memory of Whiteness*, 140–41; scientific perspectives on, 91–95, 199n29, 199n30

terraria, 136, 155–59, 161, 164, 166, 168, 178, 182

thermohaline convection, 127–28, 201–2n27, 202n28

Thomas, Lindsay, 78, 198n1, 199n24

Thoreau, Henry David, 56–57, 117, 124–26, 183

Thorn (character), 11, 44–46, 48–52

Three-Body Problem trilogy (Liu), 171

ROBERT MARKLEY is Trowbridge Professor of English at the University of Illinois, Urbana-Champaign. His recent books include *The Far East and the English Imagination, 1600–1730* and *Dying Planet: Mars in Science and the Imagination*.

MODERN MASTERS OF SCIENCE FICTION

THE UNIVERSITY OF ILLINOIS PRESS

is a founding member of the

Association of American University Presses.

———————————————————

University of Illinois Press

1325 South Oak Street

Champaign, IL 61820-6903

www.press.uillinois.edu